Penguin Books
Memory Ireland

Born in Victoria, based in Melbourne, the poet Vincent Buckley is also well known as an essayist, reviewer, and editor. His *Selected Poems* (1981) contains work from six earlier volumes, of which *Golden Builders* is the most famous. His essays range widely and include the influential and very early *Essays in Poetry, Mainly Australian*. He was at different times poetry editor for *Prospect* and *The Bulletin*, and supervised other collections.

He led appeals for imprisoned Hungarian writers, and took part in many debates central to Australian society. He has taught many generations of students at the University of Melbourne, and lectured in several countries.

His literary, critical and religious writings behind him, he now devotes all the time he can to poetry and to works of reminiscence. His last book, *Cutting Green Hay*, was written in Ireland.

Vincent Buckley

MEMORY IRELAND

Insights into the contemporary Irish condition

PENGUIN BOOKS

Penguin Books Australia Ltd,
487 Maroondah Highway, PO Box 257
Ringwood, Victoria, 3134, Australia
Penguin Books Ltd,
Harmondsworth, Middlesex, England
Penguin Books,
40 West 23rd Street, New York, NY 10010, USA
Penguin Books Canada Ltd,
2801 John Street, Markham, Ontario, Canada
Penguin Books (NZ) Ltd,
182-190 Wairau Road, Auckland 10, New Zealand

First published by Penguin Books Australia, 1985

Copyright © Vincent Buckley, 1985

Typeset in Bembo by Abb-Typesetting Pty Ltd, Melbourne

Made and printed in Australia by
Dominion Press-Hedges & Bell

CIP

Buckley, Vincent, 1927-.
Memory Ireland

ISBN 0 14 007956 4.

1. Ireland — Social conditions. I. Title.

941.5082

CONTENTS

INTRODUCTION

I write this book as a loving outsider: someone who, being pre-ponderantly Irish in ancestry, regards himself on one level as Irish but knows that on another level he is not, for he was born and has mostly lived in another hemisphere, and will always go back to it. He, I, do not claim to have the full range of Irish virtues or vices; and I do not want to think with the extravagant evasiveness of many Irish writers and intellectuals whom I know. At the same time, I try to go back to Ireland, to learn more of myself and my people, and of their life and death, as often as I can. Increasingly, these visits are inhibited by limits to time, money, and physical strength; but I shall try to continue them; and every time I leave I am already scheming with mind and voice to arrange the next return.

This book, then, is about successive goes at learning Ireland, and I restrict it as far as possible to what I have seen, heard, or learned about by immediate means; however tempting it would be to write a whole essay on the Irish churches, or brands of politicians, or history, or economic development, I have felt it only honest to resist. I have made the account in some sense a work of reminiscence, a memory-work, hoping that segments of the society will emerge in the memory's tide light. Indeed, it is a memory-work in more senses than one; for its hidden theme is Ireland's loss of its own memory, forced out by dispossessors, abandoned by ignorance, sold by jobbers, collapsed for lack of visible support, or simply leached away by the green misty weather.

Such a loss is serious; it penetrates all sections of Irish life; and it is, of course, a direct denial of the great cliché about Ireland and the Irish, that they have too much memory, are ruled by memory, worship and cultivate it and are killing themselves with it. Ireland by this account is a creature of memory who holds on to her memories past reason, is guided by the interests of centuries ago, and like the elephant never forgets a grievance. This strange anachronism is the basis of an Irish joke, and thus somewhat at odds with the other basic joke-perception: that the Irish are so stupid that they can't remember anything (e.g. any instruction formulated by the master-race) for more than a minute. No worries. Both jokes are ill-founded, like the other great ur-joke, which holds that 'only the Irish' could construct a border like that between the two separated parts of Ireland, which divides parts of towns, and even separates a bedroom from its adjoining kitchen. That border is certainly a joke, but it is not an Irish one. Some Irish refer to it as 'the English border', much as one might discuss the English 'vice'; it is not a Mick-construct but a piece of Whitehallery, and many Irish over the past sixty years have been trying to abolish it.

No, the real Irish joke is that the Irish are gullible, good natured, and inquisitive; and that, however hard they tried over the last hundred years to restore a memory which had been painfully and deliberately taken from them, they could not keep it up (poverty, migration, and economic dependence drove out the capacity for remembering before it had been fully settled); they have now abandoned the attempt. The visitor to Dublin sees gaps: the Irish memory is a structure of gaps. Gaps in the memory match those uncountable gaps in the line of a city wall, or in the contour of an estate boundary, or in the main street of a village. Nothing gets mended. When Irish country people speak of something's being 'very old', it is likely that they mean 'from my grandparents' time'. They do not like to approach time too closely or too directly, and they lack confidence in its permutations. Their whole tactic with time, and hence with the enquiring visitor, is to forget it (except for some spicy bits) and to fob him off, or at least divert him into chat ('crack') and maybe an inadvertent self-revelation.

One of the continuing tragedies of Ireland over centuries is that the conditions for sustaining corporate memory have been destroyed. Every generation of the Irish has had as one of its chief signs the phenomenon of interrupted lives, and hence interrupted memory-transmission. Families become dispersed, like leaves at the end of autumn; the 'family' remains, it is true, but as a denuded tree-stump, full of stay-put melancholy. An aunt is in Boston, another in Sydney (where in Sydney? O I can't think now. I think it begins with a 'C': Camperdown? Coogee?); an uncle has lured his two nephews to Manchester; his brother, the 'father', goes to do piecework there. He may be killed on a building-site; or he may die at a railway station in the early morning on his way back to the lost country, as Bernadette Devlin's father did. If we are to speak of memory, whose memory do we mean? Theirs? Memories of them? And with such wandering people, where is the place of memory? What sacralizes it? Irish life loses its memory because it is both too rigidly confined and too casually dispersed.

In more recent times, it has been asked to lose its national memory by a kind of policy, in which politicians of almost all parties, ecclesiastics of all religions, media operators, and revisionist historians co-operate to create (and let us hope they do not need to enforce, for if they need to, they will) a new sense of corporate identity. This sense contradicts the immediately preceding one (the one based on the rising of Easter 1916 and its aftermath), which proved first so exhilarating then so wearying to its generations, some of whom had fought to realize it. Ireland is not a nation, once again or ever, so the new story runs, but two nations: maybe several; it does not have its characteristic religion – or, if it does, it ought not; it does not have its characteristic language, as anyone can see or hear; it has no particular race or ethnic integrity. Ireland is a nothing – a no-thing – an interesting nothing, to be sure, composed of colourful parts, a nothing-mosaic. It is advertising prose and Muzak. All this revisionist thinking delivered with passion, wit, and, often, traditional song. Yet it is not a form of the realism it pretends to; it is a baring of the hindparts, as some animals bare them, to appease the myriad potential aggressors. And who are they, when they're at home? Och, you never know. But some of them doubtless live nearby.

But, as we all have reason to know, personal memory is the strongest; institutional or racial memory is nothing to it, except where either of them endorses it or contests it with disorienting force. The troops may have fought in that paddock, but you personally remember only its grass-tops, its tree, and the fearful prickling of its pond. Where were the post-war Irish to get personal memories which would not be in conflict with the corporate memory of re-birth, of the years from 1916 into the twenties? In some, a minority, personal and corporate would reinforce each other; but most of this minority are now long dead. In their children, there is an uneasy blend of pride in their accomplishment, doubt induced by the constant claims of the present-day sophisticates that nothing much, after all, was accomplished, and shame at not having completed it. For the great majority, the national memory is no memory at all, or it has no personal memory to run beside. The national memory has become a 'myth', which everyone tells them should be disregarded, discarded, for such is the way of Whitehall and Brusselian realism; the personal memory rejects it, cancels it, twists it, but not dramatically, not with sufficient force to cause a radical self-questioning; the national memory goes, and the personal twitches into self-doubt, by a process of drift and erosion.

This twisting or poisoning is one of the great sub-themes of Irish writing in this century, a perception of world and self that fills the language with plaint, with *caoine*. I will not write about that quality here, although it deserves extended treatment; I write about my Ireland, if I may be allowed to put it so possessively, the Ireland of my experience over thirty years. I have taken some care to possess it with my memory which at every point it enlightens.

Ireland is a country of extraordinary beauty, occupied by a people most of whom have in human affairs the supple tactility of a sea-anemone. This lovable quality comes of deep habit, generations old, but at the same time it is a resource for dealing with every meeting as though it were a new event; for, as I stress, they are not obsessed with history, but the carriers and victims of a history which they do not understand or which they have not been taught.

Some groups in the country have taught themselves versions of this history, however, and they offer, with startling effects in the prevailing inertia, to act out their version. Among these are the republican groups (at present, the Provisional IRA and the Irish National Liberation Army [INLA]) and their enemies the loyalist organizations (at present, chiefly the Ulster Defence Association [UDA] and the Ulster Volunteer Force [UDF]). These organizations express their sense of their own history in the tactics they use, the demands they make, and the names they give to their affiliates and campaigns. An observer who knows the history will quickly realize what republican tendency is represented by the name *An Phoblacht*, or the flag of the starry plough, and what is portended by a bombing campaign in the midst of a political initiative. All the traditional guidelines have existed, for the republicans, since the Fenians in the 1860s, and, for the loyalists, almost as long. One generation replicates the system of acts it has learned from earlier generations; or at least the moves which it uses are taken from an inherited repertoire. The loyalists do the same. Neither grouping behaves in this way because it is stupid, or obsessionally fixated on this title, that method; it does so in order to establish between the generations the continuity on which its legitimacy depends, and because these resources have proved effective in the past. The IRA, for example, seems for the past five years to have reverted to a form of military organization similar to that used by the Fenians, but much more efficient; and it is using a traditional bombing tactic, but in cities as well as the countryside, and not so much to terrorize populations as to pin down its opponents' armed forces and disable their economy. So we have a high degree of repetition and replication, with a certain adaptability. The British do not seem to understand this mixture and its provenance. If they did, it would make negotiations between the several parties easier than they are.

The central section of this book is devoted to one prolonged episode in this immensely protracted conflict; that episode is the Republican hunger-strike in The Maze Prison, also called Long Kesh, in Northern Ireland between March and October 1981. I was in

Ireland for all but the first few weeks of this tragic and moving campaign, and noted with growing horror the presentation of it by the governments of Ireland and of Great Britain, by the media of both countries, by commentators both clerical and lay, military and civil (all of them political in effect), and by the man and woman in the street, Irish and English. I say horror because on the one hand it seemed clear that the deaths of the prisoners could be avoided and some workable compromise arrived at between them and their imprisoning government; but, on the other hand, no such compromise was arrived at, largely because of a British refusal to consider one, ten men died and several others were taken off the fast at the point of dying, but the people around me for the most part expressed or affected unconcern about the whole matter.

What struck me, apart from that weary callowness, was the enormous courage of one hunger-striker after another, and the great and increasing sense of fellowship between them. Bobby Sands and his comrades seemed to me to show a fortitude and an emotional resource that put them, whatever their prior deeds, far outside the range of meaning possible to the great majority of those who watched them die.

This emotional resource was noted by several visitors to their death cells, who defined it as a growing love between them: as though they were living and dying through each other. The growing strength of this bond made it very difficult for anyone, including their political leaders, to persuade them off their fast once it had passed a certain point. Such a bond is fascinating, moving and exemplary; it is one reason why I have tried to separate their strike from their politics, their life as armed fighters outside Long Kesh from their life (and death) as unarmed warriors within it. Of course, they are not separable in the end, but it may be enlightening to contemplate the heroic endurance – the life through dying – in whatever isolation we can achieve.

In those chapters I refer frequently to 'Republicans', 'republicans' and 'nationalists'. These terms are difficult to keep distinct, but they are not synonymous and may need some explaining. Nationalists include the great majority of Catholics in the six counties, and a small number of Protestants. Nationalists may be defined as people who see themselves as Irish rather than 'British' or Scottish, tend to endorse whatever endorses or plays up to that self-image, usually have some consciousness of the antiquity of their occupancy of the land, and tend to resent all attacks on that sense of place-identity. Some Protestants meet, and some Catholics do not meet, this formula. 'Nationalist' is not necessarily a political term, either; I am not using it as the name of a political party, although such a party did until recently exist; but it entails some active desire for the unification of the country, and a dissatisfaction with the existence of the statelet of Northern Ireland. The term 'republican' is narrower; it signifies a willingness to work actively for the unification of the country, without specifying these or those means. A 'republican' might well think of himself, of his practical loyalties, and of the traditions he honours, in rather different terms from those of a 'nationalist'. Given a sufficient crisis like a hunger-strike, the differences will largely disappear. A Republican is a republican who chooses a politico-military method and organization to achieve the ends which other republicans also desire. He is either a member or supporter of the 'Republican movement', by which is meant the Irish Republican Army, its political counterpart (not 'wing', as commentators usually call it) Sinn Fein, and its organs of publicity, family support and social relief, such as Green Cross. Alternatively, he may belong to the Irish Republican Socialist Party, or to its military counterpart, INLA, or to some other group. In some conditions, Republicans may be at odds with republicans, and even more with nationalists, over questions of 'methods', for example. In other conditions, their interests may coincide. Such conditions were created, up to quite an advanced stage, by the hunger-strikes of 1981.

Such a coincidence of interests does not please some militant Republicans who believe in the separateness of the Republican movement, hate 'politics', and favour all-out military campaigns;

they reject the tendency represented by Gerry Adams and other northern leaders, who are organizing to make Sinn Fein a fully competitive political party. Two months ago, I was writing that a combination of three demographic facts in the north was changing the situation there invisibly but rapidly. In those two months, several people have been killed, and scores injured, in a series of London bombings carried out, evidently, by a dissident unit of the IRA; another IRA unit, having kidnapped a British businessman, fought gun battles south of the border with Irish police and soldiers, killing two; thousands of police and soldiers joined in the hunt for them. A journalist, Mary Holland, has reported in *The New Statesman* that the people in the border areas of the republic where the hunt and search took place soon began to treat the searchers (their own security forces) with the contempt, hatred and silence that the Belfast and Derry Catholics show to the RUC and the British army. She is a very experienced, indeed expert reporter, who understands the republican and Republican *milieux* thoroughly; she reports with astonishment the demeanour of the people in Leitrim. By the time this paragraph is printed the situation will have changed again, perhaps drastically. For it is a situation in which, while the basic issues are quite simple, the strategic and political permutations are so many and complicated that no one can predict any development at any given time.

I write as a non-party republican and, more intensely, as a writer trying to follow out an ancient ethic of showing the truth. In my view, this ethic forbids me to offer 'support' to any politico-military organization whose actions I cannot influence; such support is always offered in advance, and amounts to *carte blanche*. No writer can give *carte blanche* to any army.

In addition, I would never support the bombing, whether deliberately or by wanton inadvertence, of civilian targets, whether it is government or guerilla forces that are responsible. I have a heightened version of the normal horror of bombs and bombing; and, though it is not at all the same kind of thing, I am always horrified by death-fasts.

Part One

SETTLING IN IRELAND

Chapter One

BACK AFTER TWELVE MONTHS AWAY

When you return to Ireland after any absence, you are caught up in immediate conversation; the Irish are instant conversationalists, whether they know you or not. If they know you, the conversational form tends to be more complex. Since it is a small country, oppressed by money worries, to some degree psychologically isolated, and amazingly homogeneous in population, the subject of conversation, after a courteous enquiry about what has been happening to yourself, is sure to be what has happened in Ireland since you were last here. You will have missed great drama, they will tell you with gleaming voices, or, it may be, great boredom, they will shrug, for sure what ever happens but the same old thing. Further, the subject of all conversations is likely to be the same, although the grace-notes will vary greatly. The theme is set by consensus, the improvisations belong to the moment.

I returned in September 1983, almost exactly a year after I had left. The air was humming with subject-matter. There were urgent trivia, such as an unusually vicious football final that had just been played (Gaelic football is relatively lacking in wanton violence, and any which occurs is worthy of comment). There was the category of the *déjà vu*, such as the new government's financial bumbling ('Ah yes, and we've got a new government since you left, Vincent'). But these were not the things which provided Subject.

There were three things that did that: the increased violence in southern cities, the dramatic increase in drug addiction, mostly heroin, and the fate of the constitutional referendum on abortion. They were certainly dramatic enough, and to the returning observer deeply revealing of some dominant forces in Irish life; to me, for example, they were connected with one another more obviously than they were to my friends who endured them, and to whom they

1

appeared the more discrete the more dramatic they were. To me, for example, the heroin addiction showed a vulnerability and childishness in Irish life; this was connected with the weak authoritarianism and social detachment of the Catholic bishops, and both were surely connected with the increase in violence (muggings, burglaries, holdups, gang warfare, political violence), which was in turn surely connected with a failure to pay full attention to the nature of violence in the north. With untrustworthy leaders, the Irish had fallen into a routinism of subdued fear, and were easy prey for violent and unexpected changes in their situation. In turn, an obscure realization of that fact made them even more depressed, if extremely lively in speech, about the continuing problems.

One of these, though not really part of the Subject, was the presence and condition of the travelling people, also called itinerants or (an older term, now both inaccurate and dismissive) tinkers. Visitors often think they are gipsies, but they are almost completely native Irish; occasionally they intermarry with English or Welsh gipsies, but although they have their own version of cant, or clan language, they are Irish, one of the products of Irish history, or, more exactly, of the history of English policy in Ireland. They camp for long periods on the roads leading into Irish cities and towns, or on small areas set aside for them inside those cities. They are bitterly resented by most of the people among whom they settle, and are always in danger of being persecuted, insulted, moved on, and having their families broken, often very brutally and abruptly. I am in no position to write about the problems thus created; what struck me in September 1983 was how numerous they had grown on the roads through the area where I stayed for part of the time. Their numbers are increasing fast, the chances of housing or otherwise settling them are shrinking even faster, and they are so much more visible, in some ways more obstructive, than they used to be. The latest estimate is 15,000, increasing by 10 per cent a year. What no one told me, although I learned it months later, was that they clustered on the roads of County Dublin because Dublin City had driven them out;

the line between these entities is not very clear except to bureaucrats.

For some time I stayed with Seamus, a taxi-driver, and Christine, his wife, a nurse, in Firhouse. The rest of the time I stayed with a poet friend near the seafront, at Merrion. In the second house some of the concerns which compose the Subject came up intermittently, but it tended to be obscured by the need for recurrent doses of wisdom and gossip. In the first house, they came up repeatedly, and in an order, with an economy, which showed them to be connected not merely in social fact but also deep in the minds of my friends.

Seamus and Christine lived on a road leading from Templeogue and Rathfarnham past the large new 'complex' of Tallaght along the south-west road through the Dublin mountains into West Wicklow and on into south Kildare.

In the year since they last had seen me, they said, some things had changed, and others became clear. As I already knew, Tallaght, place of most mysterious history and prehistory, where Parthalon and the whole of his invading people were said to have lain buried for millennia in one great mound, and where from a later date a great monastery had existed, with its precious books and texts, and its more-than-millennial central tree, for nearly the whole of Christian history in Ireland, Tallaght had spread from its village and was now an estate wasteland of nearly 100,000 people. It stretched for miles to west and north; motorways and ambitious feeder-roads sped through it, joining and diverging from each other; but some of these roads were wide, and bordered by fields, and on to their verges, and the fields, and sometimes the roads themselves, hundreds of itinerants had come, with their cars, their caravans, their outdoor kitchens, their churns of water, their clothes hung on fence and hedge, their dogs, their scrap cars and other useless metal, and above all their horses: cart horses for the most part, browsing near and straying on what, after all, were major roads. None of this was a new sight or a new concept: neither the problems which the 'travellers' had, nor those which they created, could be called new; the hostility of the people among whom they had so abruptly settled was of long standing; their own misery was still not met. Some of them had 'lived' there, or thereabouts, for years; some had been driven there; some had chosen this place. What was new was that, because no one had been able to shift them, roadways completed some time before had not yet been 'opened'; the travellers were occupying them. Nowhere are misery and anomaly more visible than Ireland; and some say that the travellers' evident misery is no more than anomaly. Whatever may be said about that, the Tallaght scene was a visible and effective sign, a mad sacrament, of governmental lack of will; for even where good purposes are followed, some final weakness of will is likely to prevent their completion. So here: you finish an important road, and are then unable to open it, because you will not find housing or fielding for a few hundred people.

Purposes in Ireland are short term, and will is mostly spasmodic, lacking in stamina. Consider, said my friends, the northern shopping. Some entrepreneur has arranged weekly bus visits to Newry, in Northern Ireland. Every week a crowded bus, filled mostly with housewives, sets off from near Tallaght to travel the sixty or seventy miles into what, after all, its occupying forces, though by no means all its occupants, call a different state (foreign country, hey, different accents, different currency, a touch of danger); the southerners would spend some hours shopping, and the bus would bring them home again. What did they shop for? Meat, groceries, petrol, booze, anything electrical. They would save the price of the bus twice or thrice over. Is that why they went? Yes, said my friends. I think there is an extra thing: the outing, the togetherness, the touch of daring. Tallaght can be drab, and even Rathfarnham broody. But who would have guessed that so many people would come to think no more of going weekly into the black north of their own country than of making day trips from Wexford to do their shopping in Bordeaux? (That's a bitter joke, reader).

I don't grudge them: an outing is an outing, and Newry is a Catholic town which is therefore afflicted by chronic unemployment. The southern pound will do some good there. Yet it is chilling to think that in the relatively impoverished if uncomplaining south, prices should have gone so high.

In travelling to Newry, they are travelling to an area usually thought of as one of endless violence; but they are also travelling from a city, if not a locality, where violence increases every month. And they are increasingly worried by it.

The difference between Dublin and some other big cities is that many of the big robberies are political, as are the cases of kidnapping and extortion; they are standard ways of keeping buoyant the fighting funds of Republican military groups in the north. I have heard many suggestions over the years that there was some overlap between these activities (the actions of 'soldiers', as their perpetrators would see them) and the robberies organized by criminal gangs; but I have seen no investigation of this matter. It is possible that some criminals have republican sympathies, of course.

It is now said that, where only a few years ago Dublin was divided among four criminal families, now there are ten. As well as that, there is random violence in, for example, the inner cities, among the dispossessed and often cretinized youth who, never in work, have been breathing in almost lethal quantities of lead since they were infants. So we have a combination of automatized violence, organized gang violence, and operational political violence: the whole arising from the socio-political state of Ireland, part of which is the struggle in the north.

Into this complex comes the drug traffic. Comes, in especial, heroin. It is claimed that the subjection of Ireland to the heroin pressure results from an over-distribution of the stuff through western Europe in the last days of the Shah of Iran; his magnates, it is said, pushed huge quantities of heroin on the market in the course of getting their assets out of Iran. Certainly Scotland too has been badly affected; and in Ireland, with its many problems, heroin in great quantities was pressed on what Tom McGurk, in his brilliant article in *The Listener* (20 October 1983), called 'the most vulnerable and innocent working-class children in western Europe'. The principal distributors have been members of the leading criminal family, for whom the coming of heroin coincided with the realization that bank robberies had got very risky, and were more trouble than they were worth.

Heroin caused a trauma both in the police force, the Garda Siochana, and in the working-class areas of the inner cities. In the middle of it, sections of the respectable establishment caused a trauma in the whole country by insisting on putting to a referendum the proposition that clauses prohibiting abortion (already banned in criminal law) be written into the nation's constitution. The intention was no doubt to show sceptics, liberals, and abortionists who was boss, to elicit what the plain people of Ireland really thought, to increase the prestige of the Catholic bishops, and to restore traditional morals as a kind of absolute, shining there in its verbal reliquary as if they had been touched by magic. The actual effect was to establish that the bishops were both authoritarian and indecisive, and to throw into serious doubt the whole notion of their being leaders of the people; traditional morals may not have been affected one way or the other, for most Irish hate abortion in a way that is not much affected by referenda.

But once more, in this as in the questions of violence and drugs, the country was suffering or had suffered trauma, and no leadership had responded properly to the people's crisis. No wonder the people talked endlessly about these events. Another fact, to which they did not advert so much, is that, in two cases, the referendum and the matter of drugs, the people had to some extent taken the crisis into their own hands, and had effectively said No to those who wanted to push them around or to exploit them. There were signs that, in the twelve months I had been out of the country, some few steps had been taken back towards communal initiative.

But some of these things were told me only by way of illustration, on the way to some more substantial point. My friends could be expected to have noticed the northern bus, because it left from their vicinity, and some of their neighbours no doubt took it. The triad of violence, drugs, and referendum was far more pressing, and everyone (or at least everyone in the working-class and lower middle-class areas) was talking about its components. Ireland is a country with an enormous national debt, high inflation and very high unemployment, a high birth-rate and very high proportion of juveniles in its population; and there is now little chance of migrating. Given all this, and the weakening of religious ethics all over western Europe, and the fact that the political division of the country, having produced violence in the occupied north, will now spread it to the southern part, you have an unavoidable recipe for collapse. That collapse had become dramatically evident in the previous twelve months.

All forms of violence, from child abuse to kidnapping and extortion, had increased (though it must be said that rape is not common). Much of the violence comes from organized robberies, much from drug addicts, and much from the opportunism of street kids. Easy burglaries are the most common; I know one couple whose house had been burgled eight times in the one year; another friend had his house ransacked inexpertly by a daylight burglar whom his daughter surprised in the act. 'It's all right, it's all right,' he cried as he escaped through a downstairs window. The gardai recognized him from the description. A drug addict, aged twenty-four; no use pulling him in; the case would take forever, and he'd be dead before it finished. Any places with cash (banks, insurance companies, service stations, supermarkets) are as vulnerable in Dublin as in any other big city. They will become more so.

Seamus had seen much of the drug problem at close hand. He had driven many pushers, and seen many groups of addicts. Inner Dublin is a poor and despoliated place, full of the loneliness of lost community and the despair of failed religion. It is full of waste lots, on the one hand, and corporation flats on the other. These latter have most affecting names, St Teresa's Gardens, Fatima Mansions, and so on; but in them and in the dark streets and lanes that join them, the pushers are at work, and in five years the rate of heroin addiction among the youth in these areas has become an inflammation, so that even the Garda spokesmen, speaking of the problem on television, sometimes seem close to tears. As with so many other things in Ireland, this has happened with enormous speed: it is not just the cunning and organization of the pushers; the Irish seem to jump several phases in the assimilation of any fashion, and if something or other is the in thing, it will be commended, followed and died from with enormous if dreamy enthusiasm. Chronic addiction has made burglary endemic, and therefore produced epidemics of violence, armed robbery, family breakdown, crowded jails, hundreds of youngsters sleeping rough in the damp climate; if it is hazardous to walk the streets near O'Connell Street late in the evening, it is even more hazardous to own a car and park it near the kerb, for if it is not stolen it will very likely have its windows smashed some time in the first few months.

This means added terrorism for the poor, already terrorized by their own impotence. The old poor lived with dirt, an aged habitat, alcoholism, the absence of fathers, the prospect of migration, the appalling weakness of the health facilities, the capriciousness of government, the lack of social services, and a growing anxiety about public hypocrisy which is also, of course, an anxiety about personal identity. The new poor live with pollution, new habitats which *seem* at once unfinished and used up, drugs and the dread of drugs, a violence more brutal than before, the weariness and anxiety of parents, the virtual impossibility of escape through migration, and a network of mystifications and contradictions about medicine, law, government and social services. There is a universal conviction that those in charge are hypocrites. Many things have changed for the better, but the city fabric which needed to be restored has been rebuilt with an ugliness agreed on by land developers, town planners and profiteers. It is in these areas that the drug addict has been deliberately planted and garnered.

The last thing the Irish working class needs is heroin. Seamus has seen how 'they' hang like shades in the slum streets waiting for the pushers to deliver. Addicts? No, he didn't think so. Minor suppliers, then? Maybe. All Dublin taxi-drivers are now familiar with the 'drug run', which usually starts at St Stephen's Green and winds around by some fairly predictable addresses. Whatever the actual route, the run goes always through working-class Dublin.

The family which is publicly said to run this scene, and which is often named in print, contains many brothers. One has a mansion, with swimming pool, on the mountain. One lives in a suburban area, until recently call Holylands. One is on the run, probably in Spain, from which he continues to direct the traffic. But why go on? Every drug or prostitution racket has families like this one. What makes these a little different is that they themselves come from the Liberties, the inner Dublin area full of workers' cottages and slums, which their pushers now infest. Eight of the brothers spent long periods in 'custodial centres' when they were youngsters. They are an active slum clan of a familiar kind, lumpen shock troops. They stick together. They got into the drug racket through one of those unhappy chances that seem to afflict Ireland more than most countries; they suddenly got access to some of the vast amounts of heroin dumped in the European market by those Iranian business men in 1980. They did it because it was so easy. Thus, once again the fatalistic gullibility, the inert individualism of the Irish is seen, this time in combination with the fatal vulnerability of the whole country to the processes of dumping. Every inferior product from poor-quality baked beans to lethal preparations of hormones or antibiotics is dumped on Ireland: sometimes first, to see how it goes, and sometimes last, to see if the toxin is exhausted yet.

The family members, it is said, do not really like the heroin trade, and their next generation will not conduct it. As one reporter says, they 'are in the process of being supplanted by a larger, more ruthless criminal organization', whose members are heavily armed. So Dublin goes ahead.

The working-class victims of their pushers are in the process of booting them out, too. They have already done so in one housing complex, have almost succeeded in another, and have pushed the pushers into a narrower ellipse among the fine-sounding gardens and mansions. From there, they have, of course, gone into the streets, which is where Seamus increasingly sees them as he drives his taxi, trying to avoid the 'drug run'. It is where I have seen them, too, and where every journalist in Dublin knows them to be. As *Magill* said (November 1983):

As soon as Teresa's Gardens threw the pushers out, the trade in Dolphin House trebled, and it also increased in Fatima Mansions and Oliver Bond Flats.

When Dolphin House was recently cleared of heroin pushers, the trade spilled onto the streets and into the housing estates in the area. Last week, along an alleyway joining Cashel Avenue to Stanaway Road in Crumlin, a pusher who lives in nearby Rachland Road flats arrived every day at lunchtime and again at teatime. On each occasion he was awaited by between 40 and 50 addicts. Following heavy police activity in the area, the trade has moved elsewhere. Even the addicts are no longer sure of exactly where to find it from day to day. But it has not become less prevalent. It has just gone on the move.

But it was neither the police nor the regular politicians who forced this evil to go on the move; it was the furious residents combining to evict its agents. I have seen film of tenants' mass meetings, and noted with interest the style and accent of the speakers most vehement against pushers; they ranged from burly middle-age to almost frenetic teenage; their style might in other places be mistaken for hoodlum, but that would be a serious mistake; what they were actually expressing was a frenzy of determination born of hatred and fear at what they had seen, at close quarters, sapping the very walls of their flatland prisons. It was what Seamus had seen in their streets and in his cab, and what I had seen traces of in the streets where nearly thirty years ago I walked out with my small daughter Brigid to take the evening air of the Grand Canal.

Only one political leader was mentioned as helping in the

clear-out; and he was Provisional Sinn Fein. I have seen film of Sinn Fein members supporting a group of mothers to force a pusher out of the courtyard of their flats. It begins to seem that the 'policing' methods which the IRA has used so often in the nationalist areas of the north may eventually be used in those flats with the religious or uplifting names.

Miles further south from those riverside areas, in Tallaght and Firhouse, the local people were fighting against vandalism and organizing for such basic necessities as a youth club. They are people bothered by mortgage payments as well as by deprivations. They live not by the river or the canal but under the mountain, with the Hellfire Club standing above them at the very point from which the squalls of rain come so fiercely. They have a generalized concern with violence, but not so much intimate fear of it as the people in Dolphin's Barn. They hate drugs, but theirs is a future dread. They see the society as a whole lapsing slowly out of focus. They would love to be able to trust a government, or to sing a national song with real conviction. They observe and analyse their situation intelligently. But they are strikingly short of amenities many of us take for granted. And because no one will help them, they suffer from a partial *anomie*.

Ironically, in the early months of 1984 some of the pushers expelled by vigilantes from the area near the river have come out to operate among them; it is a fair bet that the people of Tallaght and Firhouse will in turn expel them.

There is another thing about Tallaght and Firhouse: they voted No in the referendum; and they are very proud of it. For all their own concern for respectability and responsibility, they resisted the attempt of more privileged people to force them into a respectable posture which they thought inappropriate.

In the late seventies, then with increasing urgency at the start of the eighties, a move was made to change the constitution of the Irish Republic. At first, the changes spoken of concerned the removal of clauses 2 and 3, the traditional 'republican' clauses which, by both laying claim to the six northern counties and declaring the claim in abeyance, were nervously deemed to be upsetting the northern Protestants. It was not the first time the proposal had been made, but it became a general talking-point when Garret FitzGerald, now the Taoiseach (Prime Minister) of the state, affirmed it as his passionate desire to change the constitution, and to begin by removing those clauses.

The resulting debate found people saying, 'Yes, but why stop there? Change more', and others saying, 'Review the whole constitution'; perhaps to most people's surprise, some joined in, saying, in effect, 'Don't remove: add.' And in this muted but desperate flurry of needs, a group or groups emerged whose concern was to add to the constitution a clause outlawing abortion. Ireland is passionately opposed to abortion, which is already forbidden by law; the new proposal was to make it impossible to change the law without first changing the constitution.

And, although nobody could as yet think of an appropriate wording (for constitutions need brevity as well as precision), the leaders of the two main parties, FitzGerald and Haughey, pledged themselves to enact the necessary legislation, even if it meant their *finding* the words. Elections were all the go in those days, 1981 and 1982; and the making of promises was once again becoming an art-form. Even the Labour Party was at that time thought to have endorsed the general intention, although later the press statements of its members led us to believe that they disagreed among themselves and, later still, that they had never said they would and that they would certainly not.

The thing was that both the civil liberties organizations and the Protestant churches now said that they found the proposed legislation offensive, the Protestants largely because they saw it as signalling a return to Catholic triumphalism and legalism, an insistence on writing in 'Catholic' norms as constitutional requirements, a renunciation of the ecumenical spirit, and a contemptuous willingness to drive them into an isolated enclave. Others held that a constitutional provision which no one can clearly formulate is not going to be much good in a constitution, although it might serve for a Dail debate; and others shyly expressed the view that such a constitutional desire is not necessarily 'Catholic', or anything else, at all. The matter was to be settled by referendum.

The government which mounted the referendum was a coalition between FitzGerald's Fine Gael party and the weakened Labour Party, led by an inexperienced but surprisingly strong Dick Spring. By the time they mounted it, they were opposed to it, while the chief opposition party, Fianna Fail, was vehemently for it. Smaller parties were one by one deciding against it. The battle formed up on both party and moral grounds; and it was very bitter. Actually, the main parties were split, but Fianna Fail, being traditionally the more disciplined and formulaic, was able to disguise this more easily.

The arguments became more bitter, sometimes abusive, in a word more extravagant, as it emerged that the country was split not only by party but also by occupation and region. It is true that whatever remains of the oppressively and self-consciously Catholic establishment was strongly for the amendment, while whatever exists of a pro-abortion seculariat was among those against it. But there were doctors and surgeons, obstetricians and pediatricians, grouped on both sides, just as you would expect; and lawyers, and 'personalities', and freelance commentators of various sorts; even theologians were affected. But, while the east was split, the west was for, as were the border counties and the extreme south-west. The Irish *Times* identified a 'sort of holy twilight zone west of the Shannon ...' which 'has a lot in common with the US Bible Belt except that it is Catholic rather than Tin-Chapel Protestant ...' In these counties 'there has been no real campaign at all against the amendment'. In the end, they voted more than four to one for it.

What they voted for was, in its final version, worded as follows: 'The state acknowledges the right to life of the unborn and, with due

regard to the equal right to life of the mother, guarantees in its laws
to respect, and, as far as practicable, by its laws to defend and vindicate
that right.'

As a footnote, the Nationalist members of the northern Assembly
replied in this way to the question which way they would cast their
vote if they had one: members of the SDLP, seven yes, six no, one
uncommitted; Sinn Fein members, all five against, the dread Mr
Gerry Adams declaring that 'he thought the referendum was the
result of pressure from "a small right-wing clique" on the Republic's
political parties. He would vote No because "politically it would do
nothing to deal with all the pressures that force women to have
abortions" '. The SDLP members nearly all thought the amendment
'unnecessary', but did not want to vote in a way which might
encourage the legalizing of abortion. They believed in, but would
not fight for, Occam's razor.

But what were the Catholic bishops doing? Not coming clean,
that's what. For months their priests, together with such élite, and
often secret, groups as the Knights of Columbanus, the SPUC, the
PLAC, and so on, had campaigned for the amendments; but the
bishops were late in making any concerted attempt to give formal
direction to their flock. Like the other groups, they wished to appeal
to traditions of various sorts which they felt to be threatened, as the
Irish Catholic Doctors Guild expressed 'concern about the decline in
ethical values', wishing to delay some society of the future in order to
retain one of the past; it was these doctors, incidentally, who dreamed
up the referendum, and pursued it with backing from British groups.
It was an organized campaign; and its organizers ranged from groups
with a specifically anti-abortion charter to those with a generalized
desire to control change of all sorts within the society. It is not the job
of bishops to organize such campaigns, although no doubt they often
do; but these bishops certainly sympathized with both kinds of aspiration, and it may be that they were dragged along and, in the end,
sucked in by organizers bolder than themselves.

They were unanimous, then, in giving not a clear direction but an aggressively unclear one. To judge from their public statements, the aim was to enforce an impression and create a sense of obligation without being too clear about the boundaries of the obligation, and without defining the rights of the voter at all: no comment was their view on that matter.

More than one journalist reported the hierarchy to be 'deeply divided on whether it should issue a statement telling Catholics they are free to vote No . . .' After the anti-amendment campaigners had formally requested both him and Archbishop Ryan to clarify the episcopal position, Cardinal O'Fiaich 'indicated' that they would 'probably' do so. No hope. As one bishop, 'who did not want to be named', told the journalist Joe Carroll, the bishops were in 'a serious dilemma', since not all the dimensions of the issue were within the competence that Catholic bishops claim for themselves. At the same time, some bishops had already spoken for the amendment. It was clearly not a religious, but a political situation, and whatever dilemmas arose from it were also political. As one self-effacing theologian said, 'I am sure they are all in favour of the amendment but for them to say you are free to vote No could undermine the pro-amendment campaign.' Yes, everyone could see that. And, as one anonymous expert is quoted as feeling, 'The actions of individual bishops such as Dr McNamara and Dr Ryan may have pre-empted any attempt by the hierarchy to publish a "freedom of conscience" clause at this late stage. Since the squabbles among rival prelates in the 19th century, he points out, the Irish bishops want to appear "unanimous on everything and never disagree in public".' Squabbling in public can be left to less exalted people.

Their reticence did not, in any case, stop some of those people speculating about their motives, or at least of those who 'have brought the hierarchy into this campaign as earlier, they seduced the two major political parties'. For Dick Spring, these manipulators were not pro-life but anti-life; they despised women; their real aim was to reach behind abortion and to 'outlaw' current forms of contraception, to prevent 'future change in the areas of illegitimacy, of the improved status of women, of the treatment of children and of the first tentative steps towards the growing problem of marital breakdown'.

Interestingly, Spring too saw the bishops as seduced by others more militant; yet, 'by deliberate choice in this referendum the bishops have decided to put their influence to the test'. And, no sooner had they done so, with results which have been varyingly assessed, than Joe Carroll was again reporting, in the Dublin *Sunday Tribune*, that 'Vatican officials' were not too keen on the whole business; they wished the blasted referendum had never been held; it might lead to 'serious dangers for the Catholic Church in Ireland and a greater acceptance of an "abortion ethic"'; the amendment wording was unsatisfactory, the issue was too complex for referenda, and 'there is always the possibility that some years later there will be another one which will reverse the first decision'. Besides, the bishops did not have a big enough win.

As Maud Gonne MacBride said long ago, 'Compromise never stands still.' Nor does prudence. Here we have one group of prudent politicians reproving another – for insufficient prudence. Law was estimated according to what it might lead to; present freedom was of little account compared with that. We shall see the same logic when we come to 'official' reactions to Bobby Sands and the other hunger-strikers. There was a great deal of the ethic of fear in this whole matter of the referendum; and the fears which were left to run so haphazardly were those of a destabilized society.

I arrived in Ireland, this time, a few days after the referendum results were declared, and a country which had wasted so much of its emotional substance debating before the event now settled down to debating it post factum. Individuals did this with some style. 'O the referendum,' they would cry, 'I never want to hear another word about that damned thing. Did you hear about our referendum? It was the only thing anyone ever talked about for months. I don't know myself . . .' etc. etc. The only way to short-circuit this colourful plaint was to ask, 'Which way did you vote?' It was obvious what the vote had amounted to. Those who voted followed the bishops, both in their speaking and in their not-speaking, by two to one. But almost half of the electorate did not vote at all, and the people to whom I spoke made it clear that a large part of that number was in fact a vote: a vote of non-support.

Of the slightly more than 50 per cent vote, border counties like Donegal and Cavan-Monaghan, south-western ones like Kerry South, and western ones like Mayo and Roscommon, had up to 83 per cent saying Yes; but while Cork North-West (rural) had over 80 per cent, Cork South-Central had only 55 per cent. This was the pattern throughout: the citified places have a bare affirmative majority of those voting; and Dublin actully voted No. Further, when you look carefully at the figures, you realize that there is very little difference in this respect between sophisticated, half-wealthy, cosmopolitan areas and others which might be described as petty bourgeois, or even working class. Dublin wanted nothing of any constitutional grace-notes, and it was both defiant about it and proud of it. As Seamus said to me, 'My district had the highest No vote outside Dun Laoghaire.' He and his friends who voted No are devout believers, with an attachment to the old Catholicism and many close connections to 'the religious life' through siblings who are priests and nuns. It is just that they read and discuss, and that they believe in commonsense and free speech. I hope they drew accurate conclusions about what their co-religionists think of an episcopal authority which is used in such a mystifying way, and what authority amounts to when it will not speak clearly at the proper time.

What remains of the communalism of the old Gaelic clan system is seen more vividly in politics than in other Irish ventures; and there it has an element of corruption. It survives there because of the smallness and rural provenance of the country, the fact that the civil war of 1922 provided a long-term matrix for political division, and the fact that the constituencies have from three to five seats each, filled by a complicated system of preferential voting. For all these reasons, the local machine becomes of unusual importance; an extensive business and farflung family are a great help. A friend of mine who stood as an independent claimed that he would have got a seat if only his brother, who is a local estate agent, had turned out to support him. But he did not, and he was seen not to. So parliamentary seats are passed down through the family over more than sixty years.

Dail Eireann in one year contained three pairs of brothers, one father and son, one father and daughter, several widows of former incumbents, various sons-in-law, and uncountable first and second cousins. Most Irish politicians have some rural point of reference and validation. They are the beneficiaries and bestowers of patronage; clientism is a sacrament. Such patronage has now become very public, and one young left-wing TD, Tony Gregory, won great concessions for his devastated part of north Dublin by bargaining with C.J. Haughey at the time of the formation of a government. The 'stroke', the deal, the package: there they are, waiting for their operator.

This friendly habit goes as a system and a psychology right down through the society. Like double-dipping of other sorts, which is a response to poverty, it both alleviates and creates proverty. People of inferior talent are nursed into jobs; there is not enough true competition. 'Being a postmistress', as the poet Tom McCarthy remarked, 'is a Fianna Fail job'. And so it is. In some cases, there is a residual pride of name and blood behind the nepotism; in other places, it is quite gone. It is not, for example, visible in Kildare, where the dispossession has been total.

With the south Kildare people, the big problem was how, having lost land and hierarchy, to keep any footing. No one who has not lived in an area like this can realize with what contemptuous condescension the dispossessors treat the carriers of native genius, who themselves are often grateful in a deferential and over-explanatory way for the verbal encouragements of neurotic and detached Anglos. 'Give him fair dues,' they will say, 'he didn't evict in the bad times.'

'He didn't spend all his time across the water . . . He gave a field for the youngsters . . . He built . . . sowed . . . contributed . . . He wasn't the worst.' The man of whom they speak may even have restored some of the 'monuments' his people and his caste had allowed, in their boorish ignorance, their exactions on the land, their use of 'agents', to sink into the mud and thistles.

But south Kildare is not typical; and that is by the way. With clear consciousness gone, but family patronage strong, the Irish set about creating an Ireland of the cautious. Where better than in Dail Eireann? And in the home place, where people often show a desire for two or more posts at once: the post office plus a shop or farm, or the school plus a pub, or a professor's chair plus a career in politics, or public life, or the theatre. One job, one status, is not enough. 'He wants to be himself and another', as McCarthy puts it. Each one has it in himself to be a fixer. The poet manoeuvres for a professor's job and, having got it, absents himself to work on the problem of his dual responsibility. There is clientism throughout.

It seemed to me, as a loving observer, as soon as I saw the voting figures, that the forces of traditionalism had had a serious defeat; and that among them the Catholic bishops had had the worst defeat of all, in a battle connected but not identical with that of the forces which had insisted on the amendment and the referendum and the Yes vote. For those forces may have been objectionable in all sorts of ways, but they did not fail in courage; they had fought for what they believed in. The bishops, on the other hand, had failed in courage and in purpose; and since their wavering was on the question of what might happen if they did this or that, the question must have entered the minds of some observers whether the bishops believed anything very much at all. Further, a defeat sustained by such people on such a field can never be fully compensated for. The amendment forces at least have their amendment, even if no one knows what good it will do them – or anyone. The Fianna Fail voters may have divided in the secrecy of the ballot box, but most of them will come back to heel when other issues are at stake. But what can the bishops regain?

These impressions were reinforced when I read the waiting reams of pre-referendum debate, and listened to the dozens of people only too willing to talk about it. Some of these, though not all, agreed with my impressions. Joe Carroll was one commentator who did. 'It may well be the last time,' he says, 'that Irish bishops urge Catholics how they should vote. When the votes came in, the bishops felt little inclination to triumph. For some the wrong battle had been fought at the wrong time; the church's image had been damaged by the excesses of the extremist pro-life groups; it was going to complicate the attitude of the bishops when future church-state issues would arise such as divorce, illegitimacy, reform of the contraception laws'. One bishop apparently commented, 'There were very few unaware of the attitude of their bishops and priests and yet so many voted the other way.' Yet, typically, he drew the wrong inference: the vote was 'a sign of the spirit of secularism that we have to work against'. Perhaps the attitude of the bishops themselves was the real sign of 'secularism'; for, as Carroll reports, 'By their own admission the issue was not a moral one . . . but a politico-legal one . . . In the end the bishops' statement boiled down to an appeal to vote Yes because a No vote "could well be represented as a victory for the abortion cause".'

At least three clerics gave it to me as their opinion that the bishops had been fooled by the people to whom they eventually gave such aid and comfort. One priest told me that this view was widely held among the clergy; he did not say why. He himself had managed to avoid preaching on the matter at all. A Presbyterian minister, with an impressive record on civil rights, told me that, in his opinion, Archbishop Ryan of Dublin had been trapped. My comment was that it is his business not to be trapped in these matters.

But I am an outsider, and my business was to listen. Christine, who comes from the west, talked to me at length about the traditional morality and the mores of the people. She said that the big foundling wards, 'the baby farms', were now down to a fraction of the numbers they once held. A few years ago, one place where she worked herself had held a hundred babies, aged from six days to ten weeks; all were offered for adoption. Now, there might be ten; the young mothers are keeping their babies. This, however, involves them in a wandering pattern of semi-migration. If they are country girls, and they usually are, they can't go home again. In the country, shame is the fourth cardinal virtue, or at least has a head start on cleanliness in getting next to godliness. Home is where you can't take your 'illegitimate' baby. Of one girl Christine said, 'O her father would behead her from the waist up'; an appallingly instructive phrase. Another girl had gone with her boyfriend to her local church to ask to be married; she was visibly pregnant, and this was the west, so the curate shouted at her she was not to cross the threshold of the church. 'The life of the unborn honoured everywhere save in church,' I said. Yes, said Christine; she agreed that these were barbarities; she had made the instinctive connection between the vehemence of the referendum campaign and the unresolved psychological problems of some places in Ireland. Your shame is a great nurse to your life-hatred. The proponents of the Yes vote may have unwittingly struck a blow both at Catholic authority and at wholesome farm-fed shame.

As to the violence, it was not spoken of very much, but it seemed to me that there was a permanent subterranean preoccupation with it. Anyone whom you ask bluntly enough will say that he or she expects it to grow. Many expect violence to 'spread' from the north to 'down here'. Others see the two violences as similar. Still others assign them to the same cause.

When I arrived this time, the last of the hunger-strikers was almost two years dead. No one, I noticed, offered to speak of them; when I did so, as I occasionally did, I noticed a new look come into people's eyes. This too may have been a kind of shame; for they knew I had written about it, and they generally had not. A corporate effort had been made to drive those buried men deep in the human mind again; but it had not succeeded, for they sprouted questions, doubts and dissatisfactions. The people who did not speak in 1981 had learned something by 1983; despite their silence, nothing had got better. They had no better government, no more money; no one loved or admired them more; success had not grown down to them on a golden and blessed thread. On the contrary: every week a factory closed, a ministerial promise was broken; the unemployment rate in Cork city sprang to 22 per cent, rivalling the wastelands of the north; nothing worked with complete assurance; drugs and violence became nightmares. And, in the north, not only had the armed struggle not ceased or slackened, but it had spread into the political arena; Provisional Sinn Fein had just gained 40 per cent of the total nationalist vote in the six counties elections; it had 103,000 votes, only 40,000 fewer than the much-publicized SDLP. Everyone who thought about the matter knew these facts; but there were others, less known or more specialized, to be added to them. Demographic surveys showed, for example, that the Catholic percentage of the population had 'gone up' (it may have been under-estimated earlier) from 34 to somewhere between 38.5 and 42 (depending on how the figures were computed); and there was a heavier and heavier concentration of Catholics west of the river Bann. The significance of these three sets of facts will emerge only with time; but they mean that Sinn Fein is now running on a sweeter track than it was three years ago. The nationalists are more numerous than was thought, they are grouped more densely than before, and they are voting in dramatically increasing numbers against the existence of the Orange statelet.

The people I met did not often mention these things, for they did not willingly think of the north, and were certainly not given by RTE the chance to think about it; but they were all aware that the situation there had thickened, as it were. They too had become gently but stubbornly anti-British in the intervening two years: responding to Mrs Thatcher's invitation to see her as embodying Britishness, they had not liked the dogmatic and aggressive form which the body plainly had. They did not like the British insults to their own government, they did not believe in British notions of peace, and they no longer saw Britain as having favourable intentions towards them and theirs. Anti-British feeling is now stronger than I have seen it in ten years; it is only its mode that is subdued. Underneath all this they suspect that they may have been too hasty in accepting the official British view of Irish hunger-strikers in 1981.

It is now plain that the British policy of 'criminalization' (to insist that, after a certain date, republican activity was merely a criminal conspiracy, and republican offenders merely common criminals) goes with the policy of 'Ulsterization' (which means devolving British army power on to northern Protestant police and army units). The first caused the hunger-strike, and the second led to the pattern of killings that now covers the north. From the British point of view, the joint policy may seem a sensible arrangement to minimize the oppressiveness of their own presence, and get fewer Englishmen shot: of course, it gets Irishmen shot instead. For it has the effect of delivering the whole nationalist (Catholic) population into the hands of its immediate enemies, of making police and warders targets for republican assassination squads, and of pushing the republicans into the position of being the sole targets of the security forces.

Everyone knows what the IRA is and does; the same is true of the UDA. They are political/military organizations. Everyone knows that they do not regard most of their activities as being in any way criminal, though some certainly are. Their view may be right or wrong; but it is the view they hold.

Everyone also knows that crime-fighting bodies should not commit crimes. Sometimes they do. In the north, crimes are committed by republican groups, the UDA and UVF, the British army, the police, the Ulster Defence Regiment (UDR), as well as plain criminals. But they and their crimes are not treated equally; Republicans get special treatment in the direction of severity, while troops get a bewildering range of punishments and indulgences. If it were asked why this should be so, Real-politik might put on his judge's cap and answer, 'The consequences of their crimes are worse for the *rem publicam*.' (I do not say 'the state', although Sir Real Politik might.) Again, this may or may not be true; but it is a point completely at odds with Mrs Thatcher's cry that 'a crime is a crime is a crime', that all crimes are the same. I can quite see that a given IRA operation might be regarded as a military one, morally neutral, or as criminal, or as virtuous, according to point of view; but the British always judge it as criminal, and punish it with unequal severity, not because of the deed itself but because of its supposed consequences.

It is necessary to insist that some deeds are evil, and do not admit of these alternative descriptions; it is also necessary to say that some do.

So, if between 1981 and 1983 the Irish 'forgot' the hunger-strikes, they did not forget the Falklands war. Nor did the English, both hawks and doves. They have not forgotten, and they won't. They may feel pride or anger, but they do not seem characteristically to feel shame; they are not given to crises of identity, and they have nothing to repress.

But the Irish who forget the hunger-strikes for conversational purposes also remember them on another level: they know the strikers, including those who went off the strike, were men of high calibre, and they grow more aware that the Sinn Fein activists are increasingly young people of similar calibre. As Sinn Fein spreads out through the community, engaging in community politics, this becomes more evident; that is why, a few weeks after I left Ireland, the Sinn Fein vote in a Dublin by-election went up considerably, while that of the Labour Party shrivelled.

It may be that this, and the self-confidence gained by the people of the cities from their capacity to vote No against their bishops, and the forming of co-operatives in Cork, and the anti-drug vigilantes in the slum districts, and the persistence of many Irish journalists in a free path, will provide the optimistic counter-balance to the savage deterioration I have noted elsewhere in Irish life. In the past, a sense of purpose has been maintained by Christianity (chiefly

Catholicism), nationalism, remnants of clan communalism, and the hegemony of poetry and music. Now the first two of these are weakened, the third perverted, and part of the fourth a battleground. Communalism has been destroyed psychologically, by consensus individualism plus various forms of cowardice. But behaviourally it still exists, sustained by courtesy, responsiveness to the human note, and a kind of self-renewing liveliness.

Chapter Two

ARRIVING IS ALMOST AS HARD

You tend to remember your arrivals in Ireland, perhaps because none of the points of entry, even Dublin, has anything of the huge, maze-like, heavily industrial, impersonal quality of great airports such as New York or Heathrow. Instead, it has a smalltown, even rural character, and is not divorced from its natural setting. I am not aiming to endorse sentimentality, or create an odour of ecstasy; but it is a fact that arrival in Ireland is apt to be, at first, reassuring, even if it is found later to be slightly offputting.

In any case, we may as well avoid the selective and sentimental way of the important German novelist Heinrich Böll, whose *An Irish Journal* tells of his long love-affair with Ireland. His account of his first visit opens with a girl smiling on a window-sill in the early morning as she takes in her jug of milk – that heavily symbolic milk. Ireland, we register at once, is a pastoral country, a dairying country, a land given to cattle. James Joyce's *Ulysses* also begins with a milkwoman, but somewhat older. Milkwoman, the window, the sea. Like Böll I too first arrived in Dublin in the early morning, and saw sights such as he saw. But context is all. Dublin, sleazy at the best of times (whenever they may have been), was then crammed with unemployment. It was the mid fifties, and workless men stood everywhere, as on a smaller scale they did for Böll, in O'Connell Street, along the docks, outside Westland Row station, all along Clanbrassil Street and the South Circular Road. Not so much gathered as left. Hawking and spitting. Talking and smoking. Spitting. Crying 'fecking' or 'fockin''. Murmuring from the sides of their mouths. Making their parts of Dublin which, for the visitor arriving by sea, are also his first parts, unbearably comfortless, sweat-caked and cold.

Phlegm capital of the world.

On the first or second trip, in the mid fifties, coming from Liverpool, we had a lot of luggage roped under tarpaulin on the open deck. All promises delivered in England about how and when it could be got off were obviously null and void. No uniformed person knew or would say. It was time to turn to the non-uniformed ones, the men of no property, the hawkers and spitters. On Dublin docks I approached a group of idlers, who considered my case most politely, indeed with a deference mounting to pity, before deciding whether they would release the secret. 'Go down there, turn left, then left again, and ask for Sean.' Sean! the most common name in Ireland. Still, I did it, and there was a Sean, or someone pretending for the moment, and he did get it off for me: as a favour, using brazenly uninstitutional methods, and refusing a tip. He had seen my daughter Brigid's five-year-old face, and was captivated.

On that or the next visit, we faced the customs men. Book censorship at that time in Ireland was a wonder of generalized bigotry; but I had forgotten that, and when the customs man tapped the brown paper carrier bag in my hand and demanded, 'What's in that?' I answered; 'Books!' he half-shouted, looking up sharply. 'Not banned books!' 'I've no idea,' I said. 'what books are banned here?' He was a large ageing man with a fire-red face, like the parish priest of some child's nightmare. 'Give us a look. Give us a look,' he yelled. The top exhibit was a copy of *Masses Ouvriere*, a French left-wing Catholic journal. 'What's this? What's this?' he carolled, scenting a winner. 'Well, it's a French . . .' I began, but he had already thrown it on the counter and was facing the next. This said in firm gold capitals on a black ground *Holy Roman Missal*, and I could see his mind clicking from disappointment to renewed suspicion to resignation; but he knew when he was licked. Into Ireland, fly as you please, with the help of Sean and of some unlikely Providence.

On that occasion we came to occupy an Ireland of the Poverties, just entering on its phase of half-maddened equilibrium while moving from the mentality of rural to that of urban petty-bourgeois consumerism. It was consumerism without goods. The fifties were an awful time for Ireland. Many years later, entering Dublin by air from Canada, I met another customs man. For some reason, I was through the arrival gates long before anyone else, and the customs man seated at the small desk seemed surprised to see me. Again, I was carrying an open carrier bag, this time full of small carvings and other Indian and Eskimo artefacts. 'Anything to declare?' 'No.' 'What's in the bag?', and I produced the objects one by one, to exclamations of wonder and pleasure from the youngish functionary. 'Well, isn't that grand now!', and so on. As always, I became immediately intoxicated by the whiff of simple human feeling that you get in Ireland, and expatiated light-headedly on the provenance of the articles, Cree Indians, Vancouver, and sacred ceremonies, all to the accompaniment of 'That's a lovely one now' and 'Is that a fact now?', ending with, 'Welcome to Ireland. And God bless.' In any other country you might have expected a question about value or price. The Irish are generally too courteous and, whether they are wearing a uniform or not ('Sure, it's just a job, after all'), delighted by whatever diversion comes their way. Eye to eye contact is also important, as are rhetorical and lyrical sayings, sounds and devices.

All these are features of the national temperament and value-system, but they also reflect social fact. Dublin and its airport only play at being cosmopolitan: or, perhaps I should say, they are cosmopolitan in everything but ambience. They are regional, a smalltown entry to a largely sequestered delight. The visitors for whom they are prepared are returning emigrants and casual friendly strangers: people who come to remember or to savour. They are not geared up for dignitaries, big businessmen or millionaire hedonists, although no doubt many individuals approximating to these types have passed through their doors. Air fares are now so high that at least half of each flight consists of business people. Further, the setting of the airport itself is to an extent rural; the plane descends across a deliciously small, clear coastline to a runway set among fields full of cattle, by now so modern that they do not even look up at the sound. As the writer, Tony Grey, says:

the sharpness of the east wind that slices across the tarmac at Dublin Airport
is the first intimation visitors to Ireland get that this is indeed a different
country. The freshness of the wind is another. Sharp and clean and smelling
slightly of seaweed and salt, it is different from the ersatz stuff you have
been breathing in London, as Alpine brook water from London tap.

Nearly twenty years later, this is still true. You can almost always
smell the grass and the sea through or behind the creeping reek of
benzine and diesel which afflicts the inner city, all the more savagely
since Irish petrol contains a lot of lead. That is miles away, and at the
airport, close though it is to the main Belfast road and the stupefied
high-rise flats of Ballymun, you are smelling a small rich pastoral
earth, very far from the mixture of benzine, stained cloud and door
varnish which gets to you at Heathrow. Bord Failte should call
Dublin Airport 'The Airfield of the Cows', which would go well
with the ethos of Ireland in its heroic age, based on the ownership of
cattle. It is always a joy to arrive by this means, even though you
notice straightaway that the familiar shabbiness and aimlessness are
still there: from the wandering look of the cleaners to the jaunty flat-
footedness of many of the cabs, which look as if too many returning
bums have sat on those springs. Then, if you have sent luggage ahead,
and have now to get it out of bond, the dealings with Customs come
to seem endless; more than once I have engaged in the hopeless
defensive ploy of demanding to know what is happening. Nothing,
that's what! On one occasion I said, 'If it's not ready in ten minutes,
I'm going,' and after ten minutes set off resolutely towards the defeat
of departure, only to be called back, 'Hoy there! Hoy!', and to be
called 'Sir', and to receive the stuff. They had been testing me: 'If you
go, we'll have to send it out to you.' 'That's all right.' 'It will be at
your expense.' 'Don't you believe it.' I think this slowness is a device
to give the impression of busyness, to preserve jobs in a rapidly
shrinking market, where nothing very much, after all, is now
coming into the Customs store at Dublin Airport. We did, on two
occasions in 1981, have stuff delivered. One of these deliveries turned

out to be by way of a courtesy trip. One rainy evening in Rathfarnham, a small van pulled up, a cheerful Dubliner handed over
some goods, and refused payment. 'On the house, is it?' I asked. 'I was
in Sydney for two years, so I thought I'd bring it meself.' He was
evidently a foreman, and Australia was often in his thoughts. 'Wish I
was there now.'

Such people have the adventurous disposition of minor entrepreneurs; they are not mere functionaries. The airport employee
who usually has charge of luggage lost in transit is highly efficient:
the expert operator of an inefficient system, which is inefficient
largely because of the cumbersome transfer arrangements and the
prevalence of theft at Heathrow; cases get lost (or 'lost') in the rush. It
is surprising that so few disappear entirely; after all, there is nothing
posh about the Heathrow arrangements for Irish flights. On the
contrary, as you are beckoned, searched, and led, you feel shuffled
into some corner of unimportance; you are being trained to accept
some menial role and status.

For one thing, the searchers and the searched almost never speak to
one another; this is depressing but inevitable, for whereas no one
wants to be bombed, no one wants to be demeaned, either. Once I saw
a jolly Irishman, slightly jarred, attempt a joke to two Englishmen
who were interrogating him; but the demeanour of the searchers is
that of guardians of virtue, and they insist on an inscrutability not to
be broken through by Celtic irresponsibility; the unyielding
superiority is shared by all searchers, men and women, English,
Scots, blacks and Asians (not that they exactly proliferate). When
trade is slack, they turn this to an equally inscrutable casualness, and
'joke' gutturally among themselves. The jolly Irishman could not
face this threatening system of signals, and actually failed to take the
flight. His desire to win alien hearts was unusual; generally, while
the Irish show no hostility, they show no interest, either. They are
relaxed where the searchers are tense, and the groups simply ignore
each other; the travellers almost all head straight for the tiny
duty-free shop to get their quota of booze and cigarettes. The holding

area is a place of entirely private feeling. The common mood is as distinctive, and as distinctively 'ethnic', as it was a little earlier, on the concourse, as they waited to be called through the gates into the departure areas. On the concourse, you can always tell when a Dublin or a Cork flight is about to leave. You don't even have to hear a voice; the dress, the 'racial' appearance, the air of relaxation, the informality verging on shabbiness, the lack of the hooligan look which you can see at other spots on the concourse, the casual, uninsistent, unapprehensive exchanges among strangers. My friend Jonathan White has also noticed this distinctiveness, although he has no 'Irish connection' and hence no ethnic empathy.

Anyway, it is foolish to send large quantities of luggage ahead, because then you will have to go through Ordeal by Customs, with its base in manana-thinking and its aim of testing your detachment, a virtue of which some Irish people have a lot, most people have some, and I have none at all. The rule on Irish visits is travel light, and be responsible for yourself; then customs and immigration will hardly concern you. In fact, immigration officers don't even meet the flights from Britain.

Now that the struggle in the six northern counties is so advanced, and the ties between Irish and British governments so strong and complex, if rarely visible, coming into Ireland can be fraught with prohibitions. In 1981, when I had been living there already for seven months, and had paid three months rent in advance to live in marvellous working conditions in County Kildare, I set off to go to an international writers' conference, organized for Amnesty International, in Toronto; there I was to give two papers and a poetry reading. My chosen route took me through Heathrow, my contact with English soil being limited to the bus ride from Terminal 1 to Terminal 3. Trouble arose only when I passed through the immigration desk to catch the Canadian flight. The smart young interrogator wanted to know where in England I would be living on my return and, when I told him I would be going straight to Ireland, became very 'concerned', consulted a book on the desk (*How to Look*

Concerned? Keep Them in Their Place?) and a computer list of terrorists, prohibited persons and, no doubt, Irish-Australian poets, suspended under the desk. Then, in spite of my growing impatience, and not meeting my eyes, he stamped the passport briskly and said, 'Report to the Irish authorities in Dublin.' 'What does your stamp say?' I asked. 'I have given you permission to stay in the UK for twenty-one days,' he said. 'But what has that to do with Ireland?' I asked. 'It also entitles you to stay in Air for twenty-one days,' he said; and then the row started, and he had to meet my eyes.

But it was all legal, as in my furious astonishment I found out; because of those barely visible ties between governments, an English immigration officer can determine the length of my stay in Ireland. I was told the same thing by a much nicer version of the original interrogator as I passed through immigration at Heathrow on my way home to Kildare. 'What Irish authorities?' I said. 'I'm living in Ireland. You've had a fortnight to check up with the Kildare police on whether my wife and children, my rented house and my unpaid bills, are where I said I left them. Just whom are you asking me to see, and why?' 'The Irish immigration officers,' he said. 'Have you ever flown to Dublin?' I said. No. Of course not. 'Immigration officers don't meet English flights,' I said. 'They're rarer than hen's teeth at the airport.' To the 'authorities' in Dublin Castle, then; he would give me a phone number. Special Branch, is it, I said. I imagine so, he said.

I prepared myself to 'report' to the Dublin interrogators in that seat of ancient foreign (English) power, Dublin Castle, now an administrative centre for the Irish Republic, which itself is known incorrigibly to British bureaucrats as 'Air'. Eventually I did; and I was put in touch with a superintendent whose sense of the drama and urgency of my case was so under-developed that in the end he seemed more interviewed than interviewing. When asked what legislation it was that required me, an Irishman born in Australia and an Australian national, to accept Irish residence at the say-so of an Englishman, he courteously murmured something about 'alien registration'. 'But almost all my forebears were Irish,' I said. 'I can't possibly regard

myself as an alien in this country.' 'Yes,' he said, for, unlike the
Englishman, he could see some humour in it all, and thought Necess-
ity the mother of Procrastination. 'I can see it makes you sound like a
little green man.' 'I *am* a little green man,' I said.

None of the Irish seemed to feel any sense of urgency about my
registering with them, but I came to the conclusion that I had better
do it if I were to have a clear passage into England later that year;
when I came to register, the grain of conscription in the Irish casualness came out, and I was asked for our passports, which would be
returned to me later. 'When?' 'About six weeks.' 'How?' 'By mail.'
'Certainly not,' I said, for I had started to have weekly confrontations
with the Irish mail system, 'nobody will be given possession of my
passports. If you want to register me, do it now.' And they did, with
as much ungracious impersonality as they could muster, which was
not much, for the Irish may make you wait for an hour, but it upsets
them to have you sitting there for a day (unless they have forgotten
all about you, that is).

Anyway, in 1955 all that was a long way in the future, and I was
having very few dealings with officialdom. The aim was to scrape
by, and we had very little money for amenities. Our general style was
one of poverty, and our general ethos was make-do. No university or
other institution financed my trips to the places about which I was to
write so much; I was offered no free trips, I knew no wealthy
individuals who had the makings of hosts for a married poet the
lining of whose overcoat was hanging in tatters, and of course I had
no 'private means', those resources which have a habit of becoming
public, even ostentatious, as soon as you have enough of them. Therefore, we had to choose rooms very carefully, and give some thought
to cafés, and consider a little cautiously where to move on to, and
when. There was no question of renting cars, and we would not look
for ways of 'living off the country'.

The first day of my first trip to Dublin, I left our belongings in the
B and B place we had chosen in Portobello (these B and B places have
a strange and reassuring resemblance to one another, perhaps because
so many of them were built in the same era, and the women who run

them seem to come from a common family, with marked religious opinions), and I went for a walk up South Circular Road. Phlegm capital of the world. And at least in the final judging for turds capital, too. I passed Collins Barracks, named for the famous organizer and guerrilla fighter, Michael Collins, and there I had a random, crazy thought, I wonder if Sean O'Faolain is in the phone book, for I had been reading *The Bell* and thought him in his own way a great and admirable freedom fighter. Into the phone booth, and sure enough he was in the book. I then did something I had never done before, and have never done since, I rang an eminent writer who was a complete stranger.

A woman answered, seemed uncertain what to do, said, 'O I'll see if he's in. We've just come back from the races.' When O'Faolain came to the phone, he said, 'Vincent Buckley. Your name suggests that you're Irish, and your voice suggests that you're English. What are you?' 'Australian,' I said, laughing. Ah. It was all done as easily as writing a cheque, and we met next day to spend the afternoon in the lounge of the Shelbourne, where he drank Dubonnet and looked cosmopolitan in tweeds, while I drank whiskey and gurgled Gaelic salutations. What interested me was not so much his agreeing to meet an unknown and unimportant person (for the Irish, while they are contemptuous of 'chancers', are taken with the unusual), but the fact that he enquired so acutely about Australia. He wanted to know about Australian writing, the theatre, the universities; but most of all he wanted (after having shrewdly sounded me out) to know about Catholic Action, Santamaria, Mannix, the Labor split, and how civil liberties in Australia and in the Catholic church would be affected by recent upheavals. Since his standpoint on these matters was pretty much my own, a good time was had by all. I have never seen him since, and am grateful to him for letting me know that for some Irishmen Australia mattered as a place of discourse and cultural experiment, not simply as a setting for odd holidays or a haven in which you could forget Ireland and make a lot of money.

*   *   *

'Arriving is almost as hard', says my poem. As hard as what? As leaving, for one thing. To leave a country like Ireland is peculiarly hard, and 'leave' means something different from 'leaving' America. You leave New York or San Francisco, any one of the great opposites; but leaving Ireland from any point you feel you are leaving the whole; for everything is so close together, reinforcing everything else on the mind's retina. The fifties were a period of high and poignant emigration, and a great deal of it was to England, Wales or Scotland, often to virtual disappearance in an environment so different from the place of origin, but often to establish a base from which the migrant's relationship to Ireland would be that of hungry revenant: never again totally the son or daughter, never the mere expatriate either, but the person of two homes, the lost and the chosen. It is impossible to over-stress the ambivalence of all this, for Britain had in many cases come to be chosen.

At that time I travelled always on the mailboat, from Holyhead to Dun Laoghaire or Liverpool to Dublin; and I can report without undue sentimentality that, each time, it was concertinas home and bitter silence back. More than once I saw people dancing and singing, on deck or in the saloon, in the middle of the Irish sea; but it was always *en route* to Ireland. On the way back to Britain to what was technically or really home for most of the travellers, I never heard one note of equable music. At the time I romantically thought this psychic arrangement apt; now I find it quite strange. Yet, then, many of the travellers were seriously disoriented, not even remotely up to re-orienting themselves in a new country. A Melbourne taxi-driver, a Wicklow man, told me that when he left home, at sixteen, he carried a few pound notes rolled up inside his shoe; by the time he got to Cricklewood, they had disintegrated. Yet the thought was good; it was the prior briefing that was defective. More than once I gave lifts in a taxi to young people whose cousins or brothers had failed to meet them at Euston. The Legion of Mary had volunteers boarding every ship to see to the worries of departing migrants, but they could not adequately oversee them at the point of arrival. The Irish were like seeds cast into a furrow but blown by a foreign wind into marsh or ditch; there was a limit to what anyone could do for them. Older migrants, including people in their twenties, men in the 'building trade', men and women in 'the catering trade' or 'service', sat waiting for the boat train calm, purposeful, sad. In July 1957, the day after a mass internment of republicans, picked up in hundreds after a series of police sweeps, the boat we were taking back to Liverpool was full of depressed women and agitated children. I was reading *The United Irishman*, and some of them started talking to me. They were the families of republicans, going for safety to their relations in England.

Another time, having a drink in the bar, I noticed a great tall Donegalman drinking, and singing 'Brennan on the Moor'. I remember his overcoat trailing. Half an hour later I came back, and he was fighting five men, three of whom were trying to clap him in irons. I was standing next to a wondering Englishman, who turned out to be a sales rep., or travelling salesman, as they were called in those days. 'What happened?' I said. 'I don't know,' he said. 'One minute he was singing, and the next he and his mate were trying to kill each other.' Actually, they looked like brothers, thus making the scenario more logical.

The arrivals at Dun Laoghaire at 6 am should be disconsolate, for if it's not cold it's wet, but the arriving travellers bustle off to somewhere they want to reach. If you are waiting, to meet someone, you feel like an animal hiding in a world of darkness which is furtive and scared and may itself be animal. But the spirit is one of fulfilment. And arrivals by air, however bizarre or sloppily arranged they may be in detail, can be counted on to have panache. On one occasion, flying into Shannon from Montreal, with the schedules mixed up in some way, I found myself with an overcrowded plane some hours late, and the hostesses flustered almost into incoherence. We bucketed across Ireland from west to east, at a height that seemed a couple of thousand feet, performing to an audience of every creature that lived on the island and was capable of looking up: speed, rocketing; object, to reduce lateness; demeanour of cabin crew, agitated and extraordinarily sweet; demeanour of my neighbours, gabby, self-revelatory, a little polemical (against dole bludgers): 'Well, we can't all work in the Bank of Ireland,' I said. 'I work in the Allied Irish actually,' said my nearest neighbour. 'But you must admit I'm right. You have the same in your own country,' she said triumphantly (for she had spent six weeks in Sydney). At any moment I expected a cow or a pig to point upward and cry out; you could see the shadow of the plane crossing them. It was all green, and very beautiful, and varied, and ad hoc, and there was nothing portentous about it at all.

Chapter Three

FATE AND OUTER SUBURBS

It will be understandable, however, if in a book like this I do not waste much time on leavings, since these are the occasions on which, if you are going to be rooked at all, someone will rook you. I am no stranger to the workings of that arcane truth, even though, every time it happens, I am quite disconcerted. When I said to Larry Mulryan's mother that I disliked the town of Kilcullen because, of the few people in Ireland who had tried to cheat me, three were from there, 'A few!' she exclaimed. 'You can't have been here long.' She was certainly as much in the right as I.

But settling in, with all its banalities and second thoughts, has a much larger range of possible forms, and it is likely to tell you more about the place and the people. Charm has a way of going underground, at such times, only to reappear, like a devious spring, in a still more engaging way some time on. So it was with my wife, Penelope, and our daughters Susannah and Grania.

When we arrived in 1977 (Grania not yet part of the family), it was March, in Ireland a lashing month that unravels before the blossom opens, and which can produce heavy rains, sleet, and freezing winds. It is not a month for arriving in if there is the least doubt about where you are going to stay. The poet Tom Kinsella had booked us into a guesthouse, but we did not learn until we got to his house that there was no crib or cot in the guesthouse, which was not equipped for babies and whose owner was taking us only as a favour to Kinsella. Nor did the Kinsellas have one; nor did their neighbours. We rang another poet, Seamus Deane, who alerted us to a cradle (Heaney's very own) at Seamus Heaney's house; but Heaney did not answer the phone, and the lovely old cradle, though it existed, remained out of use. We had to rush downtown to a department store and buy a portable one.

That set the pattern of our attempts to settle ourselves in Dublin that particular year. The rain lashed down, the wind blew freezing gusts at every footfall. There was nowhere to eat. Kinsella turned out and gallantly drove us to look at houses for rent. We quickly took one of these, in Dundrum, which had once been a village on the way to the Wicklow mountains but was now a suburb composed of 'estates'. Out past the mental hospital we went, wincing at its enormous stone walls, bouncing on the rutted and narrowing road, up the long steep hill from Dundrum village towards Sandyford and the mountains. Opposite the house was a small wood, Balally. Our new landlord, who later became a friend, engaged in a bit of private negotiation which by this time I suspect to be characteristic of Irish property-owners. 'What did Lisneys quote you?' he asked. 'A hundred and twenty pounds a month,' I said. 'It's worth a hundred and forty,' he said. 'That may be so,' I said, 'but I was quoted a hundred and twenty.' When owner and prospective tenant come face to face, it is common for the owner to dispense with his or her agent, the auctioneer through whom the contact was made. It had happened to me before, and was to happen again: 'If I let it to you for less than the twelve months, then Lisneys needn't be involved,' said one. 'That's between you and them,' I said. 'I'll report to them in any case that I'm taking the flat.' Things were not as crass with the Dundrum house. As we lived there, we came to realize how steep that hill was, and how close to the baby's pusher came the traffic, especially the small, rough-looking, inexpertly loaded trucks which lurched up the road shedding pieces of concrete, timber, iron, objects of various sorts, and leaving a permanent haze of cement dust in the air.

Outer Dublin is cement coloured. It colours roads, driveways, kerbs, and half of almost every house. We were in an 'estate', which contained a playground and a school, but no churches or shops; all the amenities were down in the 'village'. When it was a village, the narrowing road suited it; but as the estates grew away from that centre in irregular curves and semi-circles which became tunnels for the sweeps of the wind that blew from the hills, the more cars were needed, and the more people needed to rely on the public buses.

All of this was makeshift, almost everything had been added at the last minute. Once, we were told, a house caught fire, and it exploded as if it was built of kindling. The big advantage of the houses was that they each had four bedrooms, two fairly big, which tells something obvious about Irish life. This estate specialized in small curves and culs de sac, to slow down the traffic. On the 'main' road, however, the traffic went, lurchingly, as fast as it could. The bus ran past our place to the beautiful small village of Enniskerry, to Powerscourt demesne, and, beyond that, to the Wicklow mountains. On its way, it passed through the Dublin hills, whipping and leaning up roads which were often not much wider than country lanes or boreens. We often rode on it, marvelling that within a mile of drear Dundrum we would be attending on swelling land, hills, foothills, mountains sloping in all directions; and it was great to have a routine city bus that would get you into the mountains. For domestic purposes, however, the bus service was hopelessly inefficient, largely because the suburban roads had not been designed for large vehicles, and could hardly accommodate them. That is the charitable explanation, anyway; Dubliners blamed the public service mind, and almost every Dubliner will tell you that his is 'recognized as the worst service in Dublin'. That honour must be claimed by the Enniskerry line. Day after day a bus would be up to an hour late. Often two buses in succession would fail to arrive (cancelled, or broken-down, or forgotten), and often this would be at lunchtime, when the harassed women of Dundrum and Sandyford were lugging their shopping up the hill to get their children for lunch. Often I waited, cursing, with my own laden bags; and I learned a lot about Irish patience. The foiled passengers, whatever their needs or anxieties, would simply stand there and bear it. The rain would burst from the roofs of the cottages behind them, drenching them and their infants. They would say nothing; or the ones who essayed good cheer would gossip, and those with a touch of the rebel might venture a quiet query. Sometimes frustration would break out when women with kids at heel would clout and humiliate a child rather than complain about the transport. I was the only agitator, and once or twice I rang the bus company, CIE, to find that they too were possessors of Irish fatalism and victims of Irish fate. When a bus finally came, the dripping women would help one another aboard, and the harassed conductor would bestow pleasantries right and left as he stowed their bags and shopping jeeps for a journey of no more than a mile.

Fatalism shared is a sense of humour. It can even be charity.

My friend Seamus Deane, poet and professor, impatient Derryman, caught a bus in Ranelagh some three years after that. It was one of the bold new buses (Bombardiers, or some such Imperial name) which CIE had had made under British licence, and of which it was unrealistically proud. The bus went a mile and stopped, broken down. Everybody sat there in the Irish fashion, until after twenty minutes Deane got off and stalked away. After half a mile, the bus passed him, and the driver leaned out and called to him, 'O ye of little faith.' A furlong further on, it broke down again.

In Dundrum, however, our bus breakdowns were not small-scale, like that. Nor were we living in a city environment, strictly speaking; we were at an environmental boundary-line, where housing and wild grass encroached on each other. It was middle-class outer Dublin in its pioneering phase. Around the corner was a pub called The Lamb Doyle's, balanced on a hilly corner. Around another was the stretch of road where the British ambassador had been blown up in his car a year or so before. Around a long curve to the left was Leopardstown racecourse, beautifully set among woods, and approached between leafy fields and stone walls where, I am afraid, new estates were preparing. Around a curve to the right, somewhere near Stepaside, was a tiny broken ancient Celtic cross standing in open roadway, mica flashing modestly in its blocky trunk, outside a churchyard. Pieces of an estate edged near it. There was much concrete, cement, and grey stone growing into the patches of cold green jungle. And all the way to the right you caught the first swelling of the Dublin and Wicklow mountain system: Three Rock and Two

Rock mountains, Tibradden beyond, Glencullen to the front, and beyond them the Great Sugar Loaf, Kippure, and Djouce Mountain. Suburbia will never get into some of these areas, for they are too desolate and cold, worn down into huge gullies and rounded inaccessible mountain-mounds by too many millennia.

I said 'middle class', and so the usual demographic accounts would have it, but the title is misleading. There were so many gradations of working class and petty bourgeois that there was a general impression of classlessness. That too was misleading; for within this sameness the gradations (whatever they were) were acutely perceived and firmly insisted on by those to whom they applied, and there was much minute snobbery; further, Dundrum was a staging-point on the way upwards for people just into the profession or executive castes. It was a between land. Among those who trudged up and down the hill, seeking souls or merely listeners, were two Mormons, one tall and haughty-looking, the other short, stocky and bandy, falling further behind his mate as the hill got steeper. Both looked permanently depressed, and there was not much mateship there. There were also travelling people, members of an 'itinerant' family of professional beggars asking for food, blankets, or money. They arrived in groups of three or four women and girls, working the street. While one came to your front door, another would move nimbly towards the back, and a third would clamber over the low fence towards your neighbour's back door. If you answered the door, your beggar would be joined by the others, who would take part in the demands: 'And, chentleman, give me some blankets.' 'And, chentleman, some tea and sugar.' 'Just a pound note, chentleman.' These seemed to belong to a family of thieves, and to be much more pert and confident than most travelling people. The people of Dundrum were in no position to afford their depredations. Another woman, accompanied by a child or two, grew into the habit of calling in every so often. She was a deserted wife, who had come to live as a squatter in a ruined house down the hill. We gave her money, for we had no blankets of our own. She also sought advice on how to deal with a government welfare agency; her husband was in England, 'not a bad man, you know, but reckless'; she was always neatly dressed. When things became better for her, she came up the hill to tell us: it looked as if everything would be all right now. But where were the local support groups for cases like hers? Apart from the over-burdened St Vincent de Paul Society, they seem hardly to exist in such areas; fatalism, apathy, atomism and anxious good cheer seem to prevent them coming into existence.

To a fatalistic people, deprived neighbours are an eighth plague.

But at that time Dundrum was quietly prosperous; parents spent most of their attention holding their families and futures together. The price of petrol and of housing had not yet reached alarming size; they were just about to do so; the pound was still firm in international markets, and had not yet been placed on a devaluatory slide by being removed from parity with sterling and joined to the European currencies, which keep it chronically skinny; then, too, Ireland had not yet fallen into the electoral impasse in which, since a clear majority seems less likely at each election, people begin to wonder whether the country is governable by democratic means; and the national finances were causing worry which had not yet graduated to panic or despair.

For families, it was 'go day by day'.

A short way up the hill was the Irish Management Institute, a body full of some mysterious executive expertise, in whose grounds we used to stroll among the fallen jewel-buds of the oak, and where we discovered some lovely Australian gum trees. One building was marked Memory Ireland. No doubt it was something to do with computer banks, but it seemed to me a good symbol for a country which, far from having too much of a national or military memory, has lost whatever memory it ever had; so that Memory Ireland lives on only in a few hundred isolationist old heads wondering why the national television station has to present that imported junk. Memory is a small native animal which lives in deep wooded places, under the burying rain from England and the stifling mulch from

Brussels. Without it the living is day to day, or at any rate summer to summer.

People ascribed vices such as ignorance, prudishness and repression to 'the times'. 'O that hadn't been heard of in those times', they would say. There was no suggestion of forces of nature. As victims of change, they perceived it not as a matter of choice but as things that happened or did not. It was a way of being mentally programmed for going away, of course, for the migrant boat; but that is no longer so open to them.

On the way to Memory Ireland and the gum trees we would pass the surgery of Dr Brophy, Alo Brophy. He was one of the characters of the district, a forthright friendly overbearing man who kept a boat in his front garden, and as he came to know you would make patriotic speeches about why the west of Ireland is the best place for holidays. He would never give you a prescription or 'script' if he could find a 'sample', and to do that he would leap and clamber up to the top of a cupboard (a 'press' in Irish usage) where samples were spread like debris. He was an excellent doctor, 'especially for children', so the mothers said, for he probably told them too many home truths about Valium to be considered 'good with adults'. He was one of the fine doctors I have had over the years in Ireland.

He had one irritating habit, however. He had a security alarm system on the side of his house and, like most Dublin alarm systems, it was temperamental. One day it started shrilling, on and on, making a screech tunnel of Sandyford Road; after a couple of hours I went out and looked up and down the street, half-expecting to see some rescuer coming with pliers and screwdriver and mystery-key; for at that time I had no idea that Dubliners never interfere in or query matters of bum alarm signals, and will let them rave on for days. No one. June Rafferty was stretched out on a *chaise longue* on next door's front porch, in a bathing suit, draining up the sun. She was, as she often said, mad for the sun; and sun, as everyone knows, comes in half-hour rations in an Irish summer. 'What in God's name is that alarm bell?' I half-shouted. 'Oh,' said June, laughing, 'it's a distraction, isn't it? It's Alo, I'm afraid. He went off on his holidays this morning, and every year no sooner is he gone than the damned bell starts ringing.' I was flabbergasted. 'How long is he gone for?' I said. 'Four weeks,' she said (it turned out to be five). 'You don't mean to tell me it goes on ringing for four weeks?' I said, excited now to recklessness. 'What do you do about it? Can't someone stop it?' 'Sure, how could you stop it,' said June, 'Alo's got the key.'

We agreed it was intolerable, and while June continued to tolerate it in the sun, I went up to the house to consider the terrain. Maker's name. Ah. Phone number. Yes. Back to ring up. The security firm's phone rang and rang, much like its bell, with no answer. I rang again. I checked with directory. I rang other alarm systems, to check what they knew about this one. I got nowhere, but I was so busy that I forgot to hear the alarm. I sat down to think the matter out. The police. The Garda Siochana. I rang the Dundrum station, where the phone was answered by a man with the standard Tipperary accent. 'Sergeant,' I said. 'I want to report an alarm bell ringing. I don't think there's anything wrong in a criminal sense. I can't see any sign of burglary. Blah, blah. But the thing is driving us nuts. Do you know any way of . . .' and so on. The sergeant thanked me. His chief emotion was clearly relief. If there was one thing that man did not want to have to do, it was investigate a suspected burglary. He suggested I ring the maker. 'You won't believe this,' I said, 'but they don't answer their phone.' Ah. He could suggest nothing more. Dr Brophy had not notified the Garda station where he was going (of course he hadn't. How could I have hoped he would do such a thing?). Was I reasonably sure there had been no burglary? Ah, good. 'Thank you, sir, and God bless,' he said.

But doctors have locums, and locums have keys. With this inspiration, I rang all the local doctors until I found Brophy's locum, who cried 'Good lord!' and such things, and came up 'straightaway', having also been reassured about burglary. All this time, and four weeks of every year for years, the local residents had heard, and shrugged, and commiserated with one another, and no doubt with Alo Brophy too, and had done nothing at all. As for me, it occurred to me only much later that a probable reason for the bell's regular performance was that, in setting it before departure, Alo maladjusted it. But the moral of this episode is not only one of fatalism and patience but one of survival qualities. If you can survive Alo Brophy's alarm bell on the corner of your street for four weeks a year, you can survive anything.

The refusal to interfere, to make trouble, or to dob in ('felon-setting' is regarded as unforgivable in Ireland) is not merely cowardice but also a form of courtesy and tolerance. And they are remnants of the ancient struggle for survival. Still, the cowardice shows through. In tiny Balally Wood, soon to be sanctified by the developer into a superior estate, we used to walk among the beeches and chestnuts and the few oaks 'all fruiting away as if concrete had never been heard of. One day we noticed that rubbish was being dumped in the centre of a clearing inside it, and as a municipal garbage strike continued the pile of rubbish grew and stank with damp. Surely no local would do this. But it was no secret who was the culprit, and one day we saw a near neighbour, a middle-aged overweening woman in shorts, bustling across the road with her large parcel of leavings with the confident air of one conducting an auction. Who was she, we asked the Raffertys. So and so, a most ferocious and self-willed confronter. Why not tell her to stop it? No, it was not worth anyone's while; her record was too daunting; no one, not doctor or priest or weight-lifter, would either tackle her or dob her in to (for example) *An Taisce*. I had gone so native I did nothing, either. At least she left a fine old pile for the posh developer.

Of course, from another point of view, June Rafferty's 'fatalism' is an ability to relax. Life in Ireland can be hard, and many people find it necessary to routinize their lives in order to get a few things done. It is not common to expect that your future will be at all grand, or your achievements many or various. So, while there is a ruthlessness at the point of family survival, there is not much optimism about the expansion of your life. If you ask an Englishman about his family, he will speak of accomplishments; the Irishman will speak of origins. Then, too, the gullible streak comes out in Irish opportunism. The Irish are copyists, drawn to funny money and interested in the servicing of money. So, while men and women work hard, tediously, and decently, in the hope of managing their future, they have little sense of being able to build the future. Their ethos includes a notion of Providence as limiting the uses of what it provides. 'If you give a German a hundred thousand pounds,' said Thomas McCarthy, 'he will do research in what needs to be made, and then buy or build a factory to make it. If you give it to an Irishman he will look for somewhere to invest it. His greatest dream will be of doubling it by good luck. He will let the grass grow or the money multiply for him.' McCarthy is a poet and librarian, and he did not dare think in terms of a million. As for quadrupling, some-one else will do that for them.

A recent questionnaire showed that the Irish would prefer keeping families together to divorce; half consider they are physically fit; the great majority regard themselves as contented; and almost none declared themselves miserable. This in a deprived and materialist society. Such self-manipulation says a great deal for the spirit of the people, in whom, while most are religious adherents and 'believers', I should think a deep basic religion, and certainly mysticism, have long been merely residues.

The decadence of Irish life is of a sort which talk about religion only dimly hints at, but which is exemplified in the atomism which involves an abrupt loss of corporate feeling, a disinclination to help or to have much to do with one another unless they are actually or virtually 'family', an assuming the role of the idiot in the strict sense, a displaying feelings of fear, suspicion, and gentle, curious recessive-ness. The condition is the opposite of the 'tribal' which is so often taken to be a feature of Irish thinking. Society has been pushed to the smallest unit the mind will entertain. This is a disastrous psychology for a society large parts of which have so recently been peasant and which has always been short of a yeoman class.

The bad-tempered female polluter in shorts is merely carrying to grotesque lengths (deliberately dirtying the common space) a general Irish denial of communal involvement. Similarly, although they are excellent citizens and neighbours, the Raffertys cannot afford to confront her; they simply do not have the energy left over from the routines of living.

When you come right down to it, there is almost no civic sense at all; that concept is too wide for people's life-experience. The sense of corporate charity is focused on homes, large families, and larger extended ones. There is a distressing number of lonely unmarried people in Ireland, but even most of them have a 'family' in some sense. You get very little of that English syndrome which is represented by couples who are complacently or worriedly childless. 'We talked about it, and decided . . .' At least the Irish don't doom themselves to that kind of endless face-to-face existence. Family is the thing. There may also be some favoured charity, of church or school or drama group or football club. Whatever there is in Ireland of 'the organic community', it is not in the big towns. Reformers give up very easily, or are satisfied with minuscule or token advances.

This is not to say that the country does not enjoy the rhetoric of concern, and of the outgoing heart. 'Concern' is almost a national industry. There is endless talk on wireless and television of 'crisis', 'breakdown', and so on, in agriculture, pollution, sewage, education, local government, the meat and beef industries, tourism, health, the travelling people, and so on. The language is that of doomsday, and the rhetorical mode that of the Fianna Fail local councillor, but the focus is local, domestic, provincial. This paradox goes with a surprising failure on the part of the radio interviewers (too aggressive or too obsequious: the consensus moralists of our day) to get to the bottom of the trouble in any given case. That is one life of Ireland: anxious, self-conscious, do-gooding, striving to be self-aware and to live up to some standard of modern relevance, depressed and sympathetic ('Ah, God'). It is the mirror-opposite of that other Ireland of false community, the world in which the receptions, book-launchings, celebrations, balls, dances, public lectures, orations and presentations go on unchanged and forever, fivers are splashed thoughtlessly on bars and counters, and people portray themselves to one another as not worrying about anything, not giving a damn.

So you have conformism, reflection, formulaic thinking, versus a refusal to dob people in to the authorities, resentment of safety measures such as breathalyser tests, an anarchic streak, in which payments of car and TV licences, observance of the betting tax, reports to the police are all to be avoided. As a whole, it is petty bourgeois conformism whose other side is unmeditated anarchism. But it is, in total effect, anti-communitarian.

It is understandable too. Most people get their ethos from their grandparents, and most of the Irish people I am speaking of had grandparents who lived in country areas and were in various ways implicated in the War of Independence and the Civil War (1919–23). Then there were the British, whose length and depth of occupation are evident all through the country, in barracks and town squares, big houses and police stations, names and regulations. Then there was, and is, the Catholic church. What with grandparents, British, and bishops, it is no wonder that people defer to authority while failing to obey it, or, if you prefer another way of putting it, ignore the acts of the authority for which they have voted. Communitarianism comes to them, all the way up the well-ropes of their psyche, as an ethos laden with compulsion; the kindly Irish eyes are minatory; the songs are warnings or plaints. It is good sometimes to get away from all that inhibiting warmth, and to be yourself. If you can do it. Most can't, really, and go on to England or America, where they become not liberated Irishmen and women, but English, or Rotarians, or millionaires, or crazy boosters.

The Catholic church in Ireland preserved people's sense of identity and of a future while blocking off the natural means of their expression, which in the last two centuries involved revolutionary nationalism, and condemning the leaders who tried to lead them through the stopped passes. Revolutionary nationalism is not a creed that appeals to me much, but once large sections of the oppressed people are engaged in it as a way to their own liberation, any religious leader should consider whether it is actually immoral to use his sacred authority as a non-fiat to push them back to the sad start, to mystify and embitter the best, to demoralize and unman the others, and to lift the sanctimonious into the seats of the mighty. Further, as James Connolly pointed out with great eloquence, the selfish assumption by Catholic property owners of more property, more respectability, and greater stature became a status quo which had nothing to do with religion but which the ecclesiastics sanctified and defended against the rowdy and the landless. If selfishness and individualism are forms of the much-condemned 'materialism', then the Catholic church is partly responsible for it and them. Protestant churches, likewise. The bishops were led into the paradoxical position of supporting the anti-social (polluters and land-destroyers among them, jobbers and grabbers and fixers, practitioners of clientism and bribery) in the name of Society. Perhaps the capital letter confers some quality that society does not have of itself. But I think not; the Catholic church was riddled with a false consciousness of itself. In Australia it was more democratic, for the Catholic masses did not organize themselves so easily in 'Catholic' enterprises, unless you count the Labor Party. Irish fatalism is obviously affected by people's sense that no one will stand up for their rights, or, if he does, he can't be trusted not to sit down again in the middle of proceedings. Eventually they forget that they have any rights. The only unit of significance is the family or the club. They have little sense of a nation, and none of a *polis*. Politics is drama, in which private motives are acted out in public, or public issues are dealt with as a private preserve. As I said at the time of the second of three general elections in eighteen months, 'The elections are the only thing holding the country together.'

Then, Ireland is so local, yet so undeveloped. There can be a townland every half-mile, though the house which called 'it' into being may long have disappeared. Everything is close to everything else, yet there are great spaces between them; between Kinsella and the land of his MacMurrough ancestor, Hartnett and Donn Firinne or Fierna. From the Rock of Cashel you can see Slieve-na-mon to one side and the Slieve Bloom mountains to another. Probably on a good day you can see the mountains round Killarney. On the road to Killarney you have the Galtees on one side, the Knocknealdowns on the other, both looming like superb ranges yet feeling close enough to touch. Somebody always knows someone from any place that is mentioned. You can home in on any individual down deductions from family name or name of place of origin. Although there is little clan ideology or mythology, the traces of clan are everywhere.

Perhaps for that reason as much as anything, the people value intelligence, watchfulness, control, the ability to take a comprehensive view and to cultivate, while extending it a little, one's own garden. They despise, though sometimes while envying, excess, whether temperamental or economic, boastfulness, incivility, shows of bad temper, and snobbery without substance. They are a courteous and inhibited people. In effect, they reject what is often thought of as the basic Irish temperament and personality-type. Most of all, they admire the patrician touch, the 'decent man' with his Dickensian equability and cheerfulness combined with a Parnellian reserve. The people from whom many of us come would have called Thomas Davis 'Sir', and kowtowed to Smith O'Brien.

When I arrived in March 1981, while they were getting into position for Bobby Sands to die, I stayed in a guest room at Trinity College, at the invitation of the Provost, Professor F. S. L. Lyons. Belfast was only seventy miles away, but few people in Trinity seemed to find the situation in the northern prisons as upsetting as I did. I moved to Rathfarnham, to prepare for my family a house owned by a Trinity don on leave; I had got it through luck and the efficiency of the college housing officers. It was near schools and buslines, one of which ran past Trinity and another through University College. The suburb was under the flank of a Dublin mountain, on which you could see the pine forests and the so-called Hellfire Club of the eighteenth century, a building which can be seen dead centre if you look south up Fitzwilliam Street: a surveyor's joke, as much as anything, I suppose. As we were to learn, Tibradden Mountain has an air of lush wilderness, yet it is only about eight miles from the centre of Dublin, and a municipal bus runs to it.

So far so good. Our landmark was a pub called The Yellow House, which was a famous hostelry in Yeats's day, and is famous now. In *As I Was Going Down Sackville Street*, Oliver Gogarty intoned its name and that of The Lamb Doyle's (another famous pub, set on a hillside overlooking Dublin bay) as if they were mantras, and certainly the names are beautiful and beguiling, if the pubs are not. The Yellow House is opposite the gate of the Catholic church, behind which the Loreto Convent and the local national school are. Yeats had lived just this side of the Yellow House, evidently; we lived just the other; but I'm sure that we did not live in the same Rathfarnham. The journalists refer to it all as salubrious, opulent South Dublin, acme of middle-class comfort and amenity, the byword for what is desirable and secure. The streets have English-sounding names: Woodbrook Lawn, Gardens, Avenue. We lived in Glenbrook Park, which was a cul de sac. This effect comes about because they are parts of estates, housing developments undertaken in some recent boom period by 'speculative builders', for which the names are either brazenly made up to sound tony or based on some local 'big house'. This happens all over the world, but in Dublin it is peculiarly constricting, because there is so much of this stuff, relative to the whole. You could walk a mile in Rathfarnham, and this would be all there was. There are of course other Rathfarnhams, in one of which Yeats presumably lived.

Since these houses, lawns, streets, turnings, culs de sac, are not the remains of an old settlement, there are no amenities which have grown up gradually over a long period. There are the schools, churches, pubs, but few or no sports grounds (except attached to schools), few libraries, no youth centres that I could see. Families there are still large, by most standards, and parents are perceptibly flustered. Most of the middle-class mothers did not 'work', though some did, and to good effect. Four times a day the children trooped down or up the street, going to school or home. They either walked trimly, in small groups, or cycled in pairs. The dozens of girls who went to Loreto Convent walked pertly and with confidence. They held their heads up, but did not skylark or chase one another. The bike-riders rode absentmindedly and with panache. In good weather, they strolled or congregated in the street. During the holidays, they went away to the beach or on special projects. The general impression was one of high-minded aimlessness:

> The Mohock mountain, with its pine forest,
> as background, the air lead-blue
> for thousands of gulls to dip bright as wire
> in thermals of sunset, three geese
> assembled their triangle
> carefully, above Rathfarnham, pulled west
> away from the front porches, the cement dust,
> the Owendoher crippled on its damp bed,
> the schoolgirls pouting and crossing
> in the cul-de-sac, the boys
> tossing and turning on their bicycles,
> with the special dull
> clumsiness of daring children.
> The blue light squeezed them all flat,
> and over all the raindrops,
> unfallen, gleamed black as an alloy.

The two most disconcerting features of all this, the more-or-less permanent ones anyway, were the appearance of aimlessness, non-conviction, in such a committedly Christian people, and the virtual avoidance of play, or at least of games. The aimlessness was connected with the sense that the nation, the country, did not have a future; it had a shrinking economy with a growing national debt and a soaring budget deficit, getting or keeping a job was a matter of great anxiety; it seemed the violence in the north would never stop and the country never be unified in peace; on all sides people were terrorized by talk of 'concern', problems, and challenges beyond those they already experienced, and the old safety-valves, such as migration, were closed; indeed, trying to get a visa for Australia or Canada was a source of further anxiety; and England was no longer an alternative. The depression of fact settled down on and deepened the depression of habitual temperament.

The absence of play was very odd, and quite unexpected, even though I had seen exactly the same thing in Dundrum four years before. There was much radio and newspaper talk about sports, but people were not encouraged to seek out games which they themselves could play. In one way, it was a symptom of a certain lack of spontaneity in Irish life, though in many respects the Irish are far more spontaneous than the English. In another, perhaps the playing of games was seen as a seduction, a diverting of the valuable vital fluids, in much the way some obsessives think sex is.

For children brought up to obedience, dutifulness, and lack of purpose, was play 'dangerous'? Was it useless? Was it feared as straining something essential? Was the only image of seemliness one in which clothing was not disarranged? It could not simply be that there was no room in such a close-set urban system, for there was plenty of money for foreign holidays, school excursions, and summer schools. Perhaps it was a psychological matter, the yielding of interest in such things to the schools, the institutionalizing of games. The schools conducted sports; but I am not talking about organized sports, but about games, structures of movement into which play issues. Since the play was so truncated, so apathetic, the games did not emerge. Children rode their bicycles back and forth with idiotic confidence that no car would hit them, since they were in a cul de sac and there was no traffic by definition; although the cars tend to speed up since in a cul de sac there is no danger of cross-traffic. Yes. Or they footled around on roller skates, or booted a soccer ball idly in the middle of the road. They did not pursue any of these activities for very long; they would break off their activity to gather at this or that gatepost and talk. Whatever they were doing, riding, skating, kicking, or talking, they would not do it for long. The 'play' was casual, and stamina was not called for. They would break off their action and walk briskly in twos and threes towards some other part of the complex. They gave the image, for all the world, of people waiting without expectation, a show without content.

If they did not need to play games, if something subtly discouraged them from those creative fictions and pretences, they were not encouraged to go inside, either, until they were called. Their mothers needed their houses free of them for some reason. Perhaps there was a tacit agreement between parents and children that the parents' attitude was permissive, and that what the children were doing was playing. Perhaps boisterousness would be encouraged in another setting. But I think not.

When I reported all these things to Colette Trace, a Dubliner of slightly earlier vintage, she commented that it was also thus in her day as a chislur. The approved activities were going on walks and talking. But she would have been familiar with the idea of hobbies, of indoor crafts, of making things indoors. These children were not; or, rather, since it is hard to say what they did inside their houses when they were allowed in ('Don't be moping around the house, Liam; go out and get a bit of fresh air'), such things took a small part of their attention, and were probably regarded as ways of passing the time. Family life was warm and secure, but had too many inducements to apathy.

On one side of us, the Swifts had four strong and vigorous boys, the older ones of whom played team-sports at school, and kicked the ball with their father in their yard; but they kept themselves to themselves in a nearly English style, and aimed at a degree of privacy and self-containment which was unusual. On the other side, the Kenna children walked like starlings back and forth as long as the light held. Across the road, Grainne O'Connor was always in our place; but her father came from Kerry, her mother from Limerick, and she herself was a chatterbox and observer. Two doors beyond the Kennas were an army commandant and his family. He was a self-consciously private man, a lover of poetry, who collected every new book of Irish poetry and had two of my books. He was hardly a man for play. The first day I stopped to speak to him, he was mowing his front lawn. 'A regular job in Ireland,' I said. He agreed. 'A pity,' he said, 'they can't discover something that will . . . kill it.' 'Kill the grass,' I said. 'But they have discovered such poisons. The trouble is, they kill everything.' I was more appalled than amused. 'That's the trouble,' he said, 'you'd very likely kill the wrong things.'

The most interesting family was probably the Chamberlains, who lived two doors from us. They invited me in the first time I spoke to them, and I guessed they were country people. This was both true and false. Jim Chamberlain had been born in Dublin, but his father had come from Knocklong, the Munster town after which he named his house. It was rebel territory in the War of Independence. His wife Odran, to judge by her name, must have come from a little north of there, for her name was that of a saint who has a largely local cult.

They both thought like country people for, while they were no less private than most of the others, they would more readily invite you inside. They were full of genuine family piety, and thought equally of their parents and their children. Like everyone else, Jim would not discuss politics, especially with an election coming up, but he would agree that the northern Ireland regime was 'a bad joke', and he regretted the growing lack of national purpose. Every year he took his family by car to Scotland, where he combined their holiday with a summer task. On holiday weekends they would go to a beach-shack in Wexford, where hundreds of people from South Dublin had beach places, ranging from caravans to well-equipped houses. The sea on the Wexford coast is not turbulent, and was considered generally safe. Dubliners feel a great attraction to the pure cold Irish beaches and strands, although by and large they are not great swimmers, and the water is in any case quite cold. In the summer, the Chamberlains would try to relieve the boredom for their children in useful ways: by sending the girls to craft schools up the mountain, and the oldest girl to a school of Irish in Connemara.

But the battle against aimlessness, for those willing to undertake it, was endless, and its triumphs intermittent. Eternity must have seemed far away. We were there from April to August, through almost all of the interminable school vacation. Much of the summer had a leaden, metallic oppressiveness, like autumn without the freshness. The *Taoiseach*, C. J. Haughey, was contemplating an early election; then he called it, then everyone was fighting it, with an awful amount of made-up drama, for one of the chief issues in an Irish election is not what party, but what individual party candidates are going to be elected. Campaign songs were composed and sung endlessly. Fine Gael, the opposition party, toured the country in a brightly coloured bus, which you would see in various Dublin streets blaring its song with Garret FitzGerald nodding and waving from it, like Noddy in a pantomime. The hunger-strikers in Long Kesh prison were well into their cycle of deaths. Barmen and taxi-drivers and radio chat-show presenters proclaimed with one voice that the tourist year was ruined before it started, and they blamed the inconsiderateness of the dying men. The tourist coaches roaming Shannon and Clare were almost empty. Everyone was tense, in a form of suspended animation. It was almost as though the characteristic aimlessness had found an exact expression, or objective correlative, in the weather, which was indecisive, and so for week on week was stationary, a plateau of greyish air hovering between city and mountain.

The election debates were meaningless; very few listeners believed that the participants meant what they said, despite the fact that they were at pains to say nothing. With so little to report, the journalists had to invent special perceptions. A friend of mine, in the most original perspective I saw, told me that, although normally Fine Gael, he was going to vote for Sile De Valera because, if her vote declined, the British would say that the Irish people was now anti-Republican, and repudiated the blackmail of the hunger-strikers. Her vote did decline, but the hunger-strike candidates won their own astonishing vote. Despite it, Fianna Fail was defeated. On election day, the Fine Gael Lord Mayor spoke smiling to me from the steps of the Mansion House, and on the day of victory John Kelly, local member and a minister in the new government, smiled and addressed me from the front yard of the local presbytery. Neither of them had the least idea who I was.

A Senate election was held at nearly the same time. During it, my cousin Kevin Condon and I met a well-known candidate for the 'university panel' outside a well-known curry house in Leeson Street. He was with the well-known writer Mary Lavin. 'He's canvassing votes,' I whispered to my cousin. As we approached and greeted them, I asked him about this. 'I've started very late this year,' he said. 'I suppose neither of you fellows has a vote?' 'Afraid not,' I said, 'and if I had one I'd feel bound to give it to a hunger-strike candidate.' 'Ah,' he cried, 'there isn't one for our panel. Anyway, I've never said anything against those fellows. They've got nothing against me.' But it is useless talking elections to voteless men.

We had to start looking for another house, and for a couple of mad weeks it seemed I might have a chance of buying one. The house market was stagnant, prices were down from the previous year, and when I asked about pastoral land, just from curiosity, I found that land which would have cost 4,000 pounds an acre in 1979 was now less than half that price. The cattle herd had shrunk. There was no freshness in Dublin. We went on looking at houses, although it soon became clear that we would not be able to buy any of the country cottages we looked at, and would not be able to bear any of the overpriced suburban houses offered us to rent.

Susannah had spent a few months at her first school, the Loreto Convent. She was not exactly a pupil of it, and not exactly not a pupil. There was a problem which had to be handled with great tact: there was a waiting list for the class, and for Susannah to jump it and become a member of the class would not only be unjust but would create a furore. So she would become a person in the class without being a member of it. Sister Mary would decide this herself. But it had to be clear to all concerned that Susannah was not a member, therefore she had better not wear a uniform. Quite right, I said. But Susannah agitated for some emblem of belonging, and was allowed to wear the school's yellow smock. It was protection for her clothes, it was not a uniform; she was really still dressed in ordinary clothes.

There was obviously Jesuit blood in Sister Mary, but her decision was a wise one. She was a tiny gentle countrywoman, very outgoing and merry, who had a habit of touching your arm or elbow as she spoke. This is a common practice among Irishwomen, and so relatively obvious that Patsy Segal commented on it after one day in the country. But the summer was growing more painful; the air hovered day after day, despite visits to Cork and Clare the depression deepened, the prisoners' deaths went on with the inevitability of elections, and a sense of menace developed in the inertia. It seemed we could find nothing in Wicklow; we were unwilling to look further in Dublin; and so we fetched up in Kildare.

Chapter Four

FETCHING UP IN KILDARE

We got our house in Kildare through a mixture of irritation and curiosity. Dublin houses were out of the question, for one reason or another; and I did not really know the rules of the game; when I reported to an agent that the house I had looked at on her recommendation wasn't worth the rental, she leaned across the counter and whispered, 'My sister's looking for a tenant. Her house is much better value than that.' When I recoiled a little, she added, 'She hasn't got it on the market yet. She wants the right tenant.'

Everyone wanted the right tenant. Foiled in Wicklow, in those beautiful mountains, we started looking at houses in the Dublin mountains, nearly as desolate but much nearer town. They were scandalously overpriced, or else subject to a rule of extreme selectivity. 'My client is very particular,' said another agent. 'So am I,' I said. Despite my tieless appearance, he beamed fondly. 'O I can see that,' he said. 'I'm sure he'd let to you.' It happened that we were later to see this reserved house through another agent, and we saw at once that its owner was slob rather than snob. 'He's very particular,' said this second agent. 'You'd have to conduct the negotiations stage by stage.' 'He's not particular enough to keep the rooms clean,' I said, 'and you're making him sound bad-tempered and indecisive.' 'Exactly,' said the agent. 'He wants to let and he doesn't want to.' 'You have it.' This owner was teasing and terrorizing every agent in Dublin.

We were sick of this, and I went once more to Lisneys, of Stephen's Green, the best rental auctioneer in Dublin, to get their weekly list. Same old story, same pretentious lack of realism among half the owners. 'You'll get nothing more reasonable,' said the woman. 'That is the market price.' 'But what about houses like this?' I cried, striking an ad with photo prominently displayed under the glass of the counter. 'But that's in Kildare,' she said. 'You said nothing about Kildare.' 'Is it still for rent?' I said. 'Have you had it long? Can you tell me something about it?' She told me about it, agreed that it probably wouldn't suit me, informed me that the owner was very particular and would need to have all sorts of guarantees from the lucky tenant. She was at present in Ireland but had business interests abroad, where she resided ('France', I guessed. No. It was Hong Kong). And Lisneys would give her my name.

Things must have been going badly with such properties, for the owner was on to me quickly, and we negotiated two or three days running by phone before I arranged to meet her at the Hotel Cill Dara just outside Naas, the county town, and be conducted to the place, which she called Blackhall, although the maps add Castle. An oddity of usage, that, for I suspect that in the circles where she and her husband would seek validation 'Hall' would be preferred to 'Castle' as, quite simply, more Cromwellian gentry. 'Castle', unless it referred to a very grand structure, meant something rather too old and primitive.

Penelope, Grania and I travelled the twenty miles to Naas in a taxi, driven by our friend Seamus Allen. The rain poured in irregular sheets, and black sheets of water lay on the road verges and in the carpark of the Cill Dara. There Mrs M met me and motioned me into the passenger seat of her own small car. Thence we went, in convoy, my dear ones in the car behind, through the streets of Naas, with their usual cripplings of traffic, where a man emerged from a chemist's shop and crossed unheeding in front of us, a packet of medicine in his hand. Mrs M leaned out the car window in the rain and shouted at him, 'You'll never live to take it,' she cried. He half-turned, 'Wha?' 'You'll be dead before you take the medicine,' she roared more quietly. The centre of Naas is a good spot for exchanges like this, for traffic jams are nearly permanent there. But this episode was a good omen, I thought.

I was not quite clear where we were heading, for Blackhall was advertised as being twenty-seven miles from Dublin, and we had already come twenty-two. We bucketed on, into stud farm country, Punchestown racecourse tucked away somewhere on our left, beautiful fields introduced by a sign pointing to a school, 'Our Lady's Bower, Killashee'. It sounded a little pagan; 'Killashee,' I said. 'Church of the fairies?' Mrs M was not amused, and said she didn't know. By this time she was quizzing me as to my identity and standing. She and her husband had been to Victoria, where they had stayed with such-and-such. Did I know him? Did I know so-and-so? But, no, there was no comfort to be gained there. How to find out who I was. I can get references from several places, I said. 'Look, do you know anything about Irish poetry? I know Seamus Heaney and Tom Kinsella quite well.' Sold. Nothing about poetry, but her daughter was 'best friend' to the Kinsellas' daughter who, as I told her, used to baby-sit for Susannah.

This was indeed Ireland; and there was more to come. Having, I suppose, decided by now that, all else being equal, and so on, she would give us the lease of the house, she wanted to find out more. For example, was I a Catholic. This is a rather un-Irish form of enquiry, although I had occasionally met it before. On this occasion, after a series of delicate probes I said, 'I'm a Catholic. So are all the people in the taxi behind. Including the driver.' She was delighted, and said, 'Of course, I don't care in the slightest. People in the district get on perfectly well, whatever their religion.' A poor omen, I thought briefly; there must be lots of troubles about status and land ownership. Ah well, it won't affect me.

We splashed on into Kilcullen, down hill, over the foaming Liffey, then up the other side; on and on, taking the Athy road, then left down a sub-road, heading for Narraghmore, the taxi coming steadily behind us. The road began to rise and fall once more and, although we seemed to be running parallel to the rounded mountains on our left, we were also in some strange way getting closer to them. The country was now half-tillage, half-pasture, with patches of flat green where the walker would wade calf-deep in water; the roads were hedged and in part ditched; there were patches of wood.

Altogether a captivating if unspectacular sight, not very like the Wicklow mountains of our earlier desires; and I began to feel that if we were not in anything remotely resembling wilderness, we were pretty far back of beyond. We went through a cross-roads; 'Calverstown,' said Mrs M. The country now did not look stud-farm territory; there were cottages and bungalows on the roadside, ruins in a field, a tiny graveyard, and then we turned left through the large shabby concrete gate-posts and started splashing up a narrow drive entirely flanked by trees in an entirely untutored state: oak, beech, ash, fir, poplar and, as I later discovered, elder, hazel, and holly. Two curves, over a streamlet, up a rise, and the house was before us, its flat white Georgian front dominating the rise, and a ruined pele tower (the castle) at its right-hand corner. I think at that moment both Penelope and I separately decided to take it, no matter what it cost; and 'Janey Mac' exclaimed Seamus the Dubliner as he turned off his motor.

Now all this may seem a fussy lead-up to nothing; but the place we had come to see was eight miles further from Dublin than we had been told, it was less well kept up and comfortable than we expected, the nine acres which went with it, and which were rented by horse-owners, were not a particularly good place for children to roam in, for they consisted mainly of drive, wood, and broad dipping front lawn. The stables were built on to the house, with some more boxes in a field behind; the sheds and outbuildings were dilapidated; the grass was uncut; the back yard swirled with water; the back rooms stank of dog; cats fled from the outside kitchen window as we came near; all told, it was like an imposing outpost in a jungle, neither farmhouse nor mansion properly speaking: 'gent's residence' said Eleanor Kinsella when she saw it later.

From some upstairs windows you could see the north-west flanks of the Wicklow mountains, with their local outrider Brewel Hill; from others you could see big foothills reaching back towards Carlow, with perhaps the tip of Mt Leinster behind them. There were five usable bedrooms, two in the front, Georgian half, three in the shorter but longer and surely older back half; there was a large drawing-room and a matching dining-room, there were two bathrooms, a huge play-room, and smaller areas grouped beside the large flagged kitchen with its pantries. The two rooms behind them were now the most rudimentary kind of store-rooms; I was later told they had been (God help us!) servants' rooms. From the front upstairs you looked across a stream and up across fine tillage land to the road down which we had come. But it was summer, wet bursting summer, the hedges were uncut, and we could see no houses that might be those of neighbours. It seemed unmanageable, and we could not resist it.

Mrs M, who rang me every second day to report on her investigations of me, badly wanted us to have it, but she also wanted to implicate the male members of her family in the making of the decision for, if we defaulted with the silver and crystal which she insisted on leaving in place, it would be they who would reproach her in the time-honoured formula, 'Well, Mum (or Sheila), you've blown it again; why can't you be more sensible?' It was hard to implicate them decisively, since the husband was in Hong Kong, the sons in London and New South Wales; and she did not trust solicitors. Phone calls were made around the globe, and I was thoroughly reported on by some persons or other. Then we did the deal, and she left her daughter, who three months earlier had been a schoolgirl, to act as her agent; and, with a visit to Galway races, and a lunch to introduce us to her husband, she went back to Hong Kong where he was in charge of the race club.

More about that on some much later occasion; it comes under the esoteric heading of Business Relations in Ireland, or, Not Exactly Face to Face, or Side to Side. We went into Blackhall in late summer, among the strong almost animal smell of green, not flowers and bushes and native plants, as in Australia, but the sap and skin of the wood itself. Our job came in three phases: to manage a habitat; to learn a society; to open the terrain of a past. We did not plan it that way, but the concentration on habitat was enforced quite dramatically on our first evening, when the grand old electric stove which had been so commended to us, and the fixing of which was due to be completed the following day, went maverick and blew the whole electrical system. We learned a couple of things that evening. The first was about the neighbours' fear of trouble and their tendency to withdraw rapidly into their private heads whenever it was brought to their attention. Seeing our neighbour's lights on, I rang her to ask for advice about an electrician. She was paralysed. She knew nothing. More than once she said, beseechingly, 'How are you finding it up there? You're not finding it lonely, are you?' 'We've been here only three hours, and the electricity's gone,' I said. 'Cheerio.' When I had met her before, she had told me that I would have to watch out for loneliness in Blackhall Castle, which was an out of the way place, large and lonely (it was a mere seven hundred yards across country from her house); she was herself from another part, and had found it very lonely when she married and came to live there. It was plain that she was an instant projector of chronic worries. Only Penelope's tears succeeded in getting us an SEC electrician, who arrived a bit tipsy, found the fault, fixed it, and charged me twenty pounds, assuring me that if I had to wait for an official bill it would likely cost me twice that. A couple of days later, Larry Mulryan gave me the name of an electrician from the Curragh who would come and do jobs whenever we were in trouble, and ask me for as little as three pounds a time. Sober, too.

All this showed me that we started a bit cut off from the environment, and that not the location of the house but something to do with the characters of earlier inhabitants was having its effect on the way we were perceived. We had fetched up on a fouled shelf of land. We would have to unfoul it. That involved entering the society and learning its inner dynamism, rather than staying apart from it perched on a mound behind lines of forest from which we would emerge to lead the high life in Dublin or in Droichead Nua. We enrolled Susannah in the tiny National School at Ballyshannon, thus (although we did not know it then) absurdly pleasing all those associated with the school, for it meant that we had preferred it to the two larger, better equipped and more advanced schools which we were thought to be favouring. The fact is that we went simply for smallness and an obviously good teacher. We got Larry Mulryan in to do the carpentry at which he was so good. We employed local tradesmen wherever we could, for no other reason than that they would turn up, do the job, and charge rationally. We did our daily shopping at Narraghmore, a mile away, our weekly shopping at Kilcullen, and had a lot of dealings with the post office at Calverstown, two miles towards Kilcullen. The daily paper we got in Narraghmore; we joined the county library at Droichead Nua or Newbridge, four miles across the lovely, eerie Curragh from Kilcullen; we rented a television from a splendidly casual, accommodating and efficient dealer on the Curragh Camp; we found a young doctor in Kilcullen, and a dentist in Athy, near the Kilkenny border. We were soon spread as far as we could reasonably go, and were well known in the district before the autumn hedging began. We were plainly planted in the area, and belonged to it. The letting agreement, such as it was, required us to keep on Maura O'Rourke as 'housekeeper', which meant that she came in to clean the house twice a week for two hours. As it turned out, this was our pleasure, and we learned more about Kildare society from her than from anyone else.

But there were minor mysteries from the start. Despite my insistent questioning of my new landlord, I had not been properly briefed. Whenever I asked, 'But who has the fields and stables rented,' I was told 'a local vet', whose name was never mentioned. Only by asking others did I find that she was Fiona Hughes, wife of Leo, a commandant in the Irish army, stationed in Kildare; and only by ringing and introducing myself did I meet him. Thus I learned who rented the castle fields. But who was the driver of the small blue VW which I would sometimes see in the drive, and which once drove in and, seeing us, drove straight out again. Why, he too was a tenant of a sort; he was a farmer, Jackson, one of the relatively numerous Protestant small landowners in the district, and he rented the

buildings attached to the castle to store hay. Who let to him? Leo or
Mr M? I never found out, for Jackson never once spoke to me, and
barely acknowledged the wave of my hand; his characteristic posture
was hunched in a disappearing Volkswagen, sometimes with a bale
of hay strapped to its front or back.

> His VW, haybales strapped on
> to its waddling back,
> goes low as a badger
> back into the evening.

And who were the two men who turned up one day and, after endless
experimentation, failed to shift the horsebox which someone else
had left outside our garage? And who had taken the axe, saw, and
other necessary implements which I had seen there the first day we
came? Who kept taking and bringing back the long ladder? Who
owned the carefully trimmed treetrunks that lay in the grass of the
drive, and who stole one or two from time to time? Well, we
answered most of these questions eventually, some by raw obser-
vation, and some by asking Leo Hughes. One day I saw an expensive
car at the foot of the avenue, and a handsome tall blond woman
gazing at the horses which had begun to come back into the long
paddock. I introduced myself. She and her husband David Popple-
well were yet more renters who, so far as I could gather, rented from
Hughes. 'Perhaps you can tell me,' I said, 'who owns that long
paddock? Does it belong to Blackhall?' 'No,' she said, 'it's mine.'
When asked, Leo Hughes said it was his. Mrs Byrne, the old woman
living in the cottage near the gate, said it was Flood's, and told me
who Flood was.

There was, evidently, a dilemma about how to ascribe ownership.
It took me months to work out that, by saying the paddock was his,
Leo Hughes meant to say that nobody could take its use away from
him. It was self-fulfilling prophecy. If ownership is an indeterminate
concept, theft is a relative one. A workman told me how, after
listening to a rich woman complain about how light-fingered the

locals were, he saw her driving down the avenue holding a new and special snaffle he had just made for someone else. When the long ladder had disappeared for several months, the landlord wrote to me asking me to find out who had it and, if it was not returned, to report it to the Garda. I had no intention of doing anything of the sort; I had found out the ladder was in the hands of blue VW, as I now thought of him, and he was not in a mood to bring it back. Pursuing some ancient inarticulable grudge, I supposed. I told the story to John Tehan, who was preparing the grounds for the return of the landlord, his former boss. 'I think, he wants you to go to the Guards, John,' I said mischievously. 'No,' he said, 'I won't.' 'Well, I'm damned if I will,' I said. It was a curious situation, as anti-social as you can imagine: an unmannerly farmer 'borrowing' from a man of higher class, who was unmannerly enough to ask us to do his dirty duties, and an underling, a man of no property, put in the position of greatest strain. There was some mad mystique of ownership at work, no doubt; and only John Tehan and myself knew what we did and did not own. As two-year-old Grania said plaintively, 'What does own mean?' It was an Irish kind of question. In south Kildare everything was disguised under a filter of claim and sub-claim, emerging at times to remind you of the mystery; yet everyone except the stranger knew what was what. Nobody wanted to claim the title of tenant; even I fell into speaking of me and mine. All were proprietors in some mysterious mode, the more mysterious when three laid claim to the same patch. All was clientism, but who was client and who patron?

As summer gave into autumn, the paddocks were full of activity. Haywaggons swayed up and down the roads, and stubble began to be burnt in the hollow centres of the various holdings. Mushrooms grew in great quantities in one of Tom Walsh's fields, just behind our corrugated-iron garage; and Tom invited us in to pick whatever we wanted. The late foals were still in the long paddock with their dams, being made ready for the sales at Goff's great saleyards near Naas; their owners or mentors were coming in twice a day. Fiona the vet was bringing the adult horses into the stables for checking. The jumpers were being got ready for the National Hunt season, and the Curragh was closing down the long flat-racing season. Mares heavily in foal were being brought in, from as far away as Waterford and Tipperary; they would stay until foaling date, and some would actually foal in our stables, in the bitter winter nights. From now until we left ten months later, our lives would be filled with the shine and creak and smell of racehorses. The cats, half-feral, which had wandered off before we came in, were coming back, and multiplying, for we had found no way of catching the females to spay them. We would watch the newborn kittens dried off on the stones in the autumn sun, then carried off by one or other member of the cat coven. Sometimes a kitten would be mysteriously killed; once I found the severed head of a white kitten.

> All day the fires were stark
> on the ridge of the ploughed land.
> Next day the saw comes
> stirring and sapping, a taut side
> lopping every tree. Then
> more fires, nearer the house.
> A bit here, a bit there,
> the world disappears.
>
> And you are into the cold thrill
> of uncovery, land cleared of its humus,
> multi-coloured, cropped, paled,
> waiting the harrow of evening.
> By the end of the week they'll find
> the white kitten's head.

For it was cutting back time. Machines were out in the roads trimming some of the hedges; and, as the leaves fell to lie in great swathes, the stick-like hedges were cut back in almost every paddock. Trees too were cut down or lopped, for fencing or fires. The small hills which had seemed mere strokes in a jumble of distances became clear outlines; the shape of trees became clear; it was possible to identify hedges; houses and barns became visible, far closer to our house than I had imagined; the roots of the taken crops gave an exquisite mosaic of subtle colours; and field-systems divided themselves into rise and hollow, dry shelf and bog and marshy water; pools lay flat for days. And you could start to hear sounds over large distances – saw, bird, motorbike, playing children – as clear and distinct as at the start of summer. The land had cleared its senses, and opened ours.

Tom Walsh's cows came in a body into our paddocks, munching happily away as if they knew that in a month they would be feeding on silage; and after a few hours I rang Tom, and after another hour or two he drove them out again. Someone else's cows took a fancy to our front lawn. Dozens of other cows were fed on Tom Hickey's crop stubble. At night the owl began to moan, though we never saw the allegedly resident peregrine. The pheasants were making their starter-motor noise in thickets below the creek. The swallows, which had swooped in scores to catch whatever heat there was in the cooling evenings, had gone one day; we could almost see them going; and the rabbits which had played round and round two cypresses in front of the house were rarely seen now. The bees hummed angrily at their stone window, but did not come out. Instead, the robins started to fly in and out of the smelly stables; and it was not long before I was to see two wrens stepping on the rail outside the room where I worked.

It was then that I began to notice the trait, despondency, which I was mentally to add to those others of aimlessness and fatalism. It had been partly concealed by the cheerful stoicism of Maura, Larry, and John Tehan, whose lives were hard and imperfectly rewarded, and by having a drink with Mark Wright, seemingly so equable, or with Leo Hughes, seemingly so carefree. The darkening of the evenings brought out a melancholy in all of them; anything that anyone purposed would have to be brought to fruition in cold and dampness.

For a long time I thought this despondency a psychological trait coming from the oft-remarked fatalism, but it has to do with lack of purpose, and has a lot of resentment in it. In other words, it is social, and not simply metaphysical. I went back to that marvellously expressive book *Inishkillane*, and there saw vividly articulated much of what I had noticed in Kildare. Not that every part fitted; but a surprising amount did. Surely this was all wrong; surely I was reading in from an inappropriate text? *Inishkillane* was specifically about a rural parish in the west of Ireland, with its enormous burden of geographical and emotional loneliness, caused by rocky soil, ceaseless emigration, and distance from the validating centres of warmth, comfort, and enlightenment; it was part of the western wasteland. I was in south Kildare, thirty-odd miles from Dublin, among the lush sloping paddocks, the well-adjusted if somewhat overpowering hedges, the new bungalows, professionals and knowledgeable men and women of the turf, work (seemingly) for everyone, a land full of amenity. Surely it could not be a place of *anomie*.

Yet it was. Gradually the real map unrolled. Each road had its quota of widows and their resident bachelor sons; numbers of people had been in the asylum, for alcoholism or disorders just as vague. There was much feckless drinking. Hepatitis was epidemic twice while we were there, and according to one doctor it was in a sense endemic. The fatalism about losses of electricity, phone, public transport, and water was frightening, as was the apathy about garbage collections and politics. Then there was the lack of interest in mass injustice, such as that in the six counties. There were the scandalous rates of pay for casual work. There was the antipathy to every manifestation of government, so that many a Leinsterman or woman might have paraphrased Swift: 'Boycott everything government except its cheques.' Above all, there was the failure to look abroad for meaning (for it could never be made available to them), yet also the failure to find meaning in their own relationships.

As the months passed I was conscious that very few relationships outside the nuclear family were other than brittle, tenuous and brief. One woman with ten small children and a husband in England had to walk two miles, pushing her smallest children in a pram, to do her shopping, and two miles back; she was going from and back to a desolate bogroad; and when I asked her, she told me that no one had ever offered her a lift, not even the priest whose sermons had pressed the large family on her. Another woman, always in difficulties, was seldom offered help. 'O she has a brother in Ballitore,' people said. Implication: that's where she ought to go for help; it's his job; we have quite enough looking after our own.

The Kildare community, though reasonably affable and unaggressive, is uncommunal. There is no belief in community, as contrasted to the Romsey of my childhood, with its mixed religions but sense of corporate decency. No one in Kildare seems to believe that any corporate purpose can be fulfilled. The more you look to community, the less you will be able to do for yourself. A shopkeeper who believed that the local water, full of lime, was a cause of goitre, drank only Perrier water, but made no move to improve the general supply, although a member of her family had been one of the water co-operative's original trustees. She was a victim and carrier of despondency, although her manner was generally chirpy and ebullient. *Pace* the fluctuations in Inishkillane, seasonal movements have no effect on this depression and disbelief; there is no pattern of migration and return; nor are many people at all dependent on remittances. Nor is it affected by closeness to Dublin, a place or state which is generally both feared and scorned. Indeed, the phenomenon has its Dublin counterpart. As I have said, the desirable southern suburbs, far from validating the lives of their inhabitants, create a pattern of monotonous and meaningless semi-comfort. Walking to buy the papers, you would notice children on bikes doing all sorts of curlicues in a boredom of separate selfhood, and rushing against the walkers on the narrow footpaths, and children abstractedly eating chips, licking ice-creams, or devouring ice-pops, and throwing their wrappers with noticeable briskness on the footpaths, which were also decorated by numbers of well-fed dogs shitting in public in an astonishing range of colours. The irreligion of Ireland is seen in its radical lack even of the desire for community. Community is bad news. Communities of blood, of faith, of history, of political or national allegiance, of need; all are bad news. Do not do anything unto others.

It all has economic causes, as you might guess. The battle fought in his or her heart by the average Irish person is an economic battle, the meaning reached for and despaired of is an economic meaning. Economic pressures are unacceptably high, and rising. Ireland is big in national debt, balance of payments deficit, borrowing for government spending, inflation rate, unemployment rate, social service payments, VAT rates, prices for oil and petrol, birth-rate, crime rate, percentage of the population under eighteen, poverty, dirt, and sheer misery.

This was the Pale, the English Pale, the narrow strip of three or four counties which the Norman-English administrators had marked out in the middle ages to ensure a centre and circumference of English rule. As Patrick O'Farrell says in his *Ireland's English Question*, 'Failing to conquer Ireland, the Anglo-Normans established not so much a colony as a garrisoned province, the Pale, whose foreignness was proclaimed in law and asserted by violence.' They tried to enclose it with castles, and by a deep ditch; but its borders kept shifting. What they were able to do was to drive out the Gaelic princes, outlaw Gaeldom, at least up to a point, and instil a kind of mentality. As T.P. Coogan puts it, in his *The Irish: A Personal View*:

Whereas Dublin is very definitely Ireland, the Pale mentality is not. It is nearer in attitude to England than to other parts of the country, receiving British television programmes which are not available in fringe reception areas elsewhere, and buying more English newspapers and magazines. Its preoccupations are those of urban development, its models are British ones.

This is certainly true, and it represents the end product of the 'fossilization of Ireland' of which O'Farrell speaks. It installed the rule of copyist and chancer. It cut some counties off from the rest of the country, so that even now sophisticated people in Cork or Limerick, who have driven through this area dozens of times on their way to Dublin, have never paused in it for ten minutes, and speak of it as 'foreign' and 'remote'. The native Irish are more contemned here than elsewhere. An enormous proportion of the fertile land is owned by people with English names. There is a general shiftiness, more common here than in Munster. Deference is expected; a permanent primary school mentality is encouraged, and achieved. It is a playground which the mere Irish work to keep up to scratch.

I did not at first see much of this; I had expected to find the people divided on class lines; but the divisions were more subtle and multiple. And if I were to seek another reason for the despondency of which I have spoken, it would be that the ordinary people perceived themselves as unvalued; the owners of their country month by month enforced on them the conviction that their lives, their relationships, their feelings, were of no value. And I was interested to see that the people who resisted this pressure, who simply took no notice of it, and ignored the presumptions that landowners might have about them, were settlers from the west, from Mayo, Byrnes and Walshs and Lavins and others, who had taken Blackhall land from the Land Commission thirty years ago, and who, sustained by their enterprise, their physical strength, their network of family relationships, walked straight through the Pale mentality. But I was not to have so much to do with them as with others.

Chapter Five

LASTING A WINTER

When winter came, we learned more things about our neighbours. But when did it come? If you followed the old Celtic calendar, as the media officially did, you would find winter starting on 1 November, and certainly the air felt dark enough to make that plausible; but, as with so many other things, people accepted both this and an alternative reckoning at the same time: winter started with November, yes, but they would habitually say, 'When winter comes', projecting that condition weeks into the future. The Celtic calendar would have summer beginning on May Day, and spring on St Brigid's Day, 1 February; it would have the hawthorn as a summer, not a spring growth. None of this is true to the modern facts: not that it matters. The locals made full conversational use of their double standard, and we came gradually to join them, with me warning all and sundry that the worst was yet to come.

Autumn had been delicious, with day after day of sunshine moving in and out of moist and dry, the pheasants strutting in all directions, the horses running and gazing, the growths slowly clearing back to admit the closed emptiness of winter, and the hundreds of yards of red leaves lying underfoot, ranging in hue from fire-red to collie-red. But the days were growing inexorably shorter, the darkness more visible by mid afternoon, the air colder, the landscape barer. Racing finished on the Curragh; the Kildare hunt started to go hopefully up and down on the side roads. Not knowing how our water supply worked, but seeing, despite all reassurances, that it was clearly a risky proposition, I began to get a little scared, not merely because I had no idea how deep a breakdown in the water supply was likely to go, but also because I could not trust people who reassured me so easily on so little basis. The wren began to strut up and down on the wooden rail near the horse-trough outside my window; robins appeared in all guises, including that of marauder, flitting in and out of the horse-boxes, and having a go at the seedy straw.

I began to realize that the change in the demeanour of our neighbours represented two forces: increased depression, and new fear. What were they afraid of? Not at all clear, but there was something about the brief pagan darkness which we were approaching, that of Christmas and the winter solstice, that induced a marked psychic state. Negative feelings appeared like weedy growths in the assumed jauntiness. We were indeed approaching the year's midnight, the point of nothing, when people had nothing to look forward to; it was the time without a future tense; I felt it there as I never had in England; for England is full of towns, of people together, of social occasions, and Ireland is by contrast a place which the weather scours and fills, in one way or another. That place had grown by imperceptible degrees distinctly darker, and it was to grow darker still when the snow came.

In our part of Kildare, incidentally, close though it was to the Curragh, and full of horsy establishments, what happened to the racing did not assume great importance. Working people in particular would tell you that they had no interest in racing, or that they were very interested, and sometimes indeed had a specialized knowledge, but they preferred to stay home and 'watch it on the box'. This was not the real reason; Irish racing is seldom televised; what they would be watching would be the English racing. The real reason is that you need a lift in a car to get to the Curragh, and that it costs too much to get in. My Australian friend Dinny O'Hearn and I went to the last meeting of the flat racing season for that year; my neighbour's filly, Kazankina, a classics hope, was racing. The horses ran at all angles on the heavy ground. To an Australian, the Curragh lacked obvious amenities; there was nothing to do but lose your money, and the bookies are so timid and other-directed that you get only about ten minutes before each race to do even that. On this occasion I said to Leo Hughes that night over a drink, 'You'll never get crowds to the races while you give them so little.' 'O,' he said, 'all of us are members.' For amenity you went to the members' enclosure. He had dashed over for a couple of races, chasing information or intuition; he could do this whenever he liked. All that was fine for the few thousand members; but it meant, surely, that they did not want less formal devotees.

Anyway, with the flat racing closed down, winter was coming. In England and Ireland the great jumping races take place in the spring, not long before the spring classics. That a country should batten down so obviously is a bit surprising, since Ireland is a relatively temperate country. But people had become frightened not only of the dark gulf in time, but of snow and ice, to which they were not really used, and which the society did not have the resources to deal with speedily and effectively. When snow lay everywhere on the roads and paddocks, it turned out that Kildare County Council had no snow ploughs. There were virtually no snow ploughs in Ireland. They had never been needed. I asked Larry Mulryan how often they got snow, and what wind brought it; he replied by speaking excitedly of the snow drifts of a few years earlier. It was plain that extreme conditions were not experienced as a regular challenge to be met; at most, in this part of the country, they were an occasional threat, to be remembered with real fear.

Similarly, no one had much notion of how to cope with the other symptoms of snow storms: the ruined electricity, the exploding gas mains, the water supplies knocked out by electrical failure or frozen inside the pipes.

Two-thirds of Ireland, and most of all the south-east, will remember for decades January 1982; for then the whole area was buried under, iced into, stifled and suffused with snowfalls which looked like stopping the operations of the whole society. Some parts were not very affected, and some were affected, but in quite different ways. Mayo and Donegal by and large could not work out what all the fuss was about on the Dublin-centred radio and television services; they had had the usual weather, light impermanent falls of snow, changing winds. Sligo and North Kerry were swarming with rain while Wexford and Carlow were trying to breathe under snow. The wild Atlantic weather swept and scoured, as usual, but there was no extremity, and no disaster. But for Leinster and parts of the midlands, it was as though Ireland, temperate dampened Ireland, had become the Welsh or the Scottish mountains. And indeed it was British weather which came to its finish that month in the eastern half of Ireland.

That was January. But Kildare had had its tightening-up exercises a month earlier, as in mid December the wind swept in torrents over Brewel Hill, swinging from south-east to east to north-east, belting everything within sight for day after day, piling snow in great drifts, and showing us all what it would be like to be cut off.

The telephone went, of course, and 'came on' again, and went, in a narrowing spiral; the harassed men from Posts and Telegraphs climbed their red wrists up the same crucial pole; the same tests were done; everything as you would have expected. It was clear that even limited falls of trees or branches would bring down both electric and telephone wires, both of which on our place ran through stretches of woodland. This did not happen, but the electricity 'went' from time to time, sometimes for a day or so – a generator had been knocked out somewhere – just as you would expect. But the water did not freeze in the pipes, not yet; nor did the heating-oil freeze in its iron tank; when the water went, it was because the electricity generator which powered the pump up on the reservoir had been knocked out, and no water could be pumped up into the pipes.

It was then we started learning about the Kildare personality under stress. It had two keen symptoms. First, no one 'knew' anything, and it seemed that people preferred to be confused about what was happening, preferred not to know. Only one man in Narraghmore 'knew'; he was the president of the water co-operative, he had no phone, and the messages which he delivered standing by Mrs Hickey's store and sub post-office were so long and circumstantial that one had to misunderstand them. For the others, it seemed that there was a lesser burden, a lesser obligation, in being uninformed and confused, that indeed the best wisdom was not to know. That is, the communal mood, need, spirit, was to endure together, not to act together. The second symptom became visible as the icy conditions continued, and people passed from mouth to mouth the wisdom that the next danger was from freezing pipes, and the best way to avoid this was to leave your taps open, so that whenever the water came into them from the replenishing pump, the pipes would have water running through them all their length. The only, or the main, trouble was that the water-level was always lower anyway when the electricity was restored, and this practice lowered it still further; there might be pumps, but there was no water, and there wouldn't be any until the taps were turned off.

So notices had to be posted, to stop wantonage, and to publish whatever new regulations applied. But where could this be done? Why, where but from the pulpit, at church, during Mass and the Church of Ireland service. Some of us were thus a couple of days late getting the news. But the symptoms themselves were clear: fear of being implicated, and fear of being left behind, the two incipiently neurotic symptoms of a society which, however homogeneous it may be, is deeply non-communal, frightened to cohere, and frightened to provide the conditions which might enable it and call on it to cohere. England and Australia have their counterparts to all this; but it is particularly distressing in a place like rural Ireland, beautiful, very lacking in amenity, already full of reasons for minor depression, in which, for example, the corner shop announces that deposits may be left on Christmas chocolates or biscuits. The place cries out for community, and community, except in the way of endurance, is exactly what it denies itself.

All the time I was becoming more worried about the water supply, whose provenance and management were fast becoming clearer to me. We were getting plenty of fuel; turf delivered by Stephen Wright every Saturday night, wood which I cut with a handsaw down in the patches of forest. When the bigger snowstorms hit in January, even these small manifestations of autonomy were under threat. This time, the winds came racing and shearing from the east, straight from Siberia by way of England and Wales, which were of course suffering the heightened version of the system. They were used to it; Ireland, as I say, was not. In one coup (completely unpredicted by the meteorology bureau), Dublin was covered in snow, and all roads leading out of it were snowed in. These included the Naas road, on which we relied. Within two days it was impossible to get any closer to Dublin than Kilcullen; by the third day even that was unattainable. The highways, then, were closed, and in them hundreds of vehicles which had broken down or been abandoned. Thousands of refugees from them took refuge in the factories lining the route, and there they made do until they could be rescued by one means or another. By that time their vehicles were likely to be completely disabled; and most of them had in any case been stripped and vandalized by inhabitants of the neighbourhoods who, like a modern *jacquerie*, went out into the snow and ice to turn a pressing penny. Communications were disrupted. There being no ways of clearing the roads quickly, the media reporters were unable to assess and report on the state of affairs. People trying to get into Dublin by the back way, the Blessington road, usually bogged down within a few miles. And, despite the lack of contact, and the growing fear and mystification, it soon became clear that the areas worst affected (apart from Dublin) were Wicklow leading down into temperate Wexford, on the one side, and out into Carlow on another. The mountain system contained in this area was a frozen graveyard. People and stock had to be fed rudimentary necessities by army helicopters; sheep and cattle perished in thousands, exactly as they were doing on the Welsh side of the Irish sea; and still no way was found of shifting the masses of snow and ice except ordinary earth-moving equipment for the roads already snowed in, and salting of the surface for those under threat.

Unlike its neighbouring counties, Kildare's roads were mostly in the latter category, but they were still hard to negotiate. Oddly, while the electricity and water lasted, it was less depressing, it was even exhilarating, to be in Blackhall during this second blast than during the pre-Christmas one. Winter had done its worse, Ireland was under the worst snow in memory, but it had not wiped us out. Admittedly, there was no question of getting up to town to typist or library or copying-machine; and my daughter Brigid had arrived at a time which was disastrous for her with a strained back. But we could carry on.

Until the electricity started waxing and waning, and the water froze; for now, in this large cold rambling house, we had no water, no sure means of cooking, and no safe way of keeping the heating going. Further, although there was a village pump at Calverstown, two miles away, we had nothing to carry water in. We had to get to Droichead Nua, which involved us in going up the iced roads into Kilcullen, then left across the Curragh, with its sudden pools, ruts, icing, blundering sheep, and banks of snow. The containers we were able to buy needed to be filled twice, or even three times a day; so you could count on travelling hazardously for twelve miles every day for water alone. The wood was getting harder and harder to cut, and made a pinging noise as you put the saw in. Great branches smashed off conifers were there to be sawn up; but each was a half-day's labour. In between these efforts, I continued my attempt, which rapidly became a campaign, an obsession, to find out the nature of our water supply, the lie of the underground pipes, the siting of the stopcocks, and the obligations towards us of the water co-operative. It became an obsession because, though they were all members of the co-operative, nobody knew the answers to any of my questions and, with worries of their own, they were not about to find out. The two things which they knew, and I did not, were how the pumping system on the mountain worked, and where their own pipes ran. Even then, everybody had a different story, and a different attribution for it; there was a marked difference between this and the behaviour of an Australian small town in emergency conditions; the Irish were 'satisfied' with sketchier and less plausible answers. My neighbour, a prosperous farmer, affected not to know where our pipes ran, but he gave me, repeatedly, a gloomy prognosis, as follows: (a) they would be close to the surface, (b) the earth would be frozen right down to them, (c) they would almost certainly have burst, (d) the road stopcock, wherever it was, had probably been broken, frozen, or turned off. None of these things was true; and it turned out that he knew exactly where the pipes ran, because the laying of them had been a matter for dispute between him and my landlord; they ran for the most part under his paddocks, and he had made a bit of a profit as a side result of their laying. But he wasn't going to tell me any of this, of course. Whatever you say, speak wide of the mark.

I did not learn the answers to any of my questions until I was able to locate John Tehan, who had worked for Mr M and had laid the pipes. But he was working seven days a week for the council, clearing and salting the roads, and could not be got. My questions, by the time I did get him, had become quite anguished, because I could foresee the water coming back on for everyone but not for us, because of some simple and obvious matter on which I had not been briefed. Everyone agreed that that would be bad luck, indeed; they began to twitch every time they saw me rolling into Narraghmore looking for the waterman; they started to come up to me and commiserate with me over the fact that John Tehan had not been up to see me; soon they were blaming John, who was, it seemed, responsible for the whole debacle (which had not happened yet); and I was defending him, quite testily, for, as I said, he may have the knowledge I need, but he has no obligation towards me at all.

Eventually, he arrived and explained all. 'Ach, to hell with it,' he said, 'the pipes are a long way down; I put them there myself; the earth will be loose around them; there'll be none of them burst; the road stopcock's nothing got to do with it; you'll find it's the pipes in the yard are frozen. They do know nothing about it.' He was right on all counts. What was interesting was the tendency of his neighbours to tilt the blame towards him, for he was neither the landlord's nor my employee; perhaps some old scores were being paid off. He, for his part, could not take in the fact that I had been told nothing of any use about the water supply, and that my trouble was, simply, lack of basic information.

The taps had been left open; rationing was introduced; the snow started to melt; the electricity blazed with new constancy; the horses started to trot up the paddocks; the sound of the foxhound was heard in our land; even the phones started working again. Some of them, at any rate. One day I rang the International Airport Hotel in Dublin, and got a small town in Sligo, the other side of the country. Nearly every time I rang the hotel after that I would get a different place, all of them in Sligo, all small. This led to some interesting conversations. The Irish can make much wonderment out of these doings. Country people like it when you try to raise Dublin and get them instead. Dublin people don't reciprocate. Sometimes they pretend not to know what you are talking about. Once I asked a hotel receptionist to get me a number in Carron, in County Clare. She kept on mangling my words. 'It's in the Burren,' I kept saying, 'in Clare.' 'I've never heard of a place like that,' she said sharply. Her accent was from the west, and I said, 'But you come from the west yourself.' 'Yes,' she grumbled, 'but not from there.' Bill Hannan, who has the worst hand with a telephone of any Australian I know, used occasionally to ring me from north Limerick, where he and his family were living; for he wanted someone to check with a musician in Dublin who was making a set of pipes for him. The telephone operators used these occasions to sharpen their social skills.

'Buckley. Is it a Professor Buckley?' the call would begin.

'Yes. Yes.'

'Hold on. I have a call for you from . . . mumble crash mumble. Hold on. I've lost, mumble.'

'Is he an Australian?' I would ask desperately.

At this the operator would snap to attention; drama was in the offing; maybe gossip. 'Ah, he may well be that,' she would say. 'I took him for a mumble.' But she would be sure, then, to get Bill back on the line, both out of courtesy and concern that compatriots should be reunited, and in hope of diversion. We would oblige by exchanging subversive political innuendoes.

Dublin was slow to recover from its ordeal, as were the mountain areas to its south. In some ways they may not have recovered yet; for the shock went deep. It is not that the Irish cannot bear misfortune or reverses: quite the contrary; but this freak weather showed them their country as they had never imagined it to be, as not merely lowering but extreme in winter. Also, we proved on our pulses the old truth that adequacy of response depends on preparation, and preparation depends on money. Ireland would not have been prepared even if it had been expecting the disaster. In North America, after a snowstorm the individual clears his or her pathway with spade or broom, a machine clears the road, and a patrolling snowplough clears the highway. In Ireland, an individual with spade or broom fought through to his gate, and could go no further until the corporation workers improved the state of the pavements with whatever came to hand, perhaps spade and broom; some bulldozers shoved the snow from the road's centre to its side, but nothing could really clear the highways except the gradual heat of renewing traffic, and then the council workers would salt the cleared surface, risking in the process a new coat of icing. So Ireland was shown not to have corporate resources to deal with a disaster; Canada sent or lent six snowmobiles, and the TV showed them being put through their paces in Phoenix Park. Nor were there the corporate psychic resources; Irish people did not have the will, the habit of rousing up, the habit indeed of success, to get together on such occasions. What they did was stick it out, in the best Cockney blitz fashion. Their behaviour was not as tough and resourceful as that of Australians, and not as touchy and legalistic as that of English people. Much as I dislike national stereotypes in these matters, I think some generalizations will stand up for a while. Once I had to put up with nine hours unprovoked delay at Perth airport late on a Sunday night after a flight from London. Given that the Australian passengers had a psychological advantage in being on home soil, there were revealing differences between Australian and English sufferers. The Australians went for a walk and a drink, or they made phone calls, or they tried to sleep, or they did all three. Characteristically, they began by seeming edgy, sulky, put out. The English began by permitting themselves to seem at most a little flustered, then became brave, joky, jaunty, inclined to reassure one another and the Australians. After a few hours they started to complain, first allegedly on behalf of someone other than themselves ('this gentleman here actually paid for a first-class fare, and he's only getting sandwiches. . .'), then about deficiencies, legal or managerial, in the basic arrangements (the airport and airline becoming, for the purpose of the exercise, an unreliable coolie class). Finally, they became quite distraught, and started to think agitatedly of going for a drink, or making phone calls, or sleeping. The three or four Irish I noticed on that occasion either said nothing or continued some interminable anecdote. During a snow disaster, they do not broadcast grievances; they murmur, and their subject is the way things are.

But such imperviousness to alarm does not drive the worry away; it may set it deeper, so that relief becomes as muted as the anxiety, and no emotion can be expressed whole-heartedly, for there is no release from tension in any but trivial action. Or in prayer, or drink. The liveliness of the crowds in Grafton Street at lunchtime, or at an art opening or reception, is lovable and unaffected. So is the self-conscious merriment of the punters ('the Irish invaders', so the English press calls them) on their way to the Cheltenham Gold Cup meeting. But these are approved occasions, as Mass is the approved occasion for prayer gatherings. Outside them, and outside those sudden inducings of impromptu story-telling or song, Irish feelings are deeply inhibited. No amount of song, laughter, or wit can wish that away; it is integral to their geography, their history, their religion and their economy. The stranger sees them enduring a winter disaster, and can only marvel at so much calm, such goodwill, so little of aggression and grievance; and when he looks closer, he will see an inertia that has a sub-stratum of permanent alarm.

The profound ambivalence which can rise in a sane and intelligent person immobilized within this constricting world-system can be seen in the case of Mrs B, a woman well into her eighties, who cared for herself, tended her habitat very watchfully, and kept a weather eye on the world from the door of her cottage. She was a cheerful and lovable person, by no means a melancholic or any other sort of neurotic, yet the world mystified her into an extreme of indecisiveness in the dozens of conversations I had with her.

Is the climate good or bad? The weather is (usually) baddish, but can be apologized for one way or another. Who will win the election? Is Charlie smart or is he a rogue? Rascally, it may be. But he's smart too. Is he unique to Ireland? Both yes and no lead to some consternation. She will vote Labour, but will not say so, and if she mentions the Labour candidate at all, it will be to say that he's a hardworking man, a schoolteacher. Will an Irish horse win the Derby? Probably not, but then again . . . All of these uncertainties, concealed, feigned, rhetoricized, or flirty, have to do with Ireland itself. What is one to think of Ireland? That in turn has to do with the contradictory facts, that Ireland is said on all sides to be grand in all sorts of ways, but that it is experienced as dissatisfying and full of woe, so that the most anyone can do is wait and watch and crack a joke and not be too hard on the neighbour. Mrs B will not watch television: 'I don't want to be ruined before my time.' But is this really because of some embarrassment at not having a set, or at not wishing to involve herself with other people's houses and lives? She listens constantly to the wireless (chat shows, mostly), as many Irish do; but that is a common and intensely private habit.

She lives at the cross-point of contradiction that has its roots deep and its webs wide in Irish life: she loves animals, is curious about them, and is keen to preserve them. But all about her are people who drown kittens, hunt foxes, course live hares with greyhounds, prowl across people's fields to hunt for pheasants, treat domestic dogs with an extreme of casualness, and will beat a horse if it thwarts them. Their hardness is the mirror-image of her watchfulness. Or is it merely a form of casual acceptance of the way things are, a Camusian habit of taming the horror by playing along with its terms? The thing is, she has to talk and joke with her neighbours about their practices (live hare coursing, for example), while never letting on to the sympathetic bystander, like me, that she has any revulsion for them. If she were an Anglo-Irish gentlewoman, she might, very easily; or she might just as easily do the opposite. But she hasn't enough money or mobility to be visibly tender hearted. Then, she must have met, as I have, some examples of the clergy, manly men, to be abbots able, who speak as though opposition to blood sports were an excommunicating, if not a hanging matter. What is a body to think? She keeps deep within herself her capacity to feel, until it is, as it were, a way of thinking. But, as to human contact and disclosure on the great human issues, whatever you say say nothing.

Her feeling has not been provided with a language adequate to it. She uses many words which to me are an unfamiliar dialect – 'trock' for trough; 'shaw' for ditch – but she does not know where they come from. One is a peasant pronunciation, the second is cognate with Lallans 'sheugh', and probably comes from the Gaelic 'seoch'. They are discrete remains, just waiting for the telly to roll over them. Then there are local usages: 'set' for 'let', as in 'She won't be able to sell the house; she'll have to set it', a gently dramatic way of emphasizing the facts, as if 'she' were being put to the labour of setting a wheel or a splint, or sowing seed, or urging a horse at a fence, instead of merely finding a tenant.

The weather, which would confuse and mystify anyone, and gives haggard grins to Irish weather announcers, is the most frequent focus of Mrs B's concern for adequacy. It is Irish weather; other people joke about it; it is chancy, unpredictable, and always threatening. I contest these claims: Irish midland climate is a mild one, I say, the hawthorn stays out for weeks, long parts of the autumn are almost sultry, the snow when it comes does not last long, the volatility of the winds is in itself a safeguard against extremity, and the worst weather of the year, I remind her sternly, has come twice, both times from the east, over Brewel Hill, from England. She agrees with all this, and adds for good measure that the storms shaping up to attack Ireland in the next few days are coming from America. But the anxiety remains; for things are so chancy, and there are no meanings in them that can be latched on to. It is an anxiety about meaning and purpose; and it is thus a very disabling condition for an old woman to be in when she is tough, cheerful, charitable and intelligent in herself, but is also immobilized, unable to get around or to change her focus on the world which has so many threats. Draw back a little, the better to take out the stings; Mrs B is not in a position to do this. Her state, her situation, has its equivalent in a million different modes all over Ireland. And in each case the diagnosis has to be: lack of purpose coming from immobilization. Joyce called it paralysis. It is the existential state in which existential choices cannot be made.

What is true of Mrs B, in a mode of lovable and amusing casualness, is doubly true of many others, in quite different and more disturbing modes. But I do not pretend to sociology, or any other kind of sanctity substitute, so I shall leave them till later, till they become pertinent not to a diagnosis but to a story.

Chapter Six

ANCIENT IRELAND KNEW IT ALL

The antiquity of Ireland as a human habitat is not great by comparison with warmer and more central countries: less than 10,000 years, so far as we know; but it has two very interesting features. The population is strikingly homogeneous in that, although it is a mixture of Celts, pre-Celts, Scandinavians, Normans, and peoples of later invasions, occupations and plantations, it is a very old mix, which has been working its organic will in individuals, families and communities for several centuries. That is the first fruitful paradox, that there is an old mix and that in general terms we know what it is. The second is that, for complex reasons, the Irish have proved extraordinarily land-based, home-based. Far more than the Scots, those of mainly Gaelic provenance remain with amazing persistence in amazing proportions on or near the areas which are specified on maps as the lands of their clans from the early middle ages. There are names which are to be found almost only in Munster, or in Connaught, or in West Ulster; and, within those provinces, they may be concentrated in this or that county, or triangle joining parts of counties, or in the east or west of a province. Such facts, combined with the nature of naming in the old Irish Gaelic system, which in turn was connected with the nature of clan organization and of clan ownership of land, give a sense not only of the land, but of families, as being ancient. Most ancient of all is family-land. The repetition of national struggle against the English has a lot to do with all this.

I do not want to over-emphasize these facts, for Dublin, like every metropolis, is a magnet for people from all parts of Ireland, and it is in Dublin that most names occur in greatest numbers; but, if you look in part two of the Irish telephone book, the volume which deals with everywhere in the Republic outside Dublin, you will find the concentration I speak of. I have tested this with components of my own ancestry: Buckleys, Scanlons, and Condons are concentrated mainly in Munster, and mainly, too, in certain parts of Munster. What is interesting is that these concentrations often have a marked if unsteady resemblance to those of centuries ago. So we have in the one curious fact an unusual degree of clan-identity with an unusual degree of personal anonymity.

In Bansha, a village in Tipperary, a man was introduced to me as 'an O'Dwyer trooper', a form which he did not use himself and which my informant seemed to think was a necessary means of identification: you did not name his father, you named his clan-position. Unfortunately, he did not tell me what it means, and I still don't know. The only meaning I can assign to it is a medieval one, referring to his function in the clan as a fully working social and, indeed, military complex. The O'Dwyer trooper is now a trainer of racehorses, which I suppose is a smart adaptation to modern conditions. The clan system on which his title relies was completely destroyed at the beginning of the seventeenth century; this clan lost its lands, and its leaders went on fighting, on and off, through the succeeding hundred years. O'Dwyer troopers in a different and more desperate sense, driven from their lands, rode as outlaws against their dispossessors. Songs were written by and about them, and these songs are still sung; among them are 'Ned of the Hill' and 'Sean O'Dwyer of the Glen', two of the greatest of Munster songs. The beautiful glen of Aherlow still vibrates with their names. O'Dwyer trooper had become O'Dwyer bushranger.

That is only one example from hundreds. A people for whom identity meant clan and land had to fight against those who destroyed the nuclei of the first and stole the second, and who then, in full daily sight of those they had dispossessed, made laws forbidding them to use their language (in which their very names were conceived and born). Migration and starvation removed millions of people, but even they could not eliminate from the locality those who remained.

While they remained alive and in Ireland, they would remain there, where clan and their name were born, there ... or thereabouts, as Samuel Beckett muttered, permanent revenants, if I may coin an Irishism richly invited by English behaviour.

More prosaically, perhaps they did not move because they could not; they did not have the means. Yes, but the armies and bureaucrats of Queen Elizabeth butchered them in huge numbers, the Cromwellians six decades later ordered them to choose 'Hell or Connacht', driving them from pastoral Ireland to the stony west. Always they were squeezed or driven out; always they were to be found where their clan had begun: there, or thereabouts. My Condon ancestors, who held a dozen or more castles along the Blackwater in County Cork, committed themselves fully to the rebellion of the Catholic Confederacy in the 1640s, and those who were not executed for it are said to have been forced into Connacht. This seems unlikely to me; but, whether or no, there they are again, all over Cork, and especially around the towns on or near the Blackwater, moved by the spirit to be there or thereabouts.

Now, such people, whether their names be Norman or Gaelic, or exhibit signs of a Pictish origin, or be English or Palatine or Norse, are not members of the land-owning gentry, and are not usually called Anglo-Irish. They live in a culture quite apart from that of the 'great houses', or the 'big houses', most of which are from the seventeenth or eighteenth century. They have nothing to do with such houses, except as servants or tradespeople. They may, however, have had a great deal to do with those still older houses, the castles whose shells or stumps still rear up in hundreds, even thousands, on the long-usurped lands, which are sometimes incorporated into later buildings, and every now and again restored, as Yeats's fifteenth-century tower was, lived in by someone not afraid of cold stone. These buildings, ranging from the half-grand to the nearly domestic, are all pre-Cromwellian – medieval, products of the pre-Reformation Catholic Ireland. Most of them are Norman, some earlier; but in any case none of us can be sure that the distinction any longer has meaning, the stocks have been so inter-grafted, the cultural habits and skills so grown into one another, over 800 years. What does seem clear is that the Gaelic part of the mixture has had the greatest absorptive power, so that what remains, in stone or field or writing, of the middle ages bears a native quality of a quite distinctive sort.

This Gaelic Ireland, which lives on in the Irish language, and which can be seen and touched in innumerable remnants all over the country, is no doubt the 'ancient Ireland' of which Yeats cried, 'and ancient Ireland knew it all'. It knew it all, and it was itself the core of what it knew. But Gaelic Ireland, although ancient, is not the earliest Ireland; there were people there before the triumphal Gaels, and their memory too is incorporated in the Ireland we see everywhere before us. Ancient Ireland is also prehistoric Ireland, pre-Celtic Ireland. Over four millennia and more the remains have grown up, and four millennia of layers still grow into and out of one another with that soft green tactility, that infinitely holding and resisting softness, peculiar to a damp but temperate country.

Naturally enough the most ancient remains are thickest in parts of the country which, not being uniformly fertile enough, did not tempt the occupying magnates to de-nature them, and to remove all signs of human occupation in order to occupy themselves with cows; even so, cows, which certainly pre-date any Cromwellian in Ireland, have proved a benefit to the old culture; for, if the land is good enough for grazing, it may be saved from becoming a housing estate. Thus there are monuments everywhere; but they are more thickly grouped in areas where the 'new' landowners did not think it worth-while to attempt their civilization, beyond planting an avenue and putting up a gazebo or a fancy shed for machinery. I have seen them most in parts of Cork and Kerry, in the Burren of Clare and in Sligo. In these counties they stand or lie in thousands, waiting for the casual visitor to make sense of them.

But in July 1981, we were settling not in any of those places but in Kildare, close to Dublin, part of the English Pale from the thirteenth century, blessed with English landowners, and rich with English blood, full of small towns, affluent, and quite lacking in survivals of the old clan system. Where could I hope to find ancient Ireland there? It was there, all right, but thinner and in a different form. In South Kildare the cultural if not the genetic mingling is common, and it is remarkable that it should be so; for these are rich farmlands and breeding-grounds, dominated by Norman adventurers from the first days of the invasion, run still in many parts by or for the English. The country looks too settled and bland and richly green. In fact, it is to a striking extent a mix or amalgam; and prehistory smells strong there as soon as your senses are open.

I cannot imagine that there is any country in which you are as close as you are in rural Ireland to the prehistorical and the trans-historical: for this is not, as is often said, a land obsessed with history, but a land of largely forgotten pre- and posthistory. People there inhabit their historical past like a dreamtime. They don't care to get dates or timescales into perspective; the dimension of the not-to-be-spoken-of is so close. By this I do not mean that the country is primitive in a raw way; it has a brooding, mannered soft quality which bespeaks the long-folded corners of a civilization. It is not primitive force, but pre-human presence that meets you here. The force just stands there, as it were, half-way between light and enclos-ing twilight.

Local Kildare people have generally shouldered it away, for it is not signposted, is seldom asked after, and its importance is not validated by its being the object of visible international attention. On the road from Athy to Portlaoise you round a curve, and there on your right is a ruined rock fortress looming out of the fields, for all the world like a smaller Rock of Cashel. It is called Dunamase, a fortress for many hundred of years, contested over and over by kings, armies and adventurers. When I mentioned it to Mark Wright, a local strong farmer (and the 'luckiest man with a racehorse in Kildare', so they all said in Kilcullen), it turned out that his relations came from near there, and he was astonished by my interest in it. Sure hadn't it always been there. Always the same. Never enquired after. When you grew up you'd never notice it.

Mark did not say these things, but they do represent a common attitude. Ireland has grown up, to EEC height and with a Brussels haircut, and it did not need to notice those earthy old rocks any more. It is understandable; such an outcrop, centaur-like, part rock and part building, is a solitary and inexplicable thing; what is there to say about it? You might think of it as a pre-poetic gift of time, but what use is that either? Personally, I could never write poetry about such places. As Michael Hartnett the poet said to me, 'Cut out everything that rattles. No history, no myth, no politics, no piety.' I think that was the list; and in a way I agree with him; there has been too much 'myth', which is often a fancy name for fanciful pretending, and poetic 'history' is often mere tourism in time. The actual past is too tense for such fancifulness; each historical act took place in a land drenched in prehistory; and how do you get the multiple effects of that? In the fields around us at Blackhall, O'Connell in the 1830s addressed his vast meeting at Mullaghmast, itself the scene of slaughter of the Irish chieftains in 1577, and before that maybe a pre-literate gathering ground. In 1798, there were battles at Old Kilcullen, Narraghmore and Athy, beatings and sackings at Ballitore, floggings at Athy, and executions at Dunlavin. In the twelfth century, raths were turned into medieval castles, and some of them have now reverted to raths. Where the peasant army fought in 1798 were ancient burial grounds, sacred long stones, and other antique markers. They fought, as people in the country always seem to, over generations of their own and others' dead. And there are mysterious places to which no one seems to have the key. One of them is the exquisite little graveyard of Killeen Cormac, set near trees in a flat open paddock; it has several examples of stones engraved with ogham 'writing', and nobody knows how or why, except that other Killeens in Kerry also have ogham stones.

But writing about them is not the point; preserving them is. Inertia and self-interest lead to the erosion of the Irish past. Michael

Behan, whose grandfather had worked on the moulding on Blackhall Castle, and whose two brothers had been among the six
gardeners at Blackhall, 'in the old days', when it was 500 acres and not
nine, had run straight into them both. He had worked as a young
man at a neighbouring big house, at Calverstown, and he had been
employed there intermittently in more recent times. He too had his
Arcadia, his idyll in the mind; it concerned the Anglo-Irish who had
had the property in his youth, who had conserved and tidied, and
ridden horses, and entertained painters, and who included more than
one sensitive and considerate young lady who had taken notice of
him; so that by all these means the summer of his mind was created.
Later, the place became a stud farm, run or owned by an English
family, who kept themselves rather haughtily to themselves. Under
them, the property still includes the ruined mansion-house, which
they have misdated, and the slightly misleading archival history
which they have commissioned from some agent in Dublin, and the
great green mounds whose nature they did not know. During their
incumbency Michael was employed, in effect, excavating. There, he
said, he found in the hall of the ruined house a plaque saying ORDO
HIBERNIAE, and other things, a post incised with ogham script (very
rare in Leinster) and, while he was digging outside, a 'perfect little
archway' at ground level, leading into an underground chamber.
There was also discovered the skeleton of an elk in the largest of the
green mounds. Now, all this was startling enough to hear; but more
startling was the gentleman owner's reaction to the finds, and
especially to the sight of the archway. 'All right', he said, 'cover all
that up. There's no need to go any further.' 'Why?' said I. 'He didn't
want the quare ones coming in,' said Michael. 'You mean the
archaeologists, and so on?' I said. 'I'm a bit in favour of the quare ones
myself.' 'So am I,' said Michael, 'but you can see his point.' 'Since it
might be embarrassing for you to make the necessary enquiries,' I
said, 'I'll see that they are made.' And so I did, to the proper quarters,
and all that; but none of them has done anything.

The landowner, on this account, has an economic interest in

hiding away from the people what their ancestors have made. No one is to even mention its existence; everyone is to be mystified about the origins of the property and the nature of what is buried or concealed on it. So foreign landowners alienate not only the land but also its accumulated human meaning; and when the land comes into native hands, as it sometimes does, the treasures are lost among rubble in the corner of a ruin, or have been defaced or buried, or have been incorporated into some fabric which disguises their nature, or are lying in the long grass fertilized by cow-dung.

This last phrase gives the clue to the problem of identification and preservation: most of the antique remains are on private land, and many of them are in the hands of people who make it a point of principle to maintain a class-distance from the people in the area, especially those who, since their names are Gaelic and they are members of the shopkeeping or labouring classes, or are in service of one kind or another, are likely to show some unwelcome curiosity about shards of the Gaelic past. The landowners may not even have the faintest idea what they have in their care; local folklore in most places is fanciful and hit or miss, and archaeological societies have not often had the chance to work systematically.

Kildare is very lucky in this respect; its Archaeological Society was active and well run in the late nineteenth century, at the very time when land was beginning to change hands, and just before the proportion of land owned by Catholics began to increase. Its guiding spirit was Lord Walter Fitzgerald, of Kilkea Castle, not far from our place; so he had a particular interest in any property which the numerous Norman clan of Fitzgerald had occupied after the twelfth century, and, given the location of Kilkea Castle, he had an interest in south Kildare, the areas towards Wicklow, Carlow, and Kilkenny, rather than the now more profusely populated north Kildare. There were many other painstaking and eloquent antiquarians gathered around him; some were members of aristocratic families, some were Protestant clergymen, some were Catholic clergy, especially Jesuits. Among these last, Joycians may be pleased to recognize the name of the Rev. John Conmee, SJ.

There is of course not a single well-known medieval town which was not fought over, and fought through, decade by decade. Around us, this was true, for example, of Athy, Naas and Old Kilcullen.

The study of their layers of history, however, comes down for the most part to the dynastic toing and froing, the records of patronage and treachery, the building and letting fall, which the Norman occupation of England, too, would yield. If that was all that Ireland offered for historical understanding, it would not be much. But of course you cannot nominate one among the many time-layers at which you will stop your thought.

Besides, some places of early significance are now anonymous; Knockaulin for example, just outside Kilcullen. It was more important in pre-literate times, for on its top is Dun Ailinne, crowning-place of the Kings of Leinster. A pub nearby is named for it, but in itself it is an unremarkable hill. Less than a mile from it is the ruin and churchyard of Old Kilcullen, another mound on a hillside. Everyone knows about this, and it is in all the guidebooks, even the meanest; it can be seen for a mile or two from several directions. But it is just a graveyard surrounded by sheep paddocks; in the common manner, it is also a sheep paddock at times. It has three ruined stone crosses and a ruined high tower; it has a strange atmosphere and long views across three or four counties.

But in medieval times it was a walled town, with seven gates, which held a long stretch of the Liffey against the Danes. During this or that battle, then and later, thousands crowded inside its walls. Its function as ford-town was taken over by Kilcullen; yet even in 1798, when it was once again the scene of a battle, and an Irish victory, it had, with its church and its walls, a status which only the antiquarians know of today. Ancient Ireland exists there as deprived; elsewhere, as in Dun Ailinne, it exists as invisible. They show the point I am making, that you can live beside or on a site which was continuously occupied, recurrently sacred, for 3,000 years, and not know it: not merely because it is not signposted, but also because nobody who lives near you knows enough about its meaning in time. Perhaps this is what Professor Louis Cullen means when he speaks of 'the general poverty of tradition in Ireland'. This poverty is one of the reasons why, to use his words again, Irish people view their country 'uncertainly and apologetically'. They live without key in a superbly coded environment. And whereas a school of 'revisionist' historians was badly called for twenty or so years ago, the sense of tradition will hardly be restored when every 'reputable' historian rushes into a revisionist posture and obscurely reassures the English; soon no one will remember what it was that needed revision, and what bigotries had to be overcome for the truth to be told. I don't think anyone in Ireland is interested in Dun Ailinne.

Once you realize that there are 'antiquities' in some nearby places, you quickly find that they are everywhere. On top of Brewel Hill, just behind our place, are the Pipers Stones, a group of heavy white quartz stones arranged in some obscure but beguiling pattern. Everything about this site is enigmatic, although the stones clearly signify something ceremonial. You climb to it across the usual hilly paddocks, richly covered in cow-dung; but indeed you will not know where to start the climb unless you ask a near neighbour, for there are no signs of any kind to tell you. The 'stones' are hidden away inside an enclosure which is fenced and planted with prickly small trees; cow-dung is everywhere, and so are cows, browsing paranoiacally away beneath the branches. The enclosure may have been a fortified rath in pagan times, and seems to have had a specific sacred significance; the view from its edges is magnificent in all directions. Is it worth seeing? It is neither an historical antiquity nor a legendary matrix; for nothing of any importance is thought to have happened here, nor is it said to be 'owned' by any of the legendary heroes, by Dairmuid and Grainne, or Finn, or the Wizard Earl of Kildare. It is a slate, a *tabula rasa*; but it is clearly an important site, much more gripping to an observer like myself than Mullaghmast of the Hosting, however important its inscribed stone, or Ardscull of the Shouts and Battles. Maybe it avoided recorded battles rather than inviting them. Maybe it was established at that spot precisely because it was to be a stronghold of rear defence, where sacred objects could be safely secreted and secret ceremonies conducted. Certainly it has that feel, kept piquant among the unavoidable dung. Who or what, though, was the 'piper' whose stones these are? In what sense are the stones his 'dancers'? There are other groups bearing this name in Britain and in western Europe; one of them is a few miles further over towards the mountains, on the invisible border with Wicklow; everywhere here you are in the approaches to the desolate Wicklow mountain-system: not surprisingly a set of battlegrounds for the rising of 1798. It is all, in a sense, border country; marches, for within it two or more cultures, power-systems, encroached for centuries on one another.

Further down the Carlow road is the beautiful high cross of Moone. Again, it is set in a monastic graveyard, a few yards from the back wall of an ugly Georgian house on the one side, and fifty yards from the busy farmyard of a dairy farm on another. Again, it is unobtrusively set, but this one is a recognized national monument, and is signposted and supervised as such. What is interesting and characteristic about it is that it is one more example of culture's not being removed from nature. This is the secret and the problem of ancient Ireland as it survives in the present: it is not easy to find, it is not usually made much of, it is small-scale, it is likely to be drab or damaged; but, above all, no strict lines of reverential demarcation are drawn around it so that you focus on this one thing, are encouraged to be preoccupied with it, are led to set it in your mind's retina as still and perfected as a fly in amber. That may be an English habit, the way of an imperial conqueror, freed by conquest and its riches to contemplate things both as possessions and as objects of deliberately heightened aesthetic attention. Irish remains are not objects in that sense, unless you are seeing them in the national museum in Dublin. The high cross of Moone, which half the time is trickling with rain as the crack across its middle grows imperceptibly wider, which is perennially damp, which cannot preserve and highlight the contours of its own carvings in the face of the weather, is not isolated in that way. You take it in its context, of house, cowyard, grass, grave-stones, ruined chapel. You are not looking at, you are inside this gestalt. You are not sure when and how its component parts have come together, but you are aware of the stone buildings and crosses not as things set aside from nature but as things planted in nature, to be features of its growth. This adds to the damp, but also to the antique calm. It is very hard to take a satisfying photograph of Moone; you cannot photograph the smell of cow-shit and grass.

Irish antiquity, then, is like the country itself; it is not squeaky clean, and it is not homogenized. It is seldom spectacular, and it does not often lay claim to unusual beauty as an object-self. Moone is in any case part of a larger whole in the immediate vicinity; the lorries which speed through Castledermot on their way to the south-west or to Dublin would not be worried about the ancientness of its foundations, with their still trailing enigmas. They would be more conscious of the accident black spot near Ballitore, at which there were at least five accident deaths while we were living nearby.

Castledermot does not give an impression of decay, for this was not famine country in the way Cork was. But it was the centre of the territory taken from the O'Tooles by Strongbow himself, at the very start of the Norman settlement, and 'given' to Walter de Riddlesford. The castle itself was built by him or by Hugh de Lacy, a great one for castles. Later the Fitzgeralds, sited at nearby Kilkea, contested it with the de Burghs. In 1276, a Parliament is said to have been held here. In 1295, the town was enclosed with walls. Twenty years later the ubiquitous Edward Bruce involved it in his march; but it was left to a Butler, the Lord Justice of the time, to slaughter the uprisen Gaelic clans, the O'Mores, O'Byrnes, and the O'Tooles, whose land of course it was. By the end of that century, King Richard II had been in residence at it, and 'great councils' had been held there. At the end of the next century, a Parliament was held at Castledermot, in 1499; its laws were punitive; one was against 'those who, when they rode, used not saddles, after the English fashion'. No hibernicization in our town.

And so it went on, in the usual manner of dynastic and managerial histories, such as the Normans required and require. Such a history would be that of fiefdom. Castledermot was an important fiefdom. And if by ancient Ireland you mean these fiefdoms and their managers, Castledermot is redolent of ancient Ireland. Yet little even of that antiquity survives; you cannot read the settlement's history in its stones. By 1780, that part of its past is a matter for comment by travellers of an antiquarian bent. In that year the author of a *Tour Through Ireland* (people were always going on 'tours' through the benighted countries) wrote:

It had formerly four gates; the entrance southward still bears the name of Carlow Gate, and the other to the north, Dublin Gate, though there are not the least remains of either left . . . The inn where we dined was part of the Parliament House . . . As to the castle from which it derives its name, there are not even the vestiges to be seen.

Nowadays the account would be far more wry; we see rudimentary signs of a town wall, we are barely conscious of a town. It had been belted out of its shape, out of its very existence, in all those and in later wars. Because it was occupied so often by the losers, it no longer has an historic shape.

But is this what we mean by ancient Ireland? Are there not layers still more invisible to be caught up into the mind's eye? If a castle had not given the town its name, we might more readily ask what sort of place it was before the Normans. It was called 'disert Diarmada': the hermitage of Dermot, who came to this small version of wilderness to make it his refuge. He did so about AD 500, 700 years before the Normans swaggering in stone. We can see in a place like this just how places became significant, and dynasties were extended from the military to the religious life in ancient Christian Ireland.

In later centuries the Danes sacked the monastery (this, too, was standard); and then, in 907, Cormac Mac Cullenan 'was slain, and was interred here'. The king-bishop was no contemplative weakling; he had led his armies in battle, and had won, and slaughtered his enemies, before he was himself killed in battle. For the next three centuries, the primary clans of the area operated around Disert

Diarmada – the Fitzpatricks, the family of Dunlaing, the O'Tooles and their frequent in-laws, the O'Byrnes. I mention them to stress that the way in which the 'wild' O'Tooles and O'Byrnes are mentioned in all the histories, as wolves of the mountains marauding against the civilizing forces who were trying to nurture the rich plain, is little short of propaganda for the English dispossessors. These clans themselves came from the rich plain; every stream and mound in that marvellous country was sacred to them; and some of them were crowned as kings of whole provinces on top of that hill which I passed every day. They, and clans like them, were not preying on settlements and monasteries; they were their settlements and monasteries, taken from them and now turned into fortresses against them.

The chief book of Ireland is often entitled in translation *The Book of Invasions*; and the story of ancient Ireland seems always to come back to an invasion, an occupation, a rebellion, the settling down of some areas into marches, or border territories. Near Castledermot, south Kildare and Wicklow, starting mountain and ambitious or ambiguous 'plain' are nearly indistinguishable.

In the midst of them is Killeen Cormac, utterly mysterious in its small, compact way. It is a graveyard, set in the middle of a paddock bordering a small road that loops off the Carlow road on the way to nowhere. It is on the very border of Kildare with Wicklow, very close to Dunlavin, on whose village green, so the rebel song says, rebel prisoners captured at Ballitore were massacred in 1798. Beyond it, but unseen from the road, runs the river Greese. Burials were still being conducted here in 1900, according to Lord Walter Fitzgerald.

What is this place? The burying ground of Cormac. This man 'is said to have been a King of Munster', and when he died a 'great dispute arose as to the place of his burial'. The dispute was settled by allowing the bullocks which pulled the hearse-waggon to stop where they wished. At a certain point

a hound that lay on its master's bier made a leap forward, and landed on the Killeen, leaving the impression of one of his paws on a standing stone. The team of bullocks, proceeding on, crossed the river Greese, reached the Killeen, and refused to go further. Thus was the spot for the burial of King Cormac decided on ...

This story has an irreducibly Irish flavour: bullocks, hound, and heroic leap all swell with a Gaelic world-view. So has the magic involved in the later disappearance of the bullock team. So has the preoccupation with apt burial. So has the business of leaving a decision to the disposition of animals. We are no wiser about Cormac. He was 'a king of Munster', but South Kildare is a long way from Munster, and his death-battle is quite enigmatic.

Recounting this detail in sober prose, I feel very far from the 'ancient Ireland' of Yeats's romantic dreaming, which is full of marvellous doings and short on objects which just stay there, encapsulating their secret. Aristocratic dashers, crazed peasants and warty ramblers are nowhere in evidence – although they may, of course, lie in this very clay. Nor does anyone keep the graveyard in tourist condition, for no tourists know about it; and although I had been looking for it, I did not know it when I found it.

Given these facts, ancient Ireland, which 'knew it all', is safe from foreigners, for it sure as hell is hidden from the Irish; perhaps the endlessly draining weather will open up its secret.

Antiquity in Ireland exists, then, not as a spectacle, a sight, within a clearly defined social frame; it is, instead, a site from which the country can be seen, as presumably it was used *ab origine*. It is not an object, or a society; it is a place, often barely distinguished from the places around it. It is seldom the organizing centre of a city; usually, it exists outside cities entirely, it is not and never has been part of a city civilization, and it reveals nothing of city economy or gods. It is part of an open world, in which the sacred node does not gather things around it, but grows downward and up, to the beings of the netherworld or those of light and air. Like Tara, Dun Ailinne, or the Curragh, it was once a place of periodical gathering. The Hill of Allen, Dun Firinne, and Mullaghmast are thought to be the abode of sleeping gods or dead heroes. Others were, in effect, open air temples.

Others were defensive enclosures. If we think of the great forts of Dun Aengus, on Inismore, and the Grianan of Ailech, in northern Donegal, we are seeing ancient Ireland in its military aspect: large, commanding, defensive, perhaps built by slaves.

To me the most extraordinary scene of all is the great and mysterious complex in Sligo, of which the foci are the solitary mountains of Ben Bulben and Knocknarea, much hymned by Yeats, and the solitary prehistoric mountain graveyards of Carrowkeel and Carrowmore. Ben Bulben now has a mine on its cold top, and the poisonous muck is being drained off into Lough Gill, to sink beside Yeats's isle of Innisfree. And just as investigators are about to discover something crucial and exciting about the megaliths of Carrowmore, they also discover that the miners of gravel have been before them.

Irish antiquities, then, while free of the museum atmosphere, suffer from the paddock condition. In the fields they may be unobtrusive, even insouciant, but those fields are likely to 'belong' to someone who has little care for them, and that makes them vulnerable. If they are not capital assets themselves, they very likely lie next to resources which are; these are mined, and they are undermined. The pastoral condition of the country has preserved many of them from that fate; at the same time, the climate which creates that condition is apt to preserve them by burial; a high proportion of the artefacts in the museums have been uncovered from boglands. Metal, stone and wood become lost, or flake, or crumble in the delicate full damp of the country; if they go into the deeper dampness of the bogs, they will be preserved from erosion as well as commercial exploitation, but at the risk of staying unrecovered forever.

This climate has led to a peculiar fatalism both in the inhabitants and in commentators on Irish history; the Irish are felt, even by themselves, to be peculiarly fated by their weather patterns. This feeling, in turn, suggests that the Irish climate is in some way extreme, inhospitable, unlivable; but it is not; on the contrary, it is temperate, even equable; the trouble is that it is persistently damp, and it is changeable. So the Irish, their herds and their buildings and their towns, have been shaped by a climate which is damp, but moderate; predictable, yet changeable to the point of volatility; not dramatic so much as broody; its mean is strikingly temperate; you might feel that you need to let your bones be gathered and absorbed by a nature so beautiful; if it induces discontent (and it does), it is not because it is threatening but because it is by turns enlivening and depressing; it is a country in which the pathetic fallacy is easy to indulge.

Why the fatalism, then?

We know that waves of colonists are said to have perished, and to lie in multitudes inside the falsely welcoming hills, like Parthalon and his army in the 'plague grave' near Tallaght; and we know that well into this century tuberculosis was the plague for Irish men and women, as it still is for their cattle. But these diseases are capable of cure; and famine and massacre far outstripped natural fevers in their power to reduce the Irish. Geographical fatalism is a diversion from, and a displacement of, social and political evils. If houses are inadequately heated, the price of oil may be more to blame than some preternatural dampness of the ground. The country is no more fated, no more foredoomed, no more a premature grave, than any other. We should not read into the geography, so that it becomes inevitable, the sadness produced among the human family by history. Nor, of course, should we ignore geography in tracing history. Still, if we follow the *Book of Invasions*, or any deductions from it, we may wonder why, if the melancholia of the place assimilated, unmanned and rotted successive colonists, they rushed so hard to steal it.

No doubt, though, geographical fatalism may be expected to last among writers on Ireland for a few more decades. It is the brother of racist determinism. Both flourished in the nineteenth century, making a great excuse for landlordism and the other evils of imperial occupation: land and people are both victimized by climate; bad atmosphere and bad blood are sisters under the shawl. The people are fated to be ruled by a superior race, who are fated to be oppressed by the climate, from which they owe it to themselves to escape as much as possible. Thus, absentee landlordism is a duty for the dispossessor.

The fatalism of such commentaries is itself depressing. One wants to ask: but cannot climate be balanced by diet? No, a fatalist might say, the inertia of the country makes them incapable of agriculture. But surely they have practised agriculture for centuries, only to have their crops taken from them by landlords, and a standard crop, the potato, forced on them, despite the fact that it was bound to fail and rot periodically. Geological and geographical whingeing cannot drown out the questions. Geography, after all, means a relationship of one land mass to others. Ireland is the unmoving edge of the complicated European system of land masses. Does it serve the purpose of fending off, absorbing, or diverting the Atlantic weather bound for England? Does it belt that weather sideways, up to Scotland, through the six counties? But much of the Atlantic weather is far from enervating. Is it rational for writers like Estyn Evans to be quite so insistent on the depressing quality of Irish nature? There are moistures and moistures; and the humidity of Cork is nothing like that of Bangkok. The desolate and desolating effects of Irish landscape certainly have to do not just with chemicals in the soil, but also with the temperament of the people and their social and geographical distribution. But who, looking at Irish history in the modern era, would attribute these effects to geography instead of history? Ireland is a living testimony to the fact that its own people have absorbed history into geography, event into climate. Outside commentators should not encourage them in this history-conditioned vice.

Was it ancient Ireland that we came to live in, when we arrived in Kildare? Not immediately, at any rate. There was talk of ogham stones being found here and there, but I never saw them, any more than I saw the strange stone Ger O'Neill found on his property, or the poltergeist which had driven him to leave his starkly handsome eighteenth-century house to build a bungalow twenty yards from it. I saw no faery in the faery raths, and no incarnations of the fianna. We lived in an area whose shape, nomenclature and use were governed by its Norman occupation, by an antiquity of less than 800 years. It was a place where the fields were called by names ending in 'town' or carrying its Irish equivalent 'baile' or 'bally': Calverstown, Davidstown, Colbinstown, Ballyshannon. Narraghmore, where we shopped, had been a 'barony' – a Norman measure; and if before that it had been a Gaelic 'tuath', or minor kingdom, there were no visible signs of it.

Most of the places whose names contained 'bally' or 'town' were not by any stretch of the imagination towns, or even villages, though my friends kept telling me that 'baile' means 'town', and that's that. These places, however, were 'townlands', areas of open country demarcated by a farm, a biggish house, and maybe a few odd cottages. So 'baile' meant both town and settlement, or enclosure, like a stockade in Indian territory, or a fortified house with its enclosure or 'bawn', or a house with dependent cottages.

Blackhall, where we came to live, was such a place. The tower must have had dependent buildings, and it certainly had a bawn, or enclosure. It is hard to tell, exactly, because the houses spaced along the perimeter of the former property are bungalows less than forty years old, and some of those are small farmhouses. The tower or castle had been built by the FitzEustaces, as part of their pattern of fortified places carefully planned along the Liffey. Mr M the owner did not know of the FitzEustaces; he thought the castle must have been one of the FitzGeralds'. This was not carelessness, but lack of interest. Like others, he will make a guess if he has to, and if he does he will guess some name of importance; most of Kildare was FitzGerald country, and everyone wants to be associated with a winner. The Earl of Kildare eventually became also the Duke of Leinster. By comparison, the FitzEustaces, from being High Sheriffs of Kildare, faded out in the seventeenth century by obstinate attachment to Irishness and Catholicism; their descendants are now generally called Eustace. I found out about the FitzEustaces after ten minutes in the county library. In any case, Mr M knew that whatever

Fitz built it did not end in possession of it; and the name in the record which interested him was a much trimmer and more modern-sounding one: a name from the Cromwellian settlement, the beginning of the modern era which is also the time of free speech and no popery. One such name was Wellesley, which sounds aptly modern, even Wellingtonian, though it is in fact as Norman as any Fitz. After him, after the dispossession of some rash FitzEustace in 1641, a long succession of pseudo-squires and self-exiled gentleman farmers, until, with the War of Independence, the Free State, and Land Commission, the 500 acres were distributed among what Mrs M referred to as 'Galway farmers', though they came in fact from Mayo, and all that remained to slope down and back from the small-scale grandeur of Blackhall Castle was nine acres. Everyone in the district regarded that as so small as to be pointless.

The tower, or castle, was flanked by a house; nobody knew the age of either. One authority says the tower is thirteenth century; Mr M, during his attempt to sell it, said sixteenth; but he was almost certainly selling it short, unless of course he regarded that as a particularly dashing century. Its roots have been down certainly since the thirteenth century. You don't call that ancient? I don't myself, exactly. But it had one ancient feature, a sheela-na-gig set into its south wall, at about breast height, where the sun in winter and spring would fall fully on it and change its lichen grey to a rust-rose glow. And it was the sheela which made me fall so immediately in love with the whole place the day I first saw it.

Sheela-na-gigs are figures carved or incised in stone, and found in many parts of Ireland, England, France and Scotland. They are more numerous in Ireland, where they are to be found in the walls of church or castle. Often it seems that a figure on or in a castle wall has been brought from some neighbouring church, which was its original site. The figure may be set beside or above the door, beside or above a window, above or within an arch; it may be set vertically or horizontally. The figure is always female, and is always characterized by an enlarged vulva, which her posture is arranged to display. She is often said to be a 'fertility figure', but whether her posture asserts fertility or fends off sterilizing agencies is a matter of opinion; she may be, as some others say, a figure to ward off evil, or to warn: 'erotic display as a means of warding off evil'; she may have some further function; she may have a variety of functions.

Then again, is she a survival from pre-Christian times, a witch-figure, or a representation of a pagan goddess from the times when Celtic civilization gave great power to the female? The leading authority, Jørgen Andersen, thinks the most numerous images come from the twelfth century, are part of a medieval or romanesque fascination with and fear of female sexuality, female being, the grotesqueness coming from the ambivalence which the period felt for what was becoming central to it. On this account, sheelas would be a diversionary minor art-form within the medieval Christian complex.

But why has Ireland so many of them? Nobody seems to know. The sheela-na-gig, despite her Gaelic name, may be one more thing imposed by the Norman adventurers of the late twelfth century on the soft, protean, assimilative fabric of Irish life; and she may have frightened hell out of the clansmen; or she may have given them a good laugh.

Anyway, Blackhall Castle has one, a relatively mild, relatively symmetrical one. I don't see how anyone could regard this sheela as a figure designed to frighten, warn, or create an impression of the potency of evil. Her facial expression is faint and vague, her hands are not pulling the lips of her vulva apart (as so may sheelas do), and she is carved symmetrically, with aesthetic rather than obsessive care. She is one of the two or three sheelas known to exist within Kildare. I found her a warm, domestic *genius loci*, for even in winter the afternoon sun bathed her whole figure. But such feelings are very subjective, and whatever anyone else may have felt about her, surely she has scarcity value. Surely an owner or a tenant would see to her preservation.

My landlord showed little interest in her; she was probably too 'early' for his sense of relevance; she was not manorial. One horse-owner, a civilized man though not, I think, of very deep Irish provenance, hustled his sons away from looking at her; his view was succinctly expressed, 'Too much fertility in Ireland.' Though he was always keen on more fertility among horses.

Trinity College Dublin sent experts to take a cast of her for an exhibition which has still not been held. The experts were from Belfast, and surprisingly vague in their answers to my questions about sheelas. The owner made moves to sell the property, and as I listened to prospective buyers indulging their fantasies I became worried. None of them talked of re-roofing the castle; more than one said he found it unsightly. Grandiose plans were voiced for pulling out all the trees and planting grass, for making productive use of the space occupied by the castle, which will certainly fall down in the foreseeable future unless someone literally grasps the actual nettle. I tried ringing the guardians of culture. I will not try to remember who they were, or what authority they represented; for each was nicer and more concerned than the one before, each offered to come and see the object with the idea of putting a restraining order on it. None came. Before leaving Kildare, I said to Larry and Mary Mulryan, 'Well, you have some influence in Fianna Fail. Will you make sure that, if there is any project to pull down the castle, the question of the sheela-na-gig will be raised in Dail Eireann?' They said they would do their best. I fear they will get no thanks for it.

Irish obsessed with history, indeed.

We left Kildare at the end of July 1982. Ancient Ireland was very different in the West Cork district where we were now to spend several weeks. The village was Castletownshend, once home of the writers Somerville and Ross, and most famous of all the Anglo-Irish preserves around this long and deeply indented coast; in the popular imagination it is hardly Irish at all; and indeed the well-established people who have summer houses there are more likely to be English or any other European rather than Irish. The castle which gives the place its name is by no means antique, but a fairly recent piece of pretence; the Townshend is merely the name of a family of land-lords; but there is another castle just behind this one, and that is a look-out tower of the O'Driscolls, who were the sea-based clan of this part, and whose towers looked out to sea. From another point of view, which the Anglo-Irish naturally don't take, Castletownshend is a fishing village. From another, it is the nearest town for a tenacious farming community which, however, would shop not in it but in the nearest market-town, Skibbereen.

The town is chiefly one long, very winding, extremely steep street leading down to the tiny harbour; and this street has a dark side and a sunny side. When she got to know me, one of the native inhabitants pointed out that the likes of her tended to live on the dark side. 'You don't like to think in this way,' she said, 'but I suppose it comes down to them on one side and us on the other.' Perhaps it does. She and hers speak to the stranger with a mixture of pride, slight reserve or even testiness, but no suspicion. There is no hint of the servility which you sometimes get in Kildare. The shopkeepers take no nonsense either from visitors or from resident gentry. We lived in the Whittys' house next to the Garda station, where the Clearys had a number of children. They were models of dignity, coming obviously from personality and character, but reinforced by the fact that Sergeant Cleary is the local football coach and his son John plays for the county. 'Do you ever get yobbos here in high summer?' I said to the sergeant. Once. 'What did you do?' I asked. 'O I put on the uni-form and wandered up and down for half an hour.' I believe him.

The town which the Anglo-Irish and the English guard is an eighteenth-century preserve. That guarded by the native Irish is something far older; it is something that survived the famines of 1845–48, which brought unbearable pestilence to West Cork. The family who looked after the house we had borrowed was called McKennedy; this is an unusual name, yet while we were there I read that a McKennedy was one of the first to die of famine fever in the area, in 1845; he was a labourer, and the contents of his stomach showed that he had worked without eating for two weeks. What such people guarded is represented by the great and ancient hill-fort named Knockdrum. When I asked for directions to this wonder, naturally it was a native Irish woman I asked; but I used the anglicized form, and she gently substituted the Gaelic form. 'Do you know it well?' I asked. 'O we go up there regularly,' she said. 'We have picnics there.' She knew about the three standing stones that faced one side of the fort, but would make no comment on them. Fort and stones belonged to these people in a way in which Dun Ailinne and even Old Kilcullen have long ceased to belong to the people of south Kildare.

The Irish here live by fishing, shopkeeping, cleaning houses, farming or working for farmers, or working for the county council. None showed the slightest interest in patronage, or in currying favour, and you had the sense that they would reject any offered. Yet the village was set up for patronage. The owners of the houses on the 'sunny side' were foreigners, their cars and yachts were obtrusive, there were landowners living in full Angloid fig (though with a distinctively Irish flavour) around the visitors, and the village in a sense lived on holidays, if not tourism. Tourists would be frozen out by the summer residents. The Irish working class did not fall for the chance to get in on some corporate act and make both money and identity out of it. They already had identity, and it was in an obscure and tenuous way a clan-identity. This had all been not only famine territory but war territory; the War of Independence had been fought here in 1919 and later. A haughty old gent whom I met down at the old coast-guard station, which is now his house, was quick to tell me, 'I saw it burning when I was a young boy. I helped my father put the fire out. I'd always wanted to have the place myself.' And when I asked him, 'Who burnt it?' he said, 'O, political. In the troubles.' He was as Anglo-Irish as you could get; and he spoke more naturally of the War of Independence than any of his counterparts in Kildare could have brought himself to do.

This forthrightness seems to occur wherever the people fought and beat the British forces of occupation before 1922. All through west and north Cork, they don't have to pretend to themselves that the British are somehow better than they. So they live with them without animosity or servility, guard their antiquity with dignified reserve, and don't think too much about the sunny side of the street. I was never completely persuaded that that street has a sunny side.

Part Two

A FAST TO A DEATH

Chapter Seven

ELECTION AND DEATH OF BOBBY SANDS

When I arrived in Dublin, just before the end of March 1981, Bobby Sands had been on hunger-strike for more than four weeks. He was the first of a growing line of young men, who joined it at intervals of about ten days. They were all inmates of the prison at Long Kesh, in Northern Ireland; they were all Republican dissidents against the state which had imprisoned them; they were all Catholics, whether in belief or merely in name; most of them belonged to the Irish Republican Army, the 'Provisionals', and the rest to a smaller military group, the Irish National Liberation Army (INLA). The proportions on hunger-strike had been decided between the two bodies. The actual individuals were all volunteers. Sands, as OC of the IRA prisoners, was the prime hunger-striker, and his dying was the prime controller for the imaginations of those who watched them; although it was possible that someone who had joined the line later than he might jump the tense queue and die before him. At this time, Sands was reported to be showing signs of weakness, though not collapse; but there was no question of his dying just yet.

What was all this? I knew there had been a hunger-strike late the previous year, and that it had been called off by the strikers after certain undertakings had been given by the British government. I did not know in detail what these undertakings were supposed to have been; but both sides claimed victory, as is usually the case, and within days the prisoners were accusing the British of reneging on their promises. There were prison riots in January, and savage discontent generally. But it is hard to get firm Irish news in Australia, and, knowing that hunger-strikes are nearly impossible to resume once they have been abandoned, I didn't give enough heed to the news that another one had started in March. I was profoundly, and unreasonably, shocked to learn on arrival that Sands was already thirty days into his death-fast.

I was sick, and was hardly registering most aspects of my sur-
roundings. The day-to-day drama of the hunger-strike had yet to
touch me. One day, at Seamus Heaney's house, shortly after I arrived
in Dublin, he opened the paper and said to his wife, 'Francis Hughes
is weakening.' His tone was tense and wondering. He and Hughes
were from the same area, in South Derry; and Hughes was second to
Sands in the line of fasters. It was not only the hunger-strike as such
that was exercising people. There was also to be a by-election in one
of the northern electorates for the House of Commons at Westminster. This electorate, Fermanagh-South Tyrone, had a Catholic
majority and would normally return an anti-Unionist member, if
only one candidate of that sort, whether nationalist, independent, or
Sinn Fein, was nominated. But the electorate was much contested by
all those groupings on the anti-Unionist side. Barely known to me,
the nomination drama for the constituency of Fermanagh-South
Tyrone had itself engaged a complex of political forces in the north.
In a complicated pattern of retreat and advance, the two early
nominees, Bernadette McAliskey and Noel Maguire, both republican
but neither in a paramilitary sense, indeed both independents, had
withdrawn from the fight in order to leave only one anti-Unionist
candidate. This was Bobby Sands, IRA prisoner and hunger-striker.

There was much talk of their having been forced out of it by the
IRA to leave Sands a clear run; but nobody seemed able to give
chapter and verse for this supposition. The pressure was now on the
'moderate' anti-Unionist party, the SDLP: would they put up a
candidate against Sands? Until the last minute it seemed they would;
but then commonsense triumphed; whatever else happened, the anti-
Unionist vote must not be split. Something like this was happening
also in the Unionist side; Paisley rejected the proposed Unionist
candidate, and urged his followers not to vote for him. As for Sands,
the SDLP disowned him, as did most politicians. Priests preached
against him, newspaper editors hypothesized him into defeat.
Nobody at first gave twopence for his chances. SDLP voters were
asked to spoil their votes rather than give them to him. In the days

before the election, a census-taker, Mrs Joanna Mathers, was wantonly killed, evidently by Republicans, although the IRA disclaimed it. The Catholic Bishop Daly spoke warmly of the dead woman, and vehemently condemned her murder. It seemed to many newspaper commentators that this atrocity meant the end to Sands's campaign.

But that campaign was being expertly organized and carried out with great dedication. All the nationalist politicos of the constituency, even some SDLP ones, organized their people. From the south, this activity was not visible; it was blotted out partly by media cynicism, partly by the anti-republican policies of the Dublin government. I arrived a week before the vote, and it took me some days to realize that Sands had a chance. One day I ran into a playwright I knew, a member of Sinn Fein. After a lot of chat about other things, he asked me, 'Well, what do you think of poor Bobby?' I thought, it is unbearably poignant, coming as it does after so many deaths caused by so many various groups, including his. Like any soldier, like any schoolchild now in Northern Ireland, he must expect to die. But he is dying for a foregone conclusion; he is negotiating his life without anyone to negotiate with. He is speaking with his bones to someone who does not answer, or who answers only with insults. I never thought the death of a warrior could be so poignant. They, his enemies, never thought a terrorist could die like that, so slowly, so thin, so near the help which he must refuse. Blessed are those who hunger for justice, said the notices on the Falls Road in Belfast. Blessed are the brave, too.

All these things I thought, but I did not say them to Daithi, my questioner. There was something about the form of his question that disoriented me: why 'poor' Bobby? Why was I being asked to evaluate him, rather than his deed, his gamble, his venture? I felt sorry for him, true; but I was not an active Republican, as my friend was. 'It's poignant,' I said. 'It's very painful. He should not be allowed to die.' 'Yes,' he said, very sombre. 'It's a dreadful business.' He had picked up my implication, that anyone who was encouraging Sands's

death should cease to do so. He talked about Sands and his desires, his
personal decisions. He agreed that, whatever other Republicans
might hope by way of resolution, Sands was going to die if it were
left to Margaret Thatcher. He fell into fatalism, and went off to
his books.

Dublin became very concerned. The tourist season was just starting; a British businessman had been shot in the legs while addressing
a seminar inside the hallowed squares of Trinity; hotel bookings
were down; cancellations were up. The prospect of profits was
sinking fast. 'These madmen in the north,' said a jumpy man whom I
met at the counter at Dublin airport while we both waited to collect
our belongings, 'madmen. They have no support, you know. So-
called republicans! So-called freedom fighters!' He was an importer
of suit-lengths, and his nexus with England was virtually umbilical.
'No support at all. Everyone hates them. Nobody at all takes any
notice of them in this country.' 'Why are you so concerned about
them?' I asked. 'O you meet them everywhere,' he said. 'All the time.
They're always going on to you about the freedom fight. National
heroes!' he sneered. 'They don't go on about it on Telefis Eireann,' I
said, 'for they're not allowed to.' 'No,' said he, 'quite right, too.
Hurry up Sean, for Christ's sake, you're not inventing the forms are
you.'

His view was widely held. Taxi-drivers, for example, espoused it
with great fierceness. 'For God's sake be quiet,' I said to one who was
talking about hanging prisoners. 'Am I paying to listen to this?' They
showed a certain confusion: IRA supporters were so few that they
were a tiny sect, they barely existed, yet they were all around us,
pressing on us, threatening us, wrecking the tourist business and the
lives of cabbies. There they were, all around us: unemployed factory
workers, dismissed schoolteachers, refugees from the north, dis-
placed small farmers, victims of *anomie*, disillusion, and sheer hunger.
All around us, being harassed by police, ignored by bustling middle-
class shoppers, stared through by priests, elements of the working-
class in an unflattering posture, though whether of threat or of

beseeching it was hard to say. They were holding cardboard banners and black flags. In the Catholic areas of the north the graffiti read, 'Blessed are those who hunger for justice.' Their loyalist counterparts read, 'Die in your cell you bastard.' In Dublin they had begun to say that there looked like being no tourist season at all this year.

There they were and are, in the standardized housing estates of Twinbrook, where the Sands family died so recently, or in the dreadful makeshift of the Falls, in Strabane with its 51 per cent unemployment, in Newry rotting away with disuse, in the scrubby farms with their pious mantels, in the betting-shops, on the crumbled corners, in the churches, in the overcrowded schoolyards, at the boroo, staring across from Derry at the Grianan. There they are, and what are they doing? Why, say the British press, the British army officers, the British poets, the big spenders of Brusselian Dublin, why, they are living in the past. Their blocked drains are the past, the splintered doors, the chill winter bedrooms, the bronchitis, the heart diseases, the emphysema, the 'nerves', the visits to the doctor, the violent drinking, the attempts at migration, all these are the past, and they live in it. And it is in the past that the fifteen-year-olds walk out, trying to keep their heads high as they wait for the feel of their first Armalite, with which in the near future they will tell their tormentors what they think of their present. Lucky is the country that has a past; for it will know what it thinks about death.

On the Wednesday night after my arrival I went to Kinsellas for dinner; the talk was of the North, the house was filled with a curious, excited tension. 'Would you vote for Sands, Vincent?' 'I'd vote against the others.' Their son-in-law drove me back to Trinity: 'I hope like hell . . . I have a feeling . . . do you think it's possible?' I had the feeling, too, all the stronger because people like this, by no means IRA supporters, indeed opponents of violence, were talking like this. The next day, it was the same with Seamus Deane, professor and poet: 'I hardly dare to hope.' The feeling grew stronger, and I too began to hope; the poor bloody nationalists had decided to win this time, to ride the crippled horse into his fences, not to roll over in front of fate.

For the first time for years I was in the presence of positive corporate will.

Fermanagh-South Tyrone voted; by Friday afternoon the vote was counted. I went into the dim little television room at Trinity to check on the progress of our feelings. Telefís Eireann started giving the result. In burst a thick-set trim dark man with pugnacious jaw and a sweater blazoned 'Delgany Golf Club'. Delgany is a prosperous enclave south of Dublin; its golf club must register about .002 per cent on the republican scale. A northern Protestant, for all money. So he proved to be. 'What are you watching?' he said abruptly. 'Is it on the election?' 'Yes,' I said, 'an RTE special.' 'No, no, not them,' he cried tensely, 'let's see what the English think.' 'Certainly.' I turned the switch. 'The English' are plainly baffled. 'The English don't seem to be thinking very much,' I said. He declined to answer. There in front of him, on the live screen, the hated republicans, teagues, un-employables, racial inferiors, leaped and cheered; their man had won; they behaved as normally as English soccer players. The Delgany man leaned forward, 'Look at that. It's unbelievable.' 'What is?' I said. No answer. Later he said, 'Look at that. Have you ever seen anything like that? Would you believe that?' 'At what?' I would courteously reply, 'Seen what? Believe what?' No answer. But he raged visibly, for outrage must not only be felt but must be seen to be felt.

And contempt. He had made his point about Irish national tele-vision; how could he express this new feeling about his victorious enemies? He left, still saying, 'Have you seen anything like that?' I think he meant 'them': 'Have you seen anything like them?' Crop-pies and teagues were not supposed to win an election; the purpose of elections was to frighten them, to remind them of salutary and unpleasant truths, and generally push them under.

I wouldn't like to have been his wife and children that night, even in Delgany.

Two others came in. 'I wonder what they'll think of this on the mainland,' said one. The mainland! 'The English don't know what to think,' I said. 'Do you want me to switch to RTE?'

But mixed with my actual elation was a terrible feeling, an instinct for doom, 'Now that man is really going to have to die'. For I knew that the British government would be ungovernable. The loyalist regime had declared itself by proxy in the TV room. Delgany's tiny episode was the presage of Unionist fury; from this point they will forgive no teague any wrong, any deed or any silence; their vindictiveness will appear as a kind of disbelief: all seats in Northern Ireland are theirs; how dare anyone inferior take one? Few of them will ask why, in an area where there is much dislike as well as much support of the IRA among Catholics, they have now voted for Sands, not a local man, not known, without personal ties to the area, and without a long-standing political machine. Is Unionism so intolerable to the electors of Fermanagh-South Tyrone? It is.

By the next day, all this bullying disbelief has been translated into the well-rehearsed British propaganda rhetoric of apprehension. The Protestants are scared; the constituency had been shown to have 30,492 supporters of terrorism and murder, 30,492 tipoff men and hiders of murderers. Nobody can now feel safe with any of them, that is, any Catholic. Look at your neighbour and you may be looking at an accomplice of murderers. If Sands had got only 27,000 votes, and been beaten, would this mourning cry have been raised? Not, I think, in this form, for if there are fewer supporters of terrorism than of righteousness, they will have been reminded that it is their job to lie down. Twenty-seven thousand don't matter if the supporters of Her Majesty number 28,000. They may be regrettable, but they do not have the seat. Their having the seat is the bad thing, for it means (though no loyalist says this) that a majority of electors is saying, through the vote, that the area is kept inside the United Kingdom against its will; and no election must ever come up with that result.

The Orange card is to be played in several ways; the repeated statement of apprehension is one of them. As if to vindicate this nonsense, someone kills two Protestants associated with the UDR. They are duly buried, as so many have been, with the flourishes of grief and self-justification. Sands goes on dying. Embarrassment in the ruling circles is acute. The air is full of speculation about the end of his fast; and steps begin to be take to force, persuade, seduce or con him off it.

I am conscious in writing about all this of the need to resist any temptation to Mailerize my relation to these people and these events. My position was not that of a participant, or of the non-participant who reports from near the battle. I was nowhere near the battle; I was an isolated individual living in a milieu alienated from the issue that was so disturbing me, and barely able to follow the sequence of events because the media which presented them (I except the *Irish Times* and *Magill*) were themselves alienated, and hence mystifying. It was even hard to identify new actors as they appeared, or to distinguish what they were really up to from what they were supposed to be aiming at. The two commissions which were brought in, apparently as mediators or honest brokers, were in this category. So was the British Labour politician, Don Concannon, whom Bernadette McAliskey accused of having come to gloat over the dying Sands, and who certainly seemed to be goggling at what his government had brought about.

By mid April, Sands's mother and sister, and his election agent Owen Carron, are familiar figures on world screens. They speak no word of hatred for his enemies. The graffiti grow thicker in Belfast. 'Blessed . . .' 'Die . . .' Let Sands die. Don't let him die. It is becoming clear that he will die, and the subsequent visits, actual, proposed, or aborted, which so many people of different sorts are to make to him, appear as balletic moves in a performance in which they have only a symbolic, and no substantive role. The ESC commissioner, the Papal envoy, the charmless Don Concannon all visit him, but these visits can only pain him and his family. They will have no effect on him because they patently have no effect on the English who, by their very intransigence, make it impossible for their enemy to move. Hatred has come a long way.

Marcella Sands comes south to Dublin, to see Haughey, and is seen to see him; but he says nothing, and is seen to do so. At a certain time, he persuades her to sign a document asking for the intervention of the European Commission on Human Rights. But she is not her brother's agent in this matter, and he rejects the call, stipulating that, if he is to see representatives of the commission, the leaders of Sinn Fein inside and outside the prison must be present; for he is the OC of the republican prisoners, and prime hunger-striker, he is representing not only the other strikers, but the other prisoners, and his fellow-Republicans generally. It would not be the first time, and it will not be the last, that Sinn Fein leaders were let into Long Kesh to confer with their own members; but not this time. The commissioners make their visit, issue their statement, and depart.

I am surprised at the perfunctory nature of their performance, for like the rest of the Irish public I assume they are mediators of some importance. So they might be, but they are not inclined to take much trouble on this occasion, for they have declared against the prisoners before the hunger-strike started, and their visit is a formality. Sands knows this, but his sister has been persuaded by Haughey to hope for something more substantial. Still, for the mere observer, the whole matter of this commission's visit adds to an effect of mystification already present. There will be another, quite different commission a few weeks later, and its activities will be even more mystifying. But sufficient to the day . . .

Watching Sands die was a terrible experience, because everything and everyone we could see in the press or on the television screens or in the shops and streets was either neutral to him or bent on subverting his will. The psychology of a hunger-strike is inconceivable to me, but it is clearly the psychology of heroism. Hunger-strikers are isolated heroes because they are pitting the individual will against an enemy who is much greater, who has power over them, and is in a real sense unknown and unreachable. The striker is pitting his single resources against the anonymity of power. He often does this in a near-total isolation, in appalling circumstances, and for very long periods. His psychological isolation may also go very deep and far, into the terror caused by the humiliation of his parents, and the deaths of his siblings. On strike he is often pressured by relations, children, priests and popes. His probable weakness of will is there for every TV camera in the world to search out, predict, advise, and reveal. He suffers alone, in darkness, yet in public. People know how he is dressed, whom he has seen, what his weight is, how near his vital systems are to collapse.

What sustains him, then? The presence in his mind of the hosts of fighting men, both now, then, and in the future. The Republican movement, as he sees it. With them he is in a psychologically intimate and sacred relation, but also a formal one, a command relation. Parents, children, even priests, may appear to him under some conditions as representatives of this host. He will very likely 'believe in' his own immortality, in a traditional Catholic sense, becoming interwoven with the mystical body of the Republican movement.

He lacks the cloak of legend, the high tone of any myth but his own, and he has certainly never been to Cambridge. Yet the dirt of his world, not all of it brought there by him, cannot disguise the fact that he is at the centre of a mythopoeic universe.

Why then is he not the subject of poetic treatment? It is not that the poets are repelled by him, but that they do not understand him, and will not accept him; his bowed frame (he is almost never fit enough to be recruited for the SAS) and cheap clothes awe them.

Sands's job, then, was to survive, to last as long as possible. His jailers had an easier task, and more time for it. Their mutually supporting ideologies emerged as if by accident. For a loyalist spokesman like Harold McCusker, the issue was how to define your pound of flesh, and then get it. Republican prisoners were not only being punished by being there, they were there to get more punishment. If they do not admit their crimes regularly, after having been sentenced for them, they will not admit their need to be further punished. It is essential that errant teagues be punished and consent to their punishment. Warders are there to enforce a demeanour. Hunger-strikers are a living affront to this logic.

The British were getting a smoother act together. Sands is taking too long dying. They develop a bipartisan policy; Labour and Liberal members of parliament 'visit' Sands. Subtly, the emphasis in the media shifts: not only are the Protestants 'frightened', they have tens of thousands of fighting men, but 'only for defence'; Mr Paisley will later show us some of them. There are firearms demonstrations, but no mention of guns. UDR widows are brought out to tell how their men died. We see speaker after speaker telling the cameras why they are frightened; it is never mentioned which of them are 'part-time' armed men operating among and against their neighbours. An air of the disingenuous hangs over all. The media press gently on to change the priorities. Protestants are now 'news', in an almost childish way. Interviewers cut off objectors in mid sentence, though a few great performers like Bernadette refuse to play that game. The cells in Long Kesh are of course subject to their own logic, which it is necessary to attend to through the media exploitations of Protestants. Francis Hughes starts to weaken, but no one minds yet. The British are expert propagandists, and they have in the BBC interview techniques an expert medium for it. Yet not all their blandness can disguise the fact that the nationalists have shown all the vertu. Not one Protestant spokesman has said one big-hearted or disinterested thing. They don't have to; their Catholic counterparts are tacitly assenting to their world-picture; Cardinal Hume is meeting and sympathizing with the Anglican bishops, who of course are exhibiting and espousing what we may call government virtues.

These bishops articulated in their language what the politicians articulated in theirs. Archbishop Runcie declared the deaths of hunger-strikers 'an act of violence'. His statement was precisely timed. Sands was then in the sixty-fifth day of his ordeal. He had gone blind, and was lapsing into a coma. Remarkably controlled violence, I must say. It is strange how all these professional Christians had chanced on so happy a phrase; and their agreement on it is truly ecumenical, for Cardinal Hume also used it with gawky self-satisfaction.

The point was now given a certain theological dimension, since any deaths that might occur were declared to be suicide. Suicide, an act of violence, and causing violence: thus the high-sounding formula was arrived at, ready to meet its secular equivalent: the government cannot give in to blackmail; we cannot give political status to terrorists; a crime is a crime is a crime (Mrs Thatcher, and no one can take that away from her); these men have a choice about their deaths, their victims do not.

It is true that the victims had no choice; civilian targets seldom do, and many of them are to perish, to be murdered; as they have been perishing, from the violence of several groups, including the army. And murder is murder; many of these deaths caused by violent groups should be described as murder. But the point about blackmail is slightly unbalanced. Jailers often bargain with prisoners, rulers with subjects, especially reluctant ones, and ministers with charges, especially sick ones. This can always be described as a process of 'blackmail' and 'giving in'. Sometimes it will result in justice or in enlightened self-interest. The British did negotiate with the hunger-strikers, one minister telling them there would be no difficulty in meeting one of their five demands. It is not demeaning, nor is it dangerous, to negotiate in this way. The British do it all the time, even if with a disastrous lack of flair; it has earned them a record of giving in to the Loyalists who, far from negotiating with them, win by bullying them. The reason they will not negotiate with Republicans, beyond a certain point, is that they are against the Republicans. Yet who could be their responsibility in a fuller sense than these strikers, who are their 'subjects', their prisoners, and sick dependants.

The rivulet of platitude spread south, bearing Runcie, Hume, Concannon, the North American Episcopal bishops, Garret Fitz-Gerald, McCusker, Paisley. The Secretary of State Humphrey Atkins issued a statement 'to coincide with the funeral of Mr Sands' (and so it did), saying, 'The decision to die might not have been taken by the hunger-striker himself but rather "under the instructions of those who felt it was useful to their cause that he should die".' By my reading, Sands's intention was to fast, not to die. But many in the South nodded at the secretary's wisdom. A curious rapport of terminology grew between the men of religion and the men of policy, until Fr Denis Faul, no friend of republican paramilitaries or of hunger-strikes, was driven to say, 'The theologians of rich and powerful countries think differently from those of poor and weak ones.' True. And, as for Sands's intentions, Faul or some other commentator said, 'He intends that one night he will get a message from Margaret Thatcher or Humphrey Atkins or Cardinal Hume or Archbishop Runcie promising that the rotten condition of Northern Irish prisons will be improved.' There is a welcome absence of cliché there.

Undeterred, English clerics, and some Irish ones, developed their theology of suicide; none of them offered a theology of punishment or of penology, or speculated what in the eternal order is the responsibility of a government to and for its prisoners. The Northern priests did not buy this suicide-theology, possibly because they were the only ones who knew the alleged suicides. Nor did they buy British notions of the immorality of burying hunger-strikers whose funerals would have a military component. For the British, and the loyalists, this was an enormous cause of offence. But the Catholic priests could not see that they had any choice but to give Christian burial to someone whose family asked for it. The issues were obvious. Perhaps they regarded the English interlocutors as a bit wanting in the head. The attempt to convert political issues into 'theological' ones was a dismal failure.

Indeed, the political basis of religious utterances was obvious. On 18 May, some days after Sands's death, there was an attempt to burn down Sligo (Protestant) Cathedral; the H-Blocks committee condemned it, together with other violence and intimidation of

Protestants. Paisley was not to be conned. On the weekend of 22–24 May, he urged that petrol bombers be shot on sight. The Church of Ireland *Gazette* supported Mrs Thatcher's strategy completely, at the very time when independent conservatives were increasingly saying that she was wrong, as did the UDA and the UVF; when loyalists actually on the spot were growing quite edgy about the nature and effects of Mrs Thatcher's policy. The Unionists fought each other with great rancour in the local elections which were now held, and which the media hailed as a great Paisleyite victory, though Paisley showed some disgruntlement at it. All talked about 'the Unionist family'. Paisley's messianic nastiness had never been more evident.

There developed a curious electronic effect; which is distinctively modernist. We live through events, certainly, but for the most part through news. What arrived was announcements, and almost all of them were unsettling, frightening. We are threatened by news as our ancestors were by no news. Well, that too; for there is always a hollow of no news at the centre of the news. Take, for example, the marvellous headline:

MARGARET

FOILS IRISH

DEMO PLOT

This meant that Princess Margaret was not now to go to some place in America where, according to the English newspapers, she might witness demonstrations by the local Irish, and so would be . . . foiling . . . their . . . plot. Being smarter than the plotters, the princess simply did not go where she had intended.

The cheaper English newspapers inflamed and were inflamed by their prime minister, whose simplistic notion of a crime was, of course, a semantic instrument of her policy. Her whole treatment of the hunger-strikes was a war-tactic, concerned to gain a political-military advantage, which was not decisively gained until she had waged war in and about the Falklands as well. Her concern was not that of a government prison service, but of a punishment bureau. She did not see Sands and the others as persons, but as disgusting terrorists-trying-to-be-martyrs, insisting on dying on her doorstep. Whenever their personal circumstances, or families, were mentioned, she referred to the circumstances of their 'victims'. It was an automatic effect. Others may have seen them as martyrs; but generally republicans appreciated their individual pain. 'Others have no choice'; in a sense this is true, and it is a poignant fact. But as a polemical point it lacks something; it ignores that 'others', including Mrs Thatcher, have a choice whether these men are to die now, and that many more, including children, 'have no choice' about their deaths at the hands of the British army. And with Bobby Sands, if you lift one corner of that sagging blanket, there is still a man there.

We learn that he has long been separated from his wife and son, who are in England. On the television his sister and brother grow more gaunt every day. His election agent, Owen Carron, a fiery, gritty little man, is becoming more tremulous and downcast. The cameras are the cliché which they have to confront every day. His solicitor is thoughtful, unaggressive, dreamy. Loyalists hustle and threaten them. Waiting is boring.

Deaths go on outside the prison walls. The father of a Catholic youth run over by a British armoured car says, 'Why can't my son's life be accepted for the life of Bobby Sands?' I heard nothing as noble as that from the ranks of the Reformed. Grieving men and women sometimes speak a truth so direct and agitant that in it gesture and the deepest honesty are indistinguishable. I have heard Protestant mourners speak with similar heartfelt directness; but not during this crisis. For some months the principle of the equality of widows and of orphans was suspended.

Sands is too tough. He prolongs his dying beyond the expected flashpoint. Everyone's nerves are now in pieces, partly because the media commentators have started predicting massive sectarian fighting as soon as he dies.

All of us who have only the media to rely on are naturally affected by these speculations; we are not to know that, awake to that very danger, both Republican and loyalist paramilitary leaders are already spreading reassurances to the enemy communities, and urging their members to remain cool. Ruairi O Bradaigh, a southern Sinn Fein leader, carefully explains that IRA attacks, while they do not cease, are moderated during the fasts so that the significance of the fasting should not be obscured. But of course O Bradaigh is not interviewed or reported on the southern radio or television. In addition, as if to deny their own reassurances, the loyalists start an odd performance. The UDA puts 2,000 marchers on the streets, giving the British commentators something else to make guesses about. By 3 May, Sands is blind. Carron says goodbye to him, leaving his last days to his family. His mother, asked, 'How is he today,' replies, 'He's dyin'', in a flat Belfast accent. She asks that his death not be requited by further violence. The Pope's secretary, Monsignor Magee, a northerner, is back from Rome, leaving Sands a papal crucifix and the memory of some sympathetic remarks. He and Cardinal O'Fiaich pray beside the coffin of a Protestant killed by the IRA. The British press promises civil war, and declares that the republicans have assassination lists. Tabloid-burning lists would be more like it.

As if he had had precise warning of his reluctant subject's coming death, Prince Charles spoke in Washington on the death of his great-uncle Lord Mountbatten. According to the *Sunday Telegraph*, he attributed this death to 'blind nationalism'. Only Oxford and Cambridge graduates were present at the dinner, which the *Telegraph* described as 'glittering'. The speaker spoke with 'a mixture of seriousness and wit'. In Belfast and just outside it, in disloyal Twin-brook and unlettered South Derry, there was more seriousness than wit at that time, though in 'normal' times the proportions might be reversed.

A Martian might well regard it as odd for a British prince to 'inveigh' against nationalism. But a few seconds' reflection will see what the connection is between princehood and anti-nationalism: it is other people's nationalism he is against; indeed, the British perhaps no longer go in for nationalism, since they have settled so snugly into their mood of post-imperialism.

So Prince Charles was disclaiming nationalism, as is the way with the owners of expensive machinery, only when it became more useful to his rivals than to him.

The relative quietness of the UDA and the UVF in these oppressive days before Sands's death seemed to have something to do with self-interest. They were not in favour of the Thatcher criminalization policy; they too had many 'political prisoners' in Long Kesh and elsewhere, many of them too had conducted campaigns of disobedience within the jails. Some had even been on hunger-strike. They approved of more than one of the Republicans' five demands. They wanted segregation from the Republicans as much as the latter did from them. Yet their leaders had had many a talk with the leaders of their enemies. It would have been an appropriate paradox had they told Mrs Thatcher that they could see no objection to the five demands. Several times, as I watched, they seemed to teeter on the brink of saying something like that. Yet they never quite managed it until some weeks later.

One clue was given when the UDA's most charismatic leader Glen Barr, of Derry, mentioned that the UDA prisoners have in effect had for some time special category status, and were satisfied with it; they were able to associate with one another in the way the Republicans wanted. This agreement came from their copping it sweet within the prison system. But, since the warders are all loyalists, who had helped to sabotage earlier agreements, copping it sweet would be less sour for them than for Republicans. At any rate, said Barr, his men were not common criminals. A crime was not a crime was not a crime.

You did not see or hear Republican spokesmen or women on RTE, because Section 31 of the Broadcasting Act forbids them. In all the 217 days when their comrades were fasting to death, they could say no word about any of the issues on the national radio or television. One night, however, RTE brought a group of polemical stars before the cameras: Jim Kemmy, the bluntly anti-republican 'left-wing' parliamentarian from Limerick, faced Bernadette McAliskey (nee Devlin), of the H-Blocks committee. And there, grinning away in the group, was the abovementioned Glen Barr, he who had boasted of the privileged status of the loyalist prisoners. What was he to say? Nothing.

Bernadette placed both her opponents very adroitly. What, she said straightaway, is that man (Kemmy) doing here? And what, come to think of it, is that other fellow doing on the national TV? You cannot understand the situation of Bobby Sands, she said, unless you see the significance of the fact that RTE, which admits no member of the Republican movement before its cameras, has Glen Barr talking about the loyalist military power which he represents: 'We have been threatened or promised civil war ever since 1968. The media do all the promising. Which is well for them, for they won't be fighting it.' Civil war will not be declared by the Catholics; the loyalists may fight, for 'the guns are all on their side'. But Barr and the UDA are 'like bad trade unionists; they make none of the sacrifices but share in all the gains. If they don't want to support the five demands then the hunger-strike is none of their business; the matter is between us and the British government'. The UDA should stay right out of it. Glen Barr smiled away, and stayed right out of it. But I felt I had been allowed to see a corner of the underfelt.

Other potentates intervened in Sands's dying; the Pope, for example, sent his secretary Monsignor Magee to visit the prisoner (Prince Charles did not go so far as that). Whether or not he pressed Sands to give in is not clear; he at least had the grace not to make vacuous statements outside the Long Kesh gates, and not to carry on as if he knew he were in camera focus.

At this point, a sad paradox started to become evident: first, Sands, a man much loved by the other prisoners, had insisted on leading the fast, and on beginning it fourteen days before the second volunteer; but he proved fit enough to last longer than had been expected, and his successor, Francis Hughes, weakened by his battle-wounds and prison privations, was sinking faster than had been expected; so that Sands's design, to leave adequate time for negotiations after his death, if he should die, was to collapse. Second, the volunteers went on their fast more or less in groups, and there would therefore be time between the deaths of each group, if those deaths should occur, for the British to negotiate. Hence, they died in groups. I think they had not planned to do this, because they had not planned to die at all, but to win. However, one group died in May, and another in July. The time between was a period in which, now, at the end of May, since everyone was seen to be serious, the need for a settlement could be matched by opportunities for it. Down to business, in short. The trouble was, the negotiators were in different lines of business. After the second group died, in July, demoralization could begin, not among the hunger-strikers, but among some of those who supported them. And that is what happened, as I shall show later.

Sands died on 6 May; the next day there were riots everywhere, including Dublin, in which, according to the law by which the size of a demonstration is in inverse proportion to the size of its attendant rioting, it was more rapid and violent than anyone had expected. Crowds of youths demonstrated in O'Connell Street, then streamed across the bridge on to the south side, running up Dawson Street into Stephen's Green. On the way they smashed business windows and the windscreens of parked cars. Their attempt to reach the British Embassy was 'foiled' by the police.

As I learned later, one of the cars whose glass was broken was a secondhand Ford which Penelope and I had contracted to buy; the crowd bashed it as they ran past a secondhand dealer's yard toward their goal, whatever that was; and I mention this trivial detail because it shows how impromptu, made-up, temperamental, the demo was, how un-Republican, in a profound sense. This was an unschooled crowd whose nerves had gone decidedly twitchy. Sands's death drove them into a frenzy of impotence.

Of course, the usual taxi-driver told me the usual story how he had seen agitators handing out instructions and money to groups of youths just before the rioting started. 'Money,' I said. 'Surely not. There's no money around.' 'Ah well,' he said darkly, 'these fellers always seem able to get it when they want it.' 'Northerners, were they?' I said. 'You know the types,' he said. 'Did you recognize them?' I said. And so on. Such accounts ranged from the implausible to sheer nonsense. The real, the organized demos were still to come.

And that day of aftermath we were driven down to South Wicklow, across the silent mountain, to see a cottage for rent. The driver was a youngish auctioneer from a well-known firm whose offices were in Dawson Street. Their windows had been entirely smashed, and were now boarded up. 'Glad to be out of the place,' he said. He did not engage in the usual middle-class moralizing about the irresponsibility of the rebellious and deprived, so I assumed he did not come from Dublin, or thereabouts. In fact, he came from Cork, and Dublin was the least of his interests. His only comment on the motivation of the destructive element was, 'Why the hell did they pick us? We're a Catholic firm. They didn't touch Lisney's in the Green.' I said I doubted if denominational, not to say theological, niceties had had any part in their thinking. 'You have the better windows, anyway,' I said, 'a great display. Just made for the purpose.' He seemed to cheer up a little at this.

Dublin was slightly dangerous for a couple of days, because of the random nature of the violence. Or so I thought, from seeing the pattern of attacks. Australian visitors, David and Patsy Segal, were staying in the heart of the affected area while they paid us a visit, and they saw a little of the action. They discounted any danger, and any particular malevolence, too. This was interesting because, whereas on one side they knew nothing of Ireland, on the other they had few or no preconceptions about the inhumanity of Irish Republicans. I found the extent of the violence dispiriting, in a way; there was a pathos in the failure of protest to grow to the point where genuine mass demonstrations became possible, able to contain, muffle, and dissipate their own violence. What was needed was large, non-violent marches and meetings, whose note of sombre rejection of the British brutality would have been as evident to everyone as their size.

Sands' death day was a day of shock. There were riots in all cities, and the world's television caught something of them, even though their commentators misunderstood what they were filming: not every republican blow-out is a calculated manoeuvre. The manoeuvres were military; attacks were made on British and police forces all across the province. A Protestant milkman and his son were gruesomely killed in a riot in Derry. The media rightly grieved for them. No one except their own grieved for the republican dead. But their own now numbered hundreds of thousands. Their list of dead was mounting too. Ten people had been shot at pointblank range, usually in the face, by 'plastic bullets', heavy batonlike projectiles fired by British troops; four were teenagers, one a mother of six kneeling at an open-air prayer meeting. Of the ten, one died; he was fifteen. On 11 May, the day of Francis Hughes's death in captivity, Julie Livingstone was killed from behind by a shot fired from an armoured car. She was fourteen, and was carrying a bottle of milk; milk figured large in these barbarities. After her, sixteen more desperadoes were seriously wounded, where they were not killed, before the end of May. The score was almost one a day. One victim was five, one four and a half; one was eleven, one twelve; several others were teenagers; one was a grandmother. Two of these died.

It was while visiting Saudi Arabia that Mrs Thatcher said that 'a crime is a crime is a crime'. It did not seem to occur to her that she was in a country whose concept of a 'crime' would not bear much scrutiny. Ian Paisley opined that Sands had chosen to die, and went on from there. Other loyalist spokesmen were no more inventive in their rhetoric. Loyalists in Glasgow assaulted a group mourning Sands's death. The British army had increased forces in Catholic areas of the north. The secretary of the Alliance Party (usually called 'moderate' or 'non-sectarian', actually a mild unionist party) condemned those who 'encouraged (Sands), for their own selfish ends, to continue his fast to the death in the full knowledge that there was never any question of political status being conceded'. No need to ask who they were.

Some foreigners seemed off the desired wavelength: the Portuguese parliament observed a minute's silence; and while *Izvestia* attacked Britain, in time-solid phrases, Lech Walesa praised Sands as a hero; there were demonstrations in countries from Greece to Australia; a 'protest-wake' was held in Antwerp, and all through Belgium hourly bulletins were broadcast on the progress of his dying.

The New York *Daily News* reported the death in the words of its man on the spot:

The mother said she could not remember a time when walls and barbed wire and guard towers had not been a part of her life. During the last days of the hunger-strike, she had visited the prison every afternoon.

Standing by the bed, she had watched the colour drain from her son's face. She had seen the skin turn yellow. She had seen the muscles melt away from his arm and legs as his heart, liver and lungs cannibalized his body. She had heard his voice fade into silence.

'God has taken him,' she said. The day before, she asked that his death lead to no violence.

More eminent Christians were not misled, however. They were, as it happened, meeting in ecumenical spirit in Cork, and readily commented on events in the north. Cardinal O'Fiaich, who had been vilified in the British press as an accomplice of terrorists, said that the death 'could and should have been avoided'; he had told the British government himself how this could be done. His Protestant brothers gave him the lie, if you want to put it bluntly. The Presbyterian, Rev. Ronald Craig, said 'he could not personally see how the British government "could remain a government and yield to the demands that the prisoner was making" '. The Methodist, Rev. Sydney Callaghan, was vaguer though no less firm: 'Violence of this form must not be allowed to hold sway in the Ireland of today if that Ireland is to have a tomorrow.' (Did he mean the dying when he spoke of the violence?)

But they both did express various forms of regret, sympathy, and goodwill. The Church of Ireland Primate, Most Rev. John Armstrong, was most state-oriented of all. He too expressed sympathy with the Sands family, but none with Sands, whose death-fast was 'one of the most calculated pieces of moral blackmail in recent times'. Sands had not responded in a 'Christian' manner to the attempts to free him from his fast. Further, his actions (dying) would inflame passions and lead to further violence. Cardinal Hume had been right; this was a violence-provoking suicide. The only reference to the British government was to 'the forces of law and order', adverted to as though they were not, and had never been, parties to any dispute, but were simply the poor unfortunate cleaning ladies who had to remove the bodies.

By contrast, and possibly in some sort of dawning despair, O'Fiaich and Bishop Edward Daly appealed to the British to have some bloody sense. Of course, they also appealed to the hunger-strikers to give up.

This was not to be. The clerics did not mention the particular personality of Bobby Sands, but the northern nationalists remembered it very well: aged twenty-seven, he had spent nearly a third of his life in jail; he was sentenced to fourteen years for possession of a revolver. It was not alleged that he had ever killed anyone. He was a very personable fellow: 'A lightly-built man of about five feet nine inches, with blue-grey eyes and shoulder-length hair, he had been an able schoolboy athlete and collected several trophies.' In jail he became a fluent Irish-speaker, and translated novels into Irish for his fellow-prisoners.

Over 100,000 people were at his funeral. The *Irish Times* front page headline read:

SILENT THOUSANDS HEAR PEACE PLEAS AT SANDS FUNERAL

They waited 'in near silence and almost continuous rain'. On the TV screen they seemed like a mass of dark shoulders barely moving. Sands's parish priest 'repeatedly called for peace and deplored the deaths of the RUC man shot the previous night and that of the Markets man killed in a premature explosion'. Gerry Adams, vice-president of Provisional Sinn Fein, 'called for a dignified end to the funeral and declared that "the organization to which Bobby Sands belonged will make its own response in its own time" '. The British stayed out of it, except for trying to drown out Adams with helicopter noise.

In Dublin, many shops closed. Some towns, like Dundalk, closed for the whole day; and indeed most border towns closed completely for some hours. Tens of thousands of southern workers struck for the day. The Irish parliament, Dail Eireann, showed little more sense of the significance to it of Sands's death than did the British parliament, to which he had been elected. The Dublin cabinet shrank back to its wall, the British cabinet chained itself to its wall. It was only the first phase of the contest of wills that had closed.

Chapter Eight

Dying in Groups

The grouping effect now became evident; no sooner had the shock and anger at Sands's death reached its peak than it became evident that Francis Hughes was dying. Sands's importance was in his being a leader; Hughes's lay in his having been a fearsome guerrilla fighter. If Mrs Thatcher had not given in over Sands, she would certainly not give in over Hughes. He would certainly die; and the probability was very high that he would be followed by the next two, Raymond McCreesh and Patsy O'Hara, the latter the first of the INLA group to join the strike. We were almost certainly going to have four deaths, and then, with any luck, a few weeks of remission in which some compromise could be reached, and further deaths avoided, inside and outside the prison. If one thing was now clear, it was that both sides meant it; after four deaths, the depth of determination on both sides would be seen to be frightening. There might, of course, be a certain advantage for the negotiators in this sombre fact: where no one is bluffing, frank talking becomes possible.

As we were to learn, it did not turn out like that; only one side would negotiate, and it was not Mrs Thatcher's government. Sooner or later, on that basis, the strike was sure to be broken; but whether its breaking in those circumstances would give any lasting benefit to the British government (or, indeed, to anyone) is a matter for dispute.

Francis Hughes was undoubtedly dying. He had joined the strike fourteen days after Sands, and had shown fluctuations in health for some time. He was a different proposition from Sands who, though a natural leader, very popular, and of immensely strong will, was not a famous guerrilla fighter, as Hughes was. Hughes was from the rural area of South Derry, while Sands was from working-class Belfast. He was a loner, where Sands seems to have been a gregarious man, and a ferocious fighter, where Sands seems to have been an organizer. He had been arrested, badly wounded, after a savage gun fight, and all his time in Long Kesh he was partly crippled. People from the western counties of the north, whether republicans or not, spoke of him with awe. To the *Irish Times*, he was the 'Provisionals' hero, RUC's most wanted man'. He was serving a life sentence, with other concurrent sentences of eighty-nine years. The speed with which he deteriorated on hunger-strike was caused by muscle wastage itself caused by his wounds and his prison privations.

After Sands's death, the broadcaster and journalist Tom McGurk interviewed Oliver Hughes, the brother of Francis, who had lain awake in the cell next to Sands's listening to 'the murmur of prayer' that accompanied his death. He later said to Oliver, 'By half past one there was silence and I knew it was all over. I lay awake all night, praying myself.'

Apart from the bed and the bedside table, the only other items in (Hughes's) cell are a radio, a tray of unused cold food and a gold crucifix sent by the Pope . . .

'I was once afraid of death myself,' says Oliver, 'but now the sight of my brother Frank has put an end to that. Each time we visit him, he seems to give us strength.'

Francis Hughes too had lost his fear of death: 'He shows no emotion at all and now, with Sands gone, the biggest fear of all, the fear of death, seems irrelevant to them.' Freed of the fear of death by a 'terrorist', whom a British army doctor had described as like the piper in a Highland infantry battalion who walks before the others, leading them into battle.

But Francis Hughes was almost dead now; the three men on strike had all suffered irreversible brain damage, and his case was the worst: 'He has lost the sight of one eye,' said his brother, 'and wears a patch over it. His arms are surprisingly thick, but his thighs are thinner than his wrists. It's curious, but the bedclothes seem flat, like as if there is nothing underneath them.'

The papal envoy, Monsignor Magee, had just left. 'I met him,' said Hughes, 'and he was deeply angry'; Magee found Northern Ireland Secretary Humphrey Atkins inflexible, and said to Hughes, 'Perhaps if I was in the same circumstances I would protest too, but I couldn't agree in conscience with a hunger-strike . . . (but) . . . I wish to God I could do something for those poor fellows.'

I quote this interview because it is deeply illuminating; I cannot, of course, guarantee the accuracy of any quote, but I know and respect McGurk, who was the recipient of these comments. The point is, we did not have to watch the Hughes family harassed on television as the Sands family had been; the interviewers were not so persistent, and Oliver Hughes by no means so 'obliging'. He was not the victim of his situation as Mrs Sands was forced to be; he controlled his own responses emotionally and analytically. What he had to say tells us a lot about the psychology of young IRA leaders in extremity. I wish to God the British government would pay some attention to interviews like this.

Francis Hughes died on the fifty-ninth day. The date was 11 May. His funeral was in Bellaghy; and the television showed the swatches of youngsters running across fields to meet it; the RUC had re-routed the procession, for fear of a 'breach of the peace' if it passed through religiously divided Bellaghy. 'This was the road my brother went to church on Sunday and every morning during the week when he went to Mass', said his brother. Latecomers straggled for miles; thousands filled the fields; large parts of the crowd clapped and cheered every time Martin McGuinness mentioned the dead man's fighting prowess. The RUC ringed the town; the British army put up several helicopters, much more prominent than in the case of Sands.

And, *mirabile dictu*, the Protestant paramilitary UDA finally came out and 'urged the British Prime Minister, Mrs Thatcher, to settle the hunger-strikes in the Maze Prison, Long Kesh, within the context of general prison reform'; 'if some form of special status was granted to prisoners, loyalist paramilitary groups would not object, since their prisoners would also benefit from improved conditions'. Mr Andy Tyrie, 'supreme commander', echoed the UDA spokesman: 'It's nice to be tough. But, it would be better to be tough about other issues than this. There are special courts and special legislation, so why can't there be special prisoners?' He added that although the granting of special status would be a capitulation, 'the consequences would not be serious. The continuing violence in Catholic areas over the hunger-strikes was causing bitterness in Protestant communities and, unless the crisis was resolved, great violence could result'.

It was almost as though he was hearing Bernadette's contemptuous words uttered a few weeks earlier, to his friend Glen Barr; or as though he remembered the loyalist prisoners who had gone on hunger-strike with the Republicans the previous year. But it was late; and Mrs Thatcher had never been listening; indeed, by now most of the embattled forces wanted him not to have said such things.

The strategy of 'staggering' the hunger-strikes was having some curious effects. The two dead strikers had been replaced as soon as they died, Sands by Joe McDonnell, a close friend, and Hughes by his first cousin Thomas McElwee. Both were to die, after the regulation time, but they had some weeks to live yet. Patsy O'Hara and Raymond McCreesh were much closer to death, and since it was possible to calculate almost to the day how much longer each striker would last, the newspapers had started talking about them as if they were already dead men. The issue of the *Irish Times* which detailed the preparations for Hughes's funeral gave a brief life of O'Hara ('a life shaped by the troubles') and declared McCreesh a 'religious' man. They were already being memorialized.

This was partly because their families had got into the fatalistic habit of speaking of them in the past. O'Hara was CO of the INLA prisoners; he came from working-class Derry city where both IRA and INLA were strong. His father had been evicted twice by loyalists and had had his pub-grocery blown up once by them. Patsy, street kid, was an observer of demonstrations from before 1968. The British army shot him in the foot when he was twelve. By fourteen he was branded as 'a dedicated terrorist'. By twenty-two he had spent five years in jail. 'He never had any teenage years,' said his father. 'All he ever knew was being terrorized and lifted . . . What really makes me sick is to hear Margaret Thatcher say, "A crime is a crime is a crime." There's crime down here against the likes of me more than anywhere.' His son would fast to the death. He was serving eight years for possession of a hand grenade.

Raymond McCreesh was from Camlough, in South Armagh, the 'bandit country' of the propaganda cliché, infested by SAS, para-troopers, and undercover agents. His sentence was fourteen years for attempted murder. He had a brother and a cousin priests; he was religious in a conventional sense, attending Mass and reading the lessons. Yet he was very single-minded; he forfeited family visits 'rather than wear prison uniform for the half-hour monthly visit'. He was within a fortnight of death.

But the situation had further oddities, in church and state. In the north, the Catholic clergy was stirred up with curious force; for now it fell to them to annoint the dying and bury the dead (things they had all done scores of times), the first just out of range of the TV cameras and the second attended by crowds numbering tens of thousands. It fell to them, also, to comfort and advise the families not only of those on strike but also of the hundreds who might soon or eventually join it. They might not like any of it, but hunger-striking had become a large part of their lives, and no doubt a major part of their consciousness.

In the south, the state too was stirred up. The *Taoiseach*, Charles Haughey, having failed to meet the needs of the Sands or the Hughes family, was in the process of letting down the families of O'Hara and McCreesh. It is hard to know what he thought he could do, Mrs Thatcher being what she was; but it is also hard to know whether he tried very hard. He could wait no longer, anyhow; it was now or never to call an early general election, before more deaths sabotaged both his much advertised rapport with Mrs Thatcher and his claim to be a concerned Republican, or even republican. He called it; his opponent Garret Fitzgerald started to tour the country in a brightly decorated bus, with loudspeakers blaring a specially composed campaign song; and Haughey followed after, by a different route, alighting in town after town and declaring each of them the town of his heart.

After some confusion, the H-Blocks committee decided to run candidates, too, as did their mortal enemies of the once-republican Sinn Fein – The Workers Party, which had started off as Sinn Fein, allowed 'Official' to be prefixed to that, removed that addition, added the suffix, and were later to remove 'Sinn Fein'; that is, they are now The Workers Party, and some workers vote for them.

While they were severally considering their election strategies, the two fasters died, both on the same day, 21 May. O'Hara was buried in Derry, and the narrow city streets were seen on camera jammed with people, marching, walking, watching, crowded in shop doorways and on walls. McCreesh was given a country funeral, more ritual and compact than Hughes's, which in other respects it resembled. It had, said Fionnuala O'Connor in the *Irish Times*, 'a South Armagh mixture of Irishness and an overwhelming sense of the Catholic church'. The Mass 'was conducted almost entirely in fluent Irish, the choir sang in Irish . . .' 'The principal celebrant of the Mass was the dead man's brother, Father Brian, and in the crowded chapel whole pews of priests, young, and old and middle-aged, came from the congregation to receive communion.' The parish priest preached against violence, but Provisional leaders followed the priests up to the communion rail. Ruairi O'Bradaigh in his speech compared the dead man with 'Gandhi, Martin Luther King, Terence McSwiney, and Father Camillo Torres'.

Not that the dying had been easy. It was with McCreesh that the British decided to float their intimidation rumour. McCreesh had, so they said, asked to go off the fast, but had been urged back on to it by his attendant relations. This furphy circulated, no doubt throughout the world, for some days, and then lapsed. What he had actually said, so the questioning revealed, was in answer to the question, 'Do you want a drink of milk?'; he had replied, 'I don't know.' It then emerged that there was a bug in Patsy O'Hara's cell, and perhaps one in McCreesh's too. The presence of this device would seem to support the case of the jailers, for it would provide evidence of O'Hara's weakness and of his family's callousness. It was never asked to do so, however, and after a few days all reference to it was dropped. Possibly someone realized that it would not look too good if you produced a bug planted in the cell of a helpless prisoner dying of starvation. Was there an actual bug, or only a platonic form of the bug? No doubt we shall remain in doubt. The British had begun to suffer from the dialectical weakness of their own innuendoes. Better say as little as possible.

Both men were replaced, O'Hara by his INLA comrade Kevin Lynch, and McCreesh by Kieran Doherty. There were four prisoners on fast, as before. But it was reasonable to assume that none of these would die for some weeks; they constituted a second echelon, the whole of the first echelon having died in the expected time of little more than a fortnight. Before any of them could be expected to weaken beyond repair, there would be about six weeks of negotiating time, within which the twenty-six counties would conduct a most excitable election, and elect a new government. So far as Mrs Thatcher was concerned, there was very little for her to do except watch.

We were now well into June. The election proved bitter, and its result damaging for Haughey's Fianna Fail party, astonishingly successful for the prisoner candidates, and yet indecisive in the way nearly guaranteed by the electoral system. The nine prisoner candidates won over 42,000 votes, and two were elected to Dail Eireann with easy majorities, Kieran Doherty polling 15 per cent of the vote in Cavan/Monaghan and Paddy Agnew 18 per cent in Louth (both border constituencies each electing several members). Both of these were elected but were unable to take their seats even were they prepared to do so; Joe McDonnell in Sligo/Leitrim (another border area) was all but elected; interestingly, even in the semi-industrial area of Waterford, a long way from the border, there was a strong pro-prisoner vote. Interestingly, too, in some areas where the prisoner candidates were opposed by their former comrades and deadly enemies, the men and women of Sinn Feinn – The Worker's Party (soon to drop the Sinn Fein part), the WP candidate was eliminated before his enemy, and his votes, when distributed, showed an astonishing drift to the prisoner candidate. This happened particularly in Dublin, and there is good reason to think it happened among younger voters, who wanted to vote both for ostensibly 'radical' social programmes and for the hunger-strikers. This was, in ordinary political terms, an astonishing result, but I saw no one else comment on it; and maybe it is not so strange in Ireland, particularly if the majority of these double-think voters were young; for they could not be expected to count every nuance of a conflict which had reached the point of total breach some eleven years earlier. In any case, it showed two things: that the 'leaning' vote, as distinct from the first preference vote, for the prisoner candidates was much better than appeared, and that large numbers of the young were prepared to vote in a seemingly contradictory way rather than give their second or third preferences to an establishment party.

Friends of mine held that the pro-prisoner vote consisted almost entirely of Fianna Fail voters from the border areas who had turned round for this single occasion, and who would go back to Fianna Fail when there were no prisoner candidates. But this is a curious argument if it is intended to show that these voters are 'really' Fianna Fail people; and in any case it is almost certainly wrong. What had happened was that the hunger-strikers got a primary vote much bigger than anyone had predicted, and much bigger secondary transfers as well. The election showed that they had a surprising degree of positive support backed by a surprising degree of second and third preference sympathy.

In the formation of a new government, they were dead votes, of course; no one, including themselves, would let them take their seats. In the end, Garret FitzGerald, who had more than once inveighed against the 'five demands', took office, with Labour in coalition and the SFWP men in support. The British made appreciative noises. The hunger-strikers, now seven in number, grew older and weaker.

The talk of fear of death, the McCreesh episode, do not suggest that the strikers were somehow fanatically determined on death, fixated on martyrdom; on the contrary, it seemed that their aim was to last, to survive, and to win a contest of wills. The charge now arose with redoubled force: that the determination was not theirs; they were made to die, ordered to die; their IRA taskmasters on the outside were demanding martyrdom. This always has a certain plausibility, and I tried to investigate it. But it was a little obscured by the claims about the McCreesh family. Was Oliver Hughes, was Raymond McCreesh's brother the priest, ordering their brothers to stay on hunger-strike and to die there? Of course not, and the suggestion was withdrawn as quickly as it had been made. Were sinister IRA bureaucrats and manipulators doing it, then? After all, a hunger-strike to the death is a serious venture to undertake; when in the early seventies Sean Mac Stiofain, then an IRA leader, abandoned his fast (apparently after advice from a priest) his name was mud in Republican circles. What was the case this time? To order men to die by this fashion is not consistent with fighting for their freedom as citizens and their dignity within a penal system; that was the meaning of my remark to Daithi, in March, and he understood it very well. Now I made what enquiries I could, and the answer was the same from all informed sources: the group of strikers was in control of their own venture, which (it was hinted) was becoming something of a strain to Sinn Fein headquarters in Belfast and Dublin; I was not told why; I could mount a complicated case, but it would all be guesswork, and best left unspoken.

If what I had been told was true, it followed that it was the prisoners who would be negotiating with the British government; it would not be the IRA, or Sinn Fein, or INLA, or their political counterpart. It was also clear that the prisoners would demand the presence at any final negotiations of the leaders of their organizations both inside and outside the jail. What was not clear, but was certainly true, was that the family of any striker could take him off the strike as soon as he fell into a coma; there would be people (including their priests) advising them to that effect; some families would have promised their sons not to do such a thing, but some might not have done so. There was the beginning of split, of faction, in all this, and the British simply had to wait.

But they were also negotiating and conferring. They might keep inveighing against bargaining with criminals, but they were repeatedly at the bargaining table as, maybe, it was their duty to be. The question was, what were they doing there? Were they cynically pretending to bargain while they waited for splits to develop in their opponents' ranks? Or were they really trying to reach a settlement?

If they were doing the second, then their prime minister and her manic press barons had put them in a poor position to see the bargaining through. Both politician and editors kept intoning that the five demands made by the prisoners were not what was really at stake, were not indeed what the prisoners really wanted. What was at stake was prisoner control of the jails, what was wanted was something more and more and more. The second claim is certainly not true, and any truth in the first could have been accommodated by ceding as much of the five demands as was thought possible, but putting in a proviso specially designed to show that the person in charge of the jail was still its governor.

The British negotiators began, about August, talking as though they had realized all this, and would make a substantial counter-offer to the five demands. Were they plenipotentiaries in this matter? Yes, yes, they were. So the bargaining went on. In fact, although they may not have realized it themselves, they were not plenipotentiaries; there was always Mrs Thatcher back in Whitehall, spoiling for an easy victory; and there were always the editors in and off Fleet Street, praising her for her courage and determination, making it difficult for her to 'give in' even if she had the least inclination, and by constant abuse and insult reducing the image of the prisoners to below human level: creatures, things, you could not bargain with. These pressures, grinding away along the fault-line of Mrs Thatcher's personality, presaged splits and factions in the British camp; they were never to become evident, for she was too strong to let them show; they did lead to broken promises, but few people noticed these at the time.

By mid June the southern election was over, and the electoral strength of the hunger-strikers had been shown, to the amazement of all, the hope of some, and the horror of many. The non-Republican nationalists in the north, and their friends in the south, badly needed a bargaining counter of their own. They found it in the Irish Commission for Justice and Peace (ICJP), which was shortly to be introduced as a mediator or conduit or communications system between the embattled parties. The aim of the commission was to end the strike with some gains for the prisoners, rescued face for the British, and not too large a victory for the IRA and the INLA. Their role was not disinterested, for they were in a disguised way a political party to the dispute, and they would benefit or lose according to the way the strike ended. It was certain that it would end, and in a matter of months.

It was clear that the British government intended to sit pat and wait for the prisoners to throw in their hand, aided in this waiting policy by the feeling that the new government would be less trouble, less unpredictable in every way, than the last. It was also clear that the prisoners' protest had gone much more decisively than anyone could have expected, and that, given the nature of death-waits and of human beings, it could now be expected to begin packing up, in one way or another. If Bobby Sands, MP, and the Irish election results could not produce any change, then nothing could. And the foreign TV crews could not be expected to camp forever outside the gates of Long Kesh.

The second half of June and the first days of July were a period of hard negotiation. Hardly had the new southern government been formed than an official Catholic body went into action in the north to try to get an end to the strike. This was the Irish Commission for Justice and Peace, containing one bishop, one priest (cousin to Raymond McCreesh), one academic, one solicitor, and one SDLP politician. It worked towards producing principles for a resolution of the dispute, and it eventually agreed on these principles with the Northern Ireland Office.

One can see, without going into detail, that this was a peculiar situation; for the prisoners themselves were not represented in the making of this agreement; and, once it had been made, it became the ridiculous position of the commission to persuade the prisoners to accept a proposal which it had already arrived at with their enemies; yet in the world's eyes it would surely appear to be representing them rather than the British. The Republicans, for their part, maintained then and maintain now that the commission simply did not understand some of the concepts it was using; perhaps the reason was that the commission had a reference-group of its own, to which it kept deferring; this was the Dublin government and the opposition Fianna Fail party.

It will come as no surprise to anyone that, when agreement was reached between the commission and the British, it always turned out that they understood different things by what they had agreed: a curious trial for negotiators, leaving aside the fact that the commission was not speaking for the prisoners in any case (and the British negotiator Mr Allison only thought, and not for long, that he was speaking for Mrs Thatcher). They aimed, therefore (or so it now seems), to speak for the prisoners' families; and they bent their persuasive talents to getting into that relation with the families. At one stage, on 19 June, it hinted that the families might emerge as a pressure group in its own right; who then would feel the pressure?

Their task was made harder not only by Thatcher and her curious relations with her own spokesmen in the Northern Ireland Office, but also by the fact that, whenever they said the strikers were being manipulated by outside forces, another prisoner would volunteer for the strike. By 22 June, there were seven on fast.

The intensity of the will to join the fast was growing, therefore, in response to the increased ardour of those, whether prisoners' relations or others from the nationalist communities, who wanted an end to it. By all reasonable assessments, all the seven would last at least another five weeks. If the new government in Dublin really did have the rapport with Thatcher and her advisers which it was rumoured to have, a rapport between civilized moderates with not a fanatical bone between them, there might easily be liaison between it and the new pressure-group forming in the north; members of this group were more and more coming to Dublin, where you could hardly round a corner without bumping into one of them. If government and grouping had a common will, it might best be expressed through the commission, the ICJP; this body had, after all, briefly intervened in May, when after McCreesh's death they met and proposed a resolution. Nothing came of that, and when they entered the situation again in June, it was like a fresh intervention, and it carried that bloom of hope that renewed energy often does.

On 26 June, the British negotiator Allison assured them cheerfully that at any rate the question of prison clothing would not be an issue; they could take it for granted that one of the five demands had gone through the gap. Mrs Thatcher, however, had other ideas; and on the opposing side the H-Blocks National Committee insisted that the whole matter of terms should be left to the prisoners. The commission was by now committed to its task, or so it seems, and pressed forward.

Unfortunately, Allison's assurance about prison clothing proved vacuous, thus vindicating the earlier editorial judgement of the *New Statesman* that the government's attitude to the strike was 'implacable'. At the same time, the commission confused matters by suggesting structural changes to the prison itself; but the Republican prisoners rejected this on the grounds that it would not make any difference to their actual contact with one another.

Things were becoming urgent for everyone on the nationalist side. Another man, Laurence McKeown, had joined the fast, making eight. The British minister Humphrey Atkins made a long but vague statement, raising, in the view of the Republicans, 'hopes which when shattered would lead to demoralization'. Joe McDonnell was very close to death. The commission had still not consulted him or his fellow-strikers.

Possibly misled by the British into thinking that a settlement was imminent, the Dublin government began to consult with the prisoners' families, who travelled to Dublin for the purpose. But things were getting worse rather than better, and it was almost certain that the second group of deaths would commence within three weeks. Eventually, on 4 July, the commission met the strikers, and the next day three members of it met the prisoners' representative Brendan McFarlane, who was not on strike. But it reached no agreement with them. The British, for their part, were leaving the problem with their opponents.

The hunger-strikers at this point, on 5 July, made their most significant statement of the whole affair. Given Republican psychology, it was an open invitation to a dialogue and a settlement. They had signalled the start of this process months earlier when, instead of talking always of demanding POW status, or 'political status', they began talking of the 'five demands'. Republicans are very fixated on language formulae, as are many combative groups, and any change they make in a linguistic formula is clearly a change in attitude, or in dialectical disposition; if British Intelligence had the least interest in being intelligent, or the British government any interest in resolving disputes to the death with people it claims as its subjects, they would have learned this years ago. Republicans meant 'five demands', and it seems clear they would have settled for something a little less. Now they said:

It is wrong for the British government to say that we are looking for differ-
ential treatment from other prisoners. We would warmly welcome the
introduction of the five demands for all prisoners. Therefore, on this major
point of British policy, there is no sacrifice of principle involved.

We believe that the granting of the five demands to all prisoners would
not in any way mean that the administration would be forfeiting control of
the prison, nor would their say on prison activities be greatly diminished;
but the prisoner could have his dignity restored and cease to occupy the role
of establishment zombie.

Hardly had this gesture been made than the deaths started again. Joe
McDonnell died on 8 July, and Martin Hurson five days later. Of the
other five, Patsy Quinn gave up the fast on 31 July, and Kevin Lynch
and Kieran Doherty died in the next two days:

> And Martin Hurson on Grania's birthday,
> and Kevin Lynch and Kieran Doherty
> died shortly after the commission
> had failed to solve the English.

Thomas McElwee was to last only another six days, and Micky
Devine another fortnight. None of their replacements died:

> And another long-eyed northerner
> enrolled in their love compact.

But the whole nationalist population of the north had by this time
been destabilized, and there were initiatives being taken all over the
place. The television coverage was much shrunken, the newspaper
accounts harder to follow. When Joe McDonnell died, for example,
it was my birthday, a hot midsummer day on which I went to the
races at Phoenix Park. The middle-class suburbs showed no
awareness of his death; all the hundreds of the little black flags were
in the anonymous working-class areas; everyone had forgotten that
he had almost been elected to Dail Eireann. The prisoners' softening

of their demands, of their very tone of demand, had had no effect. It was clear that the strike would end with the jailers victorious, and it was only a question how many would die before that outcome. The new government in the south was anxious for a new and cosy relationship with the British, but it also wanted to appear to the northern Catholics as the agent of their sons' preservation.

The future course of events seemed clear; and it seemed clear that, if Mrs Thatcher were so intransigent that she would break the word of her subordinate Allison, she would actually want to force the strikers into complete submission, by death. Her stance throughout seemed a deeply racist one. What was still not clear was whether the IRA or the Sinn Fein leaders outside the prison were, as their opponents in the nationalist population alleged, forcing or in any way pressuring their members inside it to keep the hunger-strike on.

The best answer was No; the popular assumption was the opposite of the facts: the IRA leadership had never wanted the strike, and did not want it to keep going. It would not bring pressure on its members to give in, however. That was to be left to others, as the result of the process started by the ICJP, with the support of the governing groups in the south and after the pressuring of the prisoners' families.

In effect, efforts were made to convert the prisoners' families into a pressure group not against their tormentors but against them. As the Republican journal *Iris* says, 'The hunger-strike ended after four families had intervened medically to prevent their loved ones from dying and six other families had intimated that they would do likewise.' *Iris* blames Fr Denis Faul, 'an assistant chaplain to Long Kesh and civil rights activist'. He acted, it says, as the agent of the Catholic hierarchy; and certainly, without going into detailed corners of the action and counter-action, it does seem to a visitor like myself that at a certain point the Catholic bureaucracy did enter into a power-struggle with the Republican movement to see who would determine the time and mode of the strike's ending. This rivalry is ancient and fundamental, despite appearances. The Catholic hierarchy as a group never supported the five demands, although many priests and religious, even some bishops, undoubtedly sympathized with them, and held in esteem the interests of those who made them. When Faul and some priest friends of his started to put final pressure on the situation, it involved bitter confrontation both inside and outside the prison. These confrontations were coming into a bitter phase while Kieran Doherty and Kevin Lynch were dying, and the stubborn Thomas McElwee, no doubt remembering his dead cousin Francis Hughes, was preparing to die alone. Meeting after meeting took place, demoralizing many of the strikers' supporters, who simply did not know what was happening and who was ranged where, against whom.

There is no point in my giving an official Republican account of the negotiations; but such an account acknowledges and stresses the growing contest, reflecting the long-term underlying rivalry, between the Republican movement and the church. Sometimes the contest was elided or concealed, as when Cardinal O'Fiaich intervened with the British to facilitate a meeting within the prison between the Republican leader on the inside and his counterpart on the outside, the much maligned Gerry Adams, of whom it was repeatedly said that he was manoeuvring his comrades to die for strategic reasons.

A non-Provo account of this meeting is given by the editor of *Magill*, Vincent Browne, arguably the best and certainly the toughest investigative journalist in Ireland. Browne is a Limerickman of originally fairly conservative disposition until the *Irish Independent*, a conservative newspaper, sent him to Belfast in the early years of the struggle there. His years in the north not merely helped to make up his mind about the nature of that struggle but gave him many and invaluable contacts among those taking part in it. He has kept these contacts ever since, and can call on them with enviable ease, because he is sober, systematic, non-judgemental, completely trustworthy, and presents himself (justly, so far as I am concerned, whatever his many critics may say) as without *partipris*. What he has is strong opinions based on deep experience. Much of what I shall say from now on depends on Browne and his excellent article in *Magill* for August 1981.

He takes up the question whether the Sinn Fein leaders forced the prisoners to remain on strike; and his answer is an unhesitating no. In particular, he clears Gerry Adams of this charge. His account of Adams's visit to the striking prisoners is more detailed and more heartfelt than that in *Iris*. Browne, of course, was not present, and he is relying in part on Adams; but there were witnesses there, one an IRSP man, Seamus Ruddy, and the account can, I imagine, be checked. Browne claims that when, on 29 July, Gerry Adams was brought to Long Kesh to consult with the strikers, he told them that 'a meeting of relatives and churchmen the night before had asked that the army council of the IRA be asked to order an end to the hunger-strike; that the army council would not be able to meet for a few days by which time he (Doherty) would be dead'. Doherty proved unresponsive to this implicit plea, and Adams then spelt out what 'he understood to be on offer' from the British government. Doherty said that he intended to persist. Then Adams is alleged to have said, 'Doc, if you want me to, I'll go out now and announce that the hunger-strike is ended.' He had already, says Browne, told the other fasters that 'bonfires would be lit in joy at the end of the hunger-strike'. Doherty replied, 'I don't want to die but I'll only end the hunger-strike when the Brits give us our five demands . . .'; and Adams said, 'You'll never see me again.'

This account quite reverses the usual explanation of events: that the IRA prolonged their cynical exercise in 'blackmail' (blackmail by dying) in order to 'save face', or to 'create martyrs', or for some other psychotic or degenerate tactical reason. The IRA and Sinn Fein are portrayed by Browne as not wanting the strike prolonged, and as never having wanted it at all (hence, perhaps, or so the thought occurs to me, Daithi's phrasing of some months earlier: 'What do you think of poor Bobby?' Poor Bobby, the maverick, the deluded claustrophobe. Perhaps). One of their reasons for this was their belief that strikes distracted attention from 'the military struggle'; and they are notoriously suspicious of broad alliances, popular fronts, and, in general, any transfer of energy to the political area and the committee mode. Hence, while they will make use of H-Block committees and any other such broad fronts, they are not, by conviction and training, enthusiastic about them.

If, as Browne believes, that *was* their reasoning, the unfolding of 1981 must have given them a salutary shock. World reaction to Sands's death and dying was different not only in scope but also in quality and kind from its reaction to Mountbatten's death. Of course; any of us could have told them that. But, further, the abstentionists who were elected, and nearly elected, to Dail Eireann were elected as H-Block candidates, and prisoners, not for their military prowess or as representing IRA programmes. This may have been unwelcome to the Sinn Fein and IRA strategists. In any case, it was not 'martyrs' they were looking to produce; and Browne, as well as other sources, speculates that if they had tried to 'order' their members off the strike, their orders would probably have been defied. This too would have been unwelcome to them.

Browne's highly sophisticated and detailed account of the origins, development and psychology of the second (Sands) hunger-strike as it arose out of the first (McKenna) is broadly in tune with Republican accounts; but he stresses aspects of their motives which the Republican accounts underplay. It seems to be Browne's view that hunger-strikes do not suit the Republican movement for a variety of reasons, going far beyond militarism and distrust of united fronts. On his emphasis and on theirs, all the British and Dublin talk about 'blackmail', forced strikes, martyrs and addiction to martyrdom, seems not only nonsense but a cynical avoidance of the human facts: the prisoners went on strike because they found it intolerable to endure horrible living conditions passively; the strike was their traditional means of asserting a capacity and need for action, activity; and it included a large element of deep psychological bonding among the strikers. For months I marvelled that Thatcher and her advisers could not see this; in the end it became clear that they did not care enough to consider the matter at all. It was they, not the IRA, who were the utilitarians, calculating profit and loss, weighing up options, and brooding on face and its loss.

The Catholic dignitaries were not concerned with that, but with the retrieval of lives and the relief of manifold pain; but it so happened that this concern touched on their ancient rivalry with the Republicans. Living in a spiritual scarcity economy, they compete for the same lives; and rarely do circumstances allow them to share many of them. Their intervention came at a time when someone was due to come off the strike, and it hastened the process. Brendan McLaughlin, after all, had been encouraged by Sinn Fein to go off his strike on 27 May, after only fourteen days, because he was too sick to sustain its rigours or to last long enough to make his point. Martin Hurson had died after lasting only forty-six days, his condition having deteriorated dramatically. Now, in the height of the negotiations, Paddy Quinn was taken off the fast after forty-seven days by his mother, who 'could not bear the sight of him kicking and screaming in so much pain'. This event, succeeded as it was so rapidly by three more deaths, signalled the end of the strike as corporate venture. It was inevitable that the northern priests and bishops would encourage more fasters to come off strike.

Iris puts much blame on Fr Denis Faul. It accuses him of lying, misleading, manipulating, 'moral exploitation' and a curious kind of political activism. He created great enmity among the relations of some prisoners, including the Dohertys whose son had just died, and the McElwees, whose son was soon to do so. *Iris* quotes him at one meeting as suggesting 'that maybe the real issue was "the control of the voice of Irish Catholic nationalists"'. The church interventionists were both winning and losing their fight; for, while Micky Devine (the last to die) died on 20 August, the electors of Fermanagh–South Tyrone on the same day elected to the Westminster parliament Owen Carron, Bobby Sands's election agent. His vote was actually higher than Sands's, although his opponent was stronger and he himself had nothing like Sands's charisma. The people were voting against giving up, following Maud Gonne MacBride's principle, 'Compromise never stands still.' The 'moderates' were losing the internecine struggle. But so were the strikers. The same day, Mrs Pauline McGeown had the doctors take her husband off the strike.

Just the same, three men volunteered to replace him. The outline of the original strategy was being followed. It could not work for long. On 4 and 6 September, two more families acted to save their sons. The second of them had lasted for seventy days. On 25 September, another came off strike because his condition had deteriorated abruptly after thirty-two days. Next day there was another, talked into it by his mother. The strike itself was ended on 3 October.

Chapter Nine

LASTING THROUGH DEATH

The hunger-strike was called off on 3 October 1981; and three days later the British, through James Prior and his prisons' minister, Lord Gowrie, conceded parts of the five demands which had been the *casus belli*: the right not to wear prison uniform; the right not to do prison work except that involved in the maintenance of their own habitat; 'free association' between political prisoners (which, paradoxically enough, included the right for loyalists and Republicans to be segregated from each other, as both desired); proper educational and recreational facilities, including visits, letters and parcels; and the full restoration of the remissions lost during the five years in which hundreds of prisoners had been on the 'blanket protest'. Of these five, let me say in parenthesis, it seems astonishing that any government should not accede to the fourth, and not recognize the greater part of the second and fifth.

In any case, the only right fully conceded by Prior was the first one; the prisoners might now wear their own clothes. This concession ended the blanket protest, and showed that the British could have made it irrelevant five years before. In addition, the demand for 'free association' was granted in a limited way for several hours a day, and at weekends. And visits, letters and food parcels were increased. On the question of remission, the British went some distance towards the demand, but only half-way. Only on the question of prison work were they adamant.

There are several implications of this curious package; two in particular stand out. First, the enforcement of 'prison work' became a lever for splitting those who accepted this provision from those who would not; the latter were then dubbed 'hard-liners', and deprived of the concessions which their more conforming comrades were now to enjoy; there were several hundred of such hard-liners, and they were duly penalized by what I can only regard as a clever-stupid piece of manipulation. But, second, the actual granting of these concessions showed, not so much that the British government was a flexible negotiator and understanding jailer, but that it was not; for if these concessions could be made in October, they could have been made in February or March, and they could have been offered, as the basis for a settlement, at any time between those dates. It may be said of course that no government could make such concessions while it was being blackmailed with 'demands' and threats of 'suicide'; and one can understand the desire to say such things; but, apart from the fact that blackmailers and blackmailed more often than not negotiate with each other, refusal to grant such concessions, or to discuss their possibility, was what precipitated the hunger-strike in the first place. The strike, the deaths, the agony, the turmoil, the political disasters, the rancour and additional hatred, could all have been avoided; if they had not been avoided, they could all have been limited at any time between March and October. It seems that Thatcher's desire was to confront and punish, not to settle or understand.

With this curious and ambivalent settlement, the Republican press claimed that 'the focus has now shifted to the issue of segregation'. This is one which it is difficult for most of us to grasp in terms of daily living; it means that the loyalist prisoners want to be free to associate with one another, but not to be required to associate with Republicans, and the Republicans take the same attitude to them; for, while as 'political prisoners' they have a common interest, they are also enemies, who in the world outside the prison are at war with each other; yet you can put it another way, and say that, while in the world outside they are enemies, in the world inside they have a common interest. Part of this interest is in being segregated while having the same amenities. If they are not, there will be fighting. In November, a mere month after the end of the Republican hunger-strike, loyalist prisoners rioted in Crumlin Road jail, and their politicians called with renewed force for them to be separated from Republicans.

On the other hand, this truth, like all prison-truths, is partial. The British say that they will not segregate, but do segregate to a quite advanced extent. For years it has been the case that the only time that the two groups mix is 'when they are going to and from visits'. Segregation is maintained, by deliberate prison policy, government policy, most of the time. Yet the British will let men die rather than assert as policy what is already practice.

What else of an ambiguous nature did the hunger-strike produce? The Republicans were split, defeated, and split again (a signal victory for the craftiness of their opponents), yet not only has their military campaign not slackened (they have recently bombed extensively in the north and intensively in England), but their political campaign has proved more striking and successful than anyone could possibly have foreseen. In fact, Sinn Fein, which disowned the Commission for Justice and Peace, has encroached with great force on the vote and standing of the SDLP, which supported the commission and failed to make any headway with it on the British mentality. The southern government, successive governments in fact, has been shown unable to affect events in the north directly at all, and at the same time not to have the respect of the Thatcherian regime with which Haughey and his successor FitzGerald were thought to have a surprisingly sympathetic rapport. Mrs Thatcher demonstrated her 'toughness' to an electorate which welcomed that quality only when it was directed against foreigners, and was inclined to waver when it turned against themselves; but her gains were conditional, and she was obliged to demonstrate the virtue all over again the following year in the Falklands. The prisoners convicted in the closed system of 'Diplock courts' are for the most part still sweating it out in the sectarian jails, and the security forces have turned to a policy of recruiting 'supergrasses', or comprehensive informers, some of whom have gone through their paces in court and some of whom have failed at the first hurdle. The level of trust could hardly be lower all round.

Mixed with the bitterness and despair in October 1981 was a certain relief; those emotions had waxed at more than one point earlier; Irish life even in the south had been profoundly disoriented especially in the middle months, July, August, the awful dog days when men were dying as in a routine, but all sequence seemed to have ceased, and no immediate help was visible at all; by the time the commission became central to the news reports, no one seemed to know what was happening or what was important.

For myself, it was as though I were in some limbo of not understanding and not even caring, a peculiar torpor before rebirth, as it turned out.

While the ICJP was getting it so poignantly wrong in the north, and FitzGerald's government was grandstanding quietly in the south, I was embroiled in looking for a house, arranging to move into it, and finally moving in. Half of July and all of August were taken in this way. By the time Thomas McElwee died, my mood was one of despairing admiration for all the strikers and those who sustained them. People in Dublin had grown indignant and impatient with the whole affair. At least, they were the surface emotions; it is possible that quite different feelings moved beyond the threshold. In the middle-class areas there were few black flags; in the working-class areas they were numerous, but had somehow lost their bravery, their jauntiness. The activists I would see often at the roundabout in Walkinstown or in Tallaght held their flags and pictures with weary stillness. The bitter riots of two months earlier were gone; the mood was one of fatalism, with an underlying sympathy for the sufferers, even though little sympathy was expressed. In Kildare, darling of the Pale, black flags seemed anomalous; only one house showed one in the six miles between us and Kilcullen. The only permanent sign of republican solidarity was the group which kept its station day and night outside the town hall in Naas, the county seat.

This may have been a new mood among Republicans, too. It seemed that they expected the election results of June to change something; but nothing was changed. The young Sinn Fein activists who had delivered some books to me just before the election were full of buoyancy, a spirit of hopeful realism; 'Our feller will get

4,000 votes,' they said. It seemed unlikely, for it was an unpromising constituency and, although an H-Block candidate, their man was a member not of Sinn Fein but of the smaller IRSP. But he did, and he got thousands of 'transfers' (preferences) too. These two were ardent idealists of the sort whom I had known in the fifties; but they were canny with it; one gave me his name and, when I asked the other what his was, he replied in a Belfast accent: 'Liam Mumble'. 'O or Mac Mumble?' I asked. They thought that a great joke. But their hopefulness represented something that was deeply moving in elements of the urban working class at that relatively early stage; for example, when Sands was being buried, not only factories closed down, but many businesses of all sorts, including bookmakers, several of whom put paid advertisements in the paper announcing this. Up the street the bootmaker, whose window at election time had Labour Party posters, put a black flag and a poster for Sands, and closed for the day.

Perhaps they also reposed some hopes in the big march on the British Embassy in Dublin. This occurred in July, and was to be a large and orderly affair, not an IRA show; the rioting of May, which followed Sands's death, was not to be repeated. It did not turn out quite that way, for the front ranks of the marchers savagely rushed the police barricades, and the whole march was savagely counterattacked by the police. Several of my friends, all pacific, were beaten up. Some of them were very alienated not just from the police, but from the whole idea of marching. One close friend, a veteran of marches, who had walked in the front rank of marchers up to the British Embassy gates, yet was too canny to get himself beaten up, saw himself and his friends as having been set up by organizers for an operation which was aimed at undermining the southern state. 'Nobody with any sense could go on the march next Saturday,' he said. But his son, still partly in shock from the belting the gardai had given him, his body covered with bruises and welts, said, 'No, of course I'll march. I'll come down from Cavan for it. I can't let the fellows down.' And a retired politician, who had formerly been a leading minister in the Fianna Fail government, and was now an independent Republican but still a hater of the unconstitutional, said, 'I'll be marching. For partition will be broken within a few years, and history will say that the Provos broke it.' Both of these are law and order men; I agreed with parts of each statement. The fact was, mass demonstrations were not really possible in the climate of those days; you could never get the mass support you needed and at the same time guarantee peaceful assembly. Every Irish person lived out a contradiction in whatever way best suited him or her. Each of them knew subliminally what drama was being played out, and what attitude he or she might be expected to sustain. There was no keening, no air of lamentation through the warm rain-drops. There was, instead, an air of recognizing a taboo. The whole question of hunger-strike and demonstration was taboo in the south except for the vaguest and most generalized regrets. By the fourth death, the strikers had become nameless, anonymous, in the public mind. Seamus Deane's oldest son was a student at a Jesuit school; he attended demonstrations, and wore an armband for Sands, as did two or three of his classmates. He was not exactly criticized for this, though his headmaster exerted the pressure of regret. The Jesuits were pained; why couldn't this blasted thing go away? Deane himself wore an armband for Sands to a committee meeting at his university. 'Good lord,' said a colleague of his, 'why are you ... Are you ...' The colleague had once described himself to me as a 'republican', and he knew perfectly well what the armband was for.

The strike was to end in the autumn; and by September everyone was exhausted, at best busy with expressions of goodwill.

Embarrassment had become a high-minded, a quintessentially Irish emotion. The FitzGerald government, which took office in June, displayed it with unction and *elan*; they simply did not know what their British counterparts would regard as an appropriate kind of demeanour for Irish people to take in the circumstances; what the British think or affect to think is much on their minds. Dislike of Thatcher and Thatcherism was now widespread, but the expression of it was not yet licensed. This was in direct contrast to the mood which attended the strike's early days, when it was common for the Irish to think Thatcher was right, and to repeat every British cliché from, 'A crime is a . . .' to 'You can't let them take over the prisons.' The tourist season for which such fears had been expressed was 'saved' after all by Irish holidaymakers themselves who, deliberately but without fuss, turned back from the continent and headed once more for the west. There was thus less panic than at the start. Although the long-term dislike of the southerners for all northerners remained, it is possible that the commission's accusation of British dishonesty had sunk in, and even my neighbours in Kildare had taken the point that the British government had sabotaged the negotiations for a settlement. The commissionaire in one large Dublin building (a law and order man to his bootheels) greeted me one morning with, 'Well, sir, what do you think of the news?' 'If you mean Mrs Thatcher,' I said loudly and quickly, in case he had meant something else, 'I think she's bloody well mad.' 'By God,' he said, with a start of appraisal, 'that might be about it', and he launched into a bout of eloquence which entering functionaries paused a moment to hear. It included remarks about young men dying, Thatcher's own son, and her being 'a terrible bitch'. I had never known him to do such a thing before. Such faithful, decent and intelligent people, who had hated nobody and sought to subvert no nation, were scandalized that the British should have behaved so closely to the republican stereotype of them: Perfidious Albion, showing her armament for policy, and killing for effect; the great Pragmatist in front of whom no one of lesser breed or power is permitted to be pragmatic; a sniffy and racist people, whom there was no pleasing.

Specifically, they were shocked by the quite irrational hostility shown by the British press to Cardinal O'Fiaich as to Haughey, since it was plain to them that O'Fiaich was behaving pastorally and that Runcie and Hume were not.

Another subliminal force was the feeling, which had grown up by later 1981, that Mrs Thatcher was an awesome and unlikeable figure.

People who would agree on nothing else could agree on that. There was no fun in her, no give, no 'nature'. When I would say she was 'mad', that her kind of incapacity to reconsider her set position was mad, they would say yes, perhaps. Bernadette was admired, and even loved for her smallness and quality of the paradigm, but she elicited the same awe, for the warlike woman. People were impressed by funerals and elections. The economy was so bad that I kept on saying, 'Yes, the elections are the only things holding the country together.' Three elections in a year and a half. All indecisive. Immense sums wasted on them. 'One thing,' I said to a shopkeeper in Athy. 'There won't be a military coup. The Irish army is too small.' 'Yes,' he said, cleverly missing my point, 'that's the benefit of living in a democracy.' But, up to a point, the elections were the circuses which made up for the growing price of bread. The intellectual and professional classes no longer felt the circus thrill unless they were directly involved in the ringwork. A mood of doubt and revisionism throughout these classes made people ashamed to feel pride in being Irish.

But ambivalence works both ways (an Irish joke, friends).

Just to show you this from a star example: I was visiting a poet in a town in Limerick. He hated the IRA, claimed that its values were completely opposed to those of the IRA in the Tan war, and even in the thirties. He came of Republican stock, and his hatred carried, as it were, a burden of familiarity, and a special licence. On the other hand, he played cards regularly with a group, which included two republicans, 'local Provos', as he called them. One day we were walking out a gate when he greeted the driver of a truck going in. Friendly and intimate greeting; and, as the truck got past, he said, without bothering to lower his voice, 'That man's a Provo.' At that moment a Garda walked past the gate, a yard at most from us. 'O, sorry, Guard,' said Michael, affecting dismay. The Garda nodded in friendly fashion, affecting deafness or idiocy, or both. For it is live and let live in these places; and everyone knows that nobody does anything, after all. *N'est ce pas?*

These stories are not about Irish stupidity, but about Irish intelligence, and the mode which history has required that intelligence to take. One reason for ignoring the hunger-strikers, for example, is that people could represent them to themselves as commonplace; they were in a familiar tradition. The reason for continuing to ignore them after, say, the fourth death might be that the tradition had gone wrong, and the breakdown had to be met with silence and patience. To the British, such hunger-strikes are merely bizarre, grotesque. To other peoples they have been necessary historical acts. A Turkish member of Amnesty told me there had been thousands of hunger-strikers in Turkish jails; but it seemed they did not fast to the death. Indians and other peoples have gone on such strikes. Polish Solidarity members in large numbers are striking in jail right now; one of their demands is to be regarded as political prisoners.

In ancient Ireland, it was a custom for a wronged man to sit and fast at his enemy's gate; it was a form of litigation: you fasted at him. This practice may also seem bizarre to peoples who rely on large fleets, and whose intention is to punish rather than to shame an opponent. But it often had the effect of, for example, delaying the onset of tribal war. In a society like the Gaelic where the offering of food and drink was the main pledge of hospitality (as distinct from tupping daughters, or shooting snipe), it does seem odd that people should negotiate their claims by preparing to starve to death. But there is a rationale for all these practices.

The virtues of a hunger-strike as the Republicans had learned over a long period to practise it were of several kinds: first, it was active, militant, an assertion of the humanity which your prison situation denied and of the fact that your will and spirit were alert. Second, it was disciplined, communal, and organizational, although obviously there was a risk here of achieving the opposite of all three of those qualities (something that did not happen in 1980 or 1981). Third, it was a way of telling the prisoners' reference-group, whoever it was, what they really thought and felt. As such, it was an appeal for understanding, and their enemies' interest would be in either responding or refusing to do so; if they did the latter, it would be a way of reinforcing the conviction that 'these people' are *outré*, incomprehensible, and that it is a waste of time seeking a way of responding to them, because they will only. . . Fourth, it calls on an extraordinary capacity for endurance; some of the prisoners went on courses of training for their fast, and did forms of training during it. Fifth, if it is a form of 'blackmail', it also calls on the capacity to resist blackmail and threat from the imprisoning power. Sixth, it shows at its extreme the virtue of the solitary man, who expands his cell walls to re-enter the world on terms which he has chosen. He is sufferer, but not victim, warrior but not killer. He has met and broken the taboo, outfaced his own weakness, and shown himself to be capable of exerting more spiritual power than even his own priests can exert. He is redefining heroism in terms of the aspirations of the people.

Although I talked a great deal about the hunger-strike, I tried to put my political feelings from me. I went nowhere near H-Block meetings or offices, did not seek conversations with Republicans, and, while resenting the easy Dubliner and Pale cynicism or fear which repeated Thatcher's banalities, did not let my anger out.

Instead, I tried to think of the 'other side', but in my own terms, not in the clichés of government propaganda. I thought of the sheer destructiveness of the youths streaming up the glass-blown streets, I dwelt on their ugliness, I recalled my hatred of hunger-strikes, I damped down the pity I felt for the ill-dressed figures standing with black flags on the roundabouts in the 'new' working-class areas, I sympathetically entertained the Heaneys' point of view: I thought, Let it end now, quickly, for it is hopeless. It was no use. Abstract justice, once entertained, is a voracious guest, who will eat you out of house and home. Whatever pragmatism lay beneath the attitude of the IRA (and which might, for all I could know, go as far as 'they die that we may have recruits'), the British pragmatism was clear.

Whatever the arguments against 'political status', they did not necessarily apply to 'the five demands'. Those demands were debatable, and negotiable, one by one, in the way that those of any prisoners ought to be. The British were according their prisoners a special status, that of people not to be listened to. But the British government had a duty to debate and negotiate the demands, even if the plainants were starving to death in pursuit of them. To this realization, come dimly near the threshold of conscience, the British said three things: this is blackmail; they are being ordered to die; they want to die. Those with power saw the weak as being just as pragmatic and cynical as themselves.

It all illustrates a crucial difference: the managerial pragmatist says, 'Let us act as justly as is consistent with procuring the desired result', but the believer in strict and abstract justice says, 'Let us act justly, whatever the result.' The British did not go as far as even the first of these; for them, justice was institutional, and the support of it amounted to supporting the institutions in which it was enshrined, the army and the prison service, for example. Not for them the Socratic method of discovering in what justice between governor and governed consists, or between jailer and prisoner, or between administrator and plainant *in extremis*.

It did not seem to occur to them, for example, that it is clearly immoral to refuse someone justice on the grounds that the motives and intentions of his friends are impure (or that his own are), and that those friends will be advantaged by the removal of the injustice to him. They were following out an ethic which had a touch of malice in it. My judgement here is not affected by the fact that the British speculations about the strikers' motives have turned out to be wrong, and that presumptions about the effects of the strike have yet to be tested. Whenever I would ask someone, 'But what is wrong with the prisoners' demands?', I would always be answered in terms of motive and effect.

In great and thwarted passion, I wrote a number of poems, including 'Hunger-Strike', a poem in several sections, whose narrative logic ended between the death of McElwee and that of Devine, who is the only dead striker not to be mentioned in it. This poem was finished in August 1981, while the strike had six weeks to run, and it was read at an Amnesty conference in Toronto in early October, the week that its end was announced.

This is not a political poem; it is not concerned at all with party programmes or policies. It makes a number of suggestions, however: that the demands of the fasters could have been supported on humanitarian grounds; that most arguments advanced against them were bullying nonsense, designed to mystify; that the fasters confronted all this by an action which is, in old scholastic terms, contemplative, so that their role of warrior inside the hospital cell consisted in the systematic courage with which they tried, not to die, but to endure. They may have been 'gunmen' before, but now they were warriors without arms except those conferred by heroic patience. By contrast, the British cultural technicians employed slander against them.

How merely formulaic the British are when it comes to subject peoples. They are, of course, conditioned by a colonial and imperial past. Their very rhetoric shows this, with its self-righteousness blown up into the windiest kind of self-importance. ('Let me make it quite clear', 'that is what (some abstraction) is all about'.) It represents a massive and malicious withdrawal of imagination and sympathy from the sufferings they cause or have caused. Most Irish people are confused about such things as hunger-strikes because they have a sense of everyone as suffering, and of themselves as perhaps making an inadmissible claim on history. Many republicans, too, feel this way. But someone like Roy Mason or Margaret Thatcher brushes aside thoughts of all sufferings except those which serve them; they are lapsing into that phase of degeneracy which produces barbarism, a vehement irritation of the sensibility without any healing action. Hence all those TV interviews with widows, with their theme of 'kill the terrorists'; for these are increasingly the widows of armed, uniformed men; Northern Ireland is plagued not just by the IRA ('terrorists'), but by an armed-men syndrome, and by the cold cults of marching and threatening. Paisley represents this, as does the UDA.

Their statements are experienced in the south as both reproach and intimidation. Unfortunately for them, the British publicists reduced to bathos the poignant faces and speeches of the IRA's victims, and through that bathos the pitiable yet dignified cries of the hunger-strikers' women cut like a razor.

The strikers' own statements used, and grew from, a highly traditional store of concepts and attitudes, representing more than a hundred years in which their paradigm was established. The modern strikers are coding their understanding of history by replicating exemplary events. Their enemies need to decode them: which is in fact quite easy. In the case of Bobby Sands, it would have been easy for the government to find out what he wanted, why, and how much he would settle for. It did not want to find out these things; it wanted him to die or simply to surrender, so enduring another kind of death. It is possible for governments to negotiate with their prisoners; they do it all the time; why should Irish Republicans be so unusual in this regard? Everyone close to the scene, including the SDLP and the Catholic clergy, who did not want a victory for the Republicans, correctly said the dispute could easily be settled. But, as a dispute, it was in a sense a prototype for the Falklands, and perhaps for further wars, in which the Thatcherians were practising an art of not-negotiating.

The British attitude was colonizing in more ways than one. While they tested their troops and *matériel* against Belfast schoolchildren, the multi-national drug companies tested their hormonal and other drugs, their boosters and lethal sprays, on Irish livestock and plant-lands. There is much here for some skilled reporter to investigate; is Ireland, for example, unusually favoured by such testers? It is said, with what truth I do not know, that the reason the prolonged and expensive campaign to eradicate bovine tuberculosis had not worked in Ireland is that the wrong vaccine has been used: an English vaccine. Provided, recommended, sold, by whom? Ireland is a testing and dumping ground for British junk products, including TV programmes and tabloid newspapers with their racist intolerance. As the stuff pours into the country, it is sent around by a middle class that grew into degeneracy as if born to it. The Irish, the perfect complement to their ancient tormentors: choleric, agreeable, envious, and promiscuous with ideas, where the English are spiteful, reserved, self-satisfied, and formalistic (both, of course, are given to rhetoric). But the British insistence on Irish clientage relies on the obvious fact that, as Denis Donoghue has said, 'No Irishman can assume that he is at the centre of anything.' Of course not; the centre of everything is already filled with more masterful people. Similarly, in times of stress, the British High Command knows it can count on the Irish middle class to stand clear and give no trouble.

Such modes of thought are deeply traditional. So are those of their Republican enemies. Everything in the conflict over the five demands and prison conditions, from the acronyms and the titles of journals to the military tactics on both sides, and the creation of support groups, is traditional (the Anglican hierarchy, incidentally, is a support group in a way the Irish Catholic one is not). If an organization calls itself the UVF, or if Paisley mentions 'the Carson trail', or if someone mentions 'amnesty', this in itself tells everyone what conception of himself the speaker has. Naming is everything. Splits of the sort which occurred during the seventies among Republicans are predictable: IRA into Officials versus Provisionals, split from Officials into IRSP, lapsing of Officials from their original republican aims. All absolutely orthodox. So are hunger-strikes.

Irish separatists have been given savage sentences since the Fenian days of the 1860s; they have refused to acknowledge themselves as criminals, and have been given breathtakingly barbarous sentences (years of solitary, for example), designed perhaps to drive them mad. They have refused prison clothing, and been left in nakedness, re-fused amenities and been left in isolation, refused medical help and begun fasting. They have been allowed to die, or have been force-fed, as the suffragettes were, or have been pressured into submission. They have fasted in every British jail, and in every Irish one, including the southern ones. Generation after generation of pacific Irish men and women have campaigned for special status, or visits, or amenities, or basic medical care, or remission, or amnesty for prisoners. Maud Gonne MacBride campaigned from her youth to old age; Constance Markiewicz campaigned for decades; so did Maire Comerford, who died a few months ago. It was a struggle to affirm dignity against attempts to demean it.

One of the great reference-points of the War of Independence was Terence MacSwiney, Lord Mayor of Cork, who died on hunger-strike in Brixton prison. Thomas Ashe also died on fast in 1920, and it was during that strike that a British government first accorded striking prisoners political status. In the seventies, Frank Stagg died on hunger-strike, and the Price sisters, having been force-fed, abandoned their strike only after being given some assurances through Lord Fenner Brockway, a British Labour politician whom they trusted. Between these poles was a host of strikes, some by individuals, some with a mass basis.

The biggest of these latter was the civil war hunger-strike in 1923, of which James Healy, SJ, has written in the Autumn 1982 issue of *Studies*. This strike involved 8,000 strikers in more than ten prisons and similar establishments. It lasted forty-one days. The strikers were republicans protesting against the policies of their former comrades now leading the Free State government. Kildare was full of strikers; there were 1,700 in Newbridge and over 1,000 in the Curragh, both recent stamping-grounds of mine.

The demand was for release. Most strikers ceased, individually or in groups, within a month; about 200 strikers continued and two died around the fortieth day. Then the rest agreed among themselves and ceased together on 23 November. Many ex-strikers were released within a month, on the condition that they be loyal to the Irish Free State. About 100 remained in prison for a further year or more.

Decisions were taken according to 'democratic procedures'; some Republicans, including the writer Frank O'Connor, refused to go on strike, and met some intimidation. Those who gave in 'resented those who continued to hold out' (an interesting reversal of what we might have expected). In some places there were food-stampedes as the fasters came off strike. An amnesty to '3,000 of the prisoners, including all the women', was granted because of fear of influenza. Healy thinks it more likely that the strike was finally called off following 'political discussion' among the prisoners than that they were ordered off.

Then, as now, righteous public figures disowned the strikes. The poet and artist AE 'furiously denounced it'. The Catholic Archbishop Dr Cohalan 'would not allow religious exercises which constitute Christian burial to take place at the burial of Denis Barry' in Cork, for he had 'deliberately taken his own life', despite Cohalan's having officiated, with seven other bishops, at the funeral of the apparently more acceptable MacSwiney. This by itself illustrates how fiercely political the decisions are that governments take towards their prisoners; and, as Healy comments, a hunger-strike may mean winning a government or a war; its defeat therefore can void a government or lose a war.

It seems, too, that the contest is starkly between prisoners and governments; mediators and public opinion are of small account. According to *Iris*, trade union support for the prisoners in 1981 was overwhelming, and even a government-sponsored poll in December 1980 found that '68 per cent of those polled thought that the British should concede the five demands'. This support can be effective only if it is made real through three media: the pulpit, the broadcasting and TV channels, and mass demonstrations. The first in Ireland is closed by fiat, the second by law and cowardice combined, and the third will be available only if everyone knows in advance that the demonstration will be non-violent. Then goodness knows how many marchers might be brought out.

Of the men who went on hunger-strike between 1 March 1981 and the end of September, ten died, two were persuaded off the strike by their comrades because they were too sick to last long enough to make the necessary point, several were taken off by their families when they went into coma, and several more were still on strike until the end. A profile of these strikers would make a fascinating study, and I hope some qualified person undertakes it. But, even if you restrict yourself to making a few simple points about those who died, some interesting suggestions come out.

Their fathers' occupations were invariably sub-middle class: retired small farmer, small publican and grocer, retired local council worker, steel erector, tiler, builder, small hill farmer, retired builder, and so on. Their families were big; only Sands had as few as three siblings, and Devine had one; the rest had between five and eleven. They themselves had a schooling restricted to primary and inter-mediate or primary and secondary; O'Hara seems to have been edu-cated on the streets, and McDonnell had a trade training; none attempted tertiary education. Similarly, their occupations were mostly in manual work: coach builder, painter and decorator, engineer, upholsterer, builder, fitter and welder, motor mechanic, draper's assistant. Most of them were still apprentices when they were first imprisoned, and some never completed their apprentice-ships; several, including Sands, McCreesh, McDonnell and McElwee, were forced from their jobs by loyalist harassment; Doherty was laid off.

In all this, we have so far a picture of modest, family-based, intelligent working-class respectability, with the added touch that they tried to pursue their trades in a society which might at any moment beat them out of their livelihood; so that humiliation and failure were among their job entitlements. Further, they seem, if one reads between the lines of their comrades' stereotyped accounts, to have been active and fun-loving young men, ranging from the stereo-typical singer, dancer and whistler (Francis Hughes), and the mad hatter, practical joker stance claimed for three of them, to the shy, reserved, caring one claimed for another three. Several, including Sands, were keen sportsmen, two or three, especially McCreesh, were fluent in Irish.

Nothing out of the ordinary here – I might say, the engaging ordinary. Yet they met extraordinary deaths. How does this come about? Were they programmed in some extraordinary way? By whom? Not one single portrait is that of a fanatic, a neurotic itching for martyrdom. Did someone de-nature these lads, then? Were they driven mad by some catastrophe? Did they at some point grit their teeth and decide to become the ruthless subhuman killers of the British propaganda cartoons?

Not at all. What happened is that each was both harassed and invited into a response to a situation which he found demeaning to him as a man; and that response had its own logic. No fewer than nine of the ten joined Republican groups after being brutally assaulted by the northern police or the British army. O'Hara had been assaulted since the age of twelve, McCreesh and McDonnell were driven from home, interned, and beaten in prison; and so on. Hurson was even said to have been arrested to keep up the rate of 'self-incriminating statements' in his home area. Three of them lived for periods on the run, while four others lived at home while keeping a low profile.

When they were finally arrested, six were remanded in custody for up to a year. All went on the blanket protest in jail. Four volunteered for the 1980 hunger-strike. Two refused to recognize the authority of the warders. Two were elected to parliament: Sands to the House of Commons, Doherty to Dail Eireann; both were MPs when they died.

But what was it all about, so far as they were concerned, and what were their crimes? They came, as might have been expected, from anti-Unionist backgrounds, but these were not necessarily Republican, or even republican; in a couple of cases, politics was avoided in the family. This was allegedly true of Hurson, for example, whose family lived in a tight-knit enclave of some 200 families in a rural hill society. Sands's family was not republican, in the sense of those of Hughes and McElwee, and the two latter lived moreover in a republican townland. O'Hara came from a family of Republican activists, whereas McCreesh's family, although nationalists in a strongly nationalist area, had no record of republican activism. McDonnell was from a republican area, incessantly harassed by the army. Poor Devine seems to have come from the abandoned fringes of the working class. Several, then, were not brought up as republicans, never mind Republicans; it was not propaganda that made them, but harassment, not Dublin but Stormont. Some others were of Republican provenance, and acted just as their uncles, fathers and grandfathers had. There is a double lesson in this for the British authorities, or, indeed, for anyone who cares to listen: that you cannot kill republicanism, for there are too many males in those battered republican families, and they will not stand for continued oppression; and that the effort to kill it by suppressing those families creates more recruits because it involves suppressing others. That is obvious. A close view of the strikers' minds can not be given by an outsider like me.

These men learned a particularly intense comradeship both in the IRA (and INLA) and in the jails. The attempt to portray them as vicious criminal types (or 'ordinary decent criminals', to quote the old Irish joke) is ridiculous, as is the astonishment displayed by British newspaper editors on learning that they regard themselves as political prisoners, and not criminals at all. I can find no record of what most of us would regard as non-political criminal offences in the past of any of these men; there may be some, but if so they cannot be of much significance. Apart from their political violence, they had remarkably clean records.

As to that political violence, while it was common to berate them as a gang of murderers, few of them were even accused, much less convicted, of murder; few indeed were accused even of attempted murder. Francis Hughes was convicted of murder, and Raymond McCreesh of attempted murder (for which he got fourteen years), while Hurson was found guilty of conspiracy and McElwee of manslaughter (which, combined with possession of explosives, got him twenty years). Many of these sentences were savage even if you trusted the judicial process which produced them. The dreaded

Bobby Sands got fourteen years for possessing a revolver, the self-same weapon of which I think three of his comrades were found to be in possession, and for which they were given long prison terms. O'Hara, possessing a hand grenade (eight years); possessing Bobby Sands's revolver (McDonnell, fourteen years); Doherty, possessing arms and explosives (eighteen years); taking part in a raid on an armoury, Devine, twelve years.

Most of these were certainly armed men, therefore, and several of them had seen military action; but hardly any was the hardened, habitual, death-loving, fanatical 'gunman' beloved of hostile legend, living only to put the fiftieth notch on his gun and then die like a wolf. They were mostly ardent but inexperienced guerrilla soldiers; they were in prison too long to gain more experience. And it may be said that their chief experience of the warrior life was the one which they had in their death-cells, and of which the motif was sheer endurance.

Part Three

POETS, HOPES AND FEARS

Chapter Ten

POETS AND THE POOR

Since Sean O'Faolain proved so easy to meet, I was encouraged to expect that lesser Irish writers would be even more amenable. And so they were; the world of poets and writers is very small in some ways, even if you include 'writers'. In a social or a reverberative sense, Ireland is very small, Dublin even smaller; so it seems to follow that the world of Dublin writers and writing will be smaller still. I found it exhilaratingly much more informal and easy than its Cambridge counterpart, yet disablingly much more discontinuous. Where Cambridge men and women had ambition without leisure, the Dublin ones had aspiration without ambition. They were always on the lookout for 'diversion' and diversions, many of which were discovered in and through booze. They were very much in the position of those actors who are always between engagements. Lots of them were said to be nasty – spongers, bullies, and blackguards. And perhaps they were.

I met only nice ones. This may have been partly by luck, since Patrick Kavanagh was in London feeding material to Anthony Cronin, the friend who was to write such a devastating account of him many years later; Brian O'Nolan (the 'real' Flann O'Brien) was incapacitated in some way, and Brendan Behan I was prevented from meeting except for two brief chats. I have the feeling that to the luck was added deliberate management, conducted by the young poet Richard Weber. The Bohemians of the mid fifties were swarming in London, and Bob Brissenden, who had homed in on Soho and treated all inside that heartland without fear or favour, had introduced me to a couple of denizens. Unable to raise Dylan Thomas, he said to me on one occasion, 'I think I can do you George Barker', whom he had met. Barker also proved a non-starter, though among the poets whom Brissenden provided for chat was a fellow who bravely struggled out of bed, to which he had gone pretty pissed, to represent Thomas and his values to us for an hour or two before closing-time.

Anyway, Kavanagh and Behan mixed in those (Romantic) circles when they were in London. But now Behan was in Dublin; where his second latest escapade involved his waving a loaded revolver at the Gardai during a demonstration against the closing of a performance of *The Rose Tattoo*; and his latest involved his being knocked around and thrown out of a bar on the south side by 'a lady cattle dealer from the County Meath' (so it was reported to me) who objected to his profanity. I wanted to meet him, for I had read *Borstal Boy*, which I thought a lovely innocent book, and seen *The Quare Fellow*; I also knew some lesser writings. And I was in a fair way to do this, for both in 1956 and 1957 I was living on or near the South Circular Road, between Dolphin's Barn and Harcourt Street, we were close to the city, and I was always going down there to work, look, talk, and so on. I was often in the National Library, the National Museum, and of course, a few yards away from both of these, Trinity College, which, with the Bank of Ireland building, has an awesomely central position in the cultural geography of Dublin. Not only do all roads seem to lead to it, but many lead through it; and it was then, as it still is, an indispensable talking-ground.

It was there that I met Weber, who was the best informed poet of a group which belonged to Trinity; he himself did not, but he had made it his place of talk, and the first day I met him he led me into the refectory, nodding and joking to the doorman placed especially to keep out such as he and I ('the cheapest good meal in Dublin, Vincent', he whispered as we got into the great hall). Up the queue to the women serving meals, who greeted Weber with warmth and a more than academic respect, as he introduced me (as Doctor Buckley, perhaps?) and commended them and me to one another's care. Nobody could have penetrated his disguise, for he was very tall and looked fragile; his head had a noble birdliness and his bearing was distinguished; he was about twenty-three; and so far as those around him were concerned, if he wasn't a distinguished young don he was something even grander, a musician or an architect perhaps, and a credit to the whole establishment. He ate his lunch in Trinity most days, and was probably their most popular customer.

He introduced me to signal individuals, as I shall relate; but he went to some lengths to avoid introducing me to Behan. He was himself no roisterer, in fact rather abstemious and contemptuous of drunken folly, but he would stand in a bar and stand his round, and endure the conversation, until the thought of Behan's arrival would blanch his face and put a cold sweat into his voice. He was particularly insistent that Behan not meet me. Why, for God's sake?

'He'll insult you. He'll kill you.' 'Why?' 'He'll think you're English. He can't stand meeting Englishmen.' 'Easy enough to tell him I'm Australian.'

There was more at stake in this matter than I could fathom, however; and whenever he would hear the great Rahahooa lada noise in the entrance to Jammets, or outside the Bailey, he would say, 'Ah God, there's Brendan', and we would move on, with me expostulating mildly in disbelief, Behan (or whoever it was) going 'Rahooa', and Weber explaining unconvincingly the root of the matter. Plainly Behan was a nuisance to him, and Behan does seem to have tried to give a mythic stature to his own aggressiveness. I never saw this in action, and many years later a cabby told me that he had known Brendan well, they came from the same district, they used to drink together on the north side, they were butties and chums, and it was all wrong about Brendan's being violent. 'He'd never hit anybody,' he said piously. 'There wasn't a punch in his whole body.'

In any case, when I did meet him, he was in no condition to throw punches; it was in the morning, and both times he was badly hungover; he was friendliness itself, in a detached way, to Weber and to me; and he seemed to have no interest in my nationality. His conversation might be described as gentlemanly-disoriented. Why, then, was Weber so apprehensive of him? Was it a form of extremist aestheticism, which found it impossible to remain in the presence of so gross a social disorder? Was he afraid that he might see in Behan's

countenance the features of Ireland as a whole? The real Brendan
Behan (the cabby's was only one among many versions) had been
standing up in a variety of places for decades; and always the disguise
is a new one. Cronin's account of him in *Dead as Doornails* is a most
desolating one; and I am told that it is of a desolating accuracy. It's
possible he did not know who he was.

But, dead or alive, he has to act the character; and if he's not
available for well-known reasons, his widow, or brother, or still
sprightly mother, will be roped in to do it for him. The trouble is,
this media concentration on Behan is often ostensibly for the sake of
someone or something else. Last time I saw it, it was for James Joyce,
and in the interests of the centenary celebrations, from February to
June 1982 (of which, too, more later). Joyce was, it seems, the
Brendan Behan of his day, the archetypal, the quintessential
Dubliner, the stroller and irreverent roister, the prankster, the
portrait of the artist. Both were 'lovely men'; any Dubliner will be
proud to count them among his kind. And so Dublin survives the
destruction of its own fabric: slop about Joyce and Behan will
do it.

Through Weber I became a part of the vaguely drifting talk-
culture that nested in Trinity. Duncan was an Ulster Scot who edited
Icarus, the college literary journal. He lived in college, in conditions
of a cold lack or failure of furniture; his rooms, based on those of a
Cambridge college, were by comparison with their prototype lacking in amenity, comfort, decoration. Not that Duncan cared. Among
his friends were the poet Anne Cluysenaar, Meryl Gourlay,
Christopher FitzSimons, who became well known in theatre, Kate
Lucy, who as a relation of the Catholic bishop of Cork ought not to
have been there at all, but who was, actress and singer. Also representing the Gael was Tommy MacGloin, a hard-working romantic
poet who had been born, I think, in New York of parents from
Donegal, and who had been the junior bagpipe champion of all
Ireland. It was with talk and, occasionally, booze and song that they
warmed the cold squares of Trinity. They were far more relaxed, far

wittier and more melancholy, than the Cambridge performers to whom I would have to return, after each Irish visit.

Weber also introduced me to Austin Clarke, at that time an ageing man if you took one perspective, but from another an original poet at the height of his powers and achievement. Dublin took little notice of him, for despite his *fin-de-siècle* hat and coat he was a quiet and scholarly man. Yet two or three mornings a week he would hold court, at a fixed time, in Bewley's Oriental tea and coffee shop in Grafton Street. It was not every day that a court assembled, and I never saw more than three at the one time; and that is counting myself, Weber, or both; so perhaps the monarchy was in process of converting itself into a banana republic. Weber at any rate was faithful. He was an imaginative man, who could see some filiation or other link between the old Clarke and the young Kinsella, and between the latter and my barely apprenticed self. Being free of malice (for he vented all his aggressions in witty gossip and asides), he wanted to bring such people together; his affection for poetry, while sardonic, was pure (in this, it resembles the attitude of a much younger poet, Denis O'Driscoll, now a few years out of his own apprenticeship).

That Bewley's tea-shop should have been the site of the court was a tribute to many factors: Clarke was an abstemious man, and a poor one, as were those who went to see him; none of us could have afforded the Shelbourne or the Royal Hibernian, where I would occasionally have afternoon tea with Denis Donoghue. As well as that, the Grafton Bewley's is just down the street from the pubs, particularly McDaid's, where Clarke's rivals and enemies, Kavanagh, and so on, would growl and profane over their booze and their betting-guides; so his occupancy of that spinsterly seat was a symbolic rejection and rebuke of whatever was happening up the street, inside or outside those feckless adversary heads.

Bewley's was far too crowded and clattery for that sort of thing; but no doubt it was a point of contact rather than anything else. Clarke needed to recruit acquaintances; he was courteous but lonely.

He could satisfy nobody: Weber was far too sardonic to play courtier, and I was far too garrulous. But I would be happy to visit him at Templeogue.

There he lived in the Bridge House, by a small bridge over the River Dodder just off Firhouse Road; I saw the last stages of the house's demolition only three years ago, and I heard everybody comment what a pity was the destruction of the home of such a fine poet (Austin Clarke the poet, as the local people always refer to him), a landmark. There I went, on two or three Sunday afternoons, on a bus trip which seemed interminable, though it took only half an hour. Templeogue was then a village in the 'country'. It was bare, a little desolate, lacking both in innocence and improvement. Clarke's house also had a touch of desolation; he was living far short of the sage's comfort, and entertained us in a room almost as bare of furniture as Duncan's room in Trinity. His hospitality, and that of his wife, was abundant. But there was no court here, either. Had the word got out on Austin Clarke? What word? Was he dangerous? Who would listen to serious detraction? But who would listen to Clarke, either, in his slightly desolated house down among the trees, by the faintly leaping water, in his bit of old Ireland among the cement dust future of Templeogue and Tallaght?

One of his recurrent subjects was James Joyce, whom he had known well and whom, by his own account, he had had to endure in Paris: Joyce the sponger and hypocrite, and not the roistering Joyce of the RTE programmes. Clarke's Joyce was writing whingeing letters home at the very time the admiring American women were sending him crates of fine wine. Another subject was the Catholic church in Ireland, which was, of course, the chief subject or sub-topic of Clarke's later poetry. Through his scalding anti-institutionalism I thought I could detect something like religious faith, if that strange creature of the centuries can be distinguished from religious belief; there was no question of allegiance.

Censorship was still in force, and every Irish writer of any quality was harmed by it, in one way or another; a sour piety lay about the streets, next to the stout-like puddles. Bookshops battled on, trying to promote and sell Irish literature; so, oddly, did the municipal libraries, which were an obvious target for the *bien-pensants*. Over it all was an air of hopelessness and of time-wasting, the permanent effluvium of a world which was isolated and had no money. Old writers such as Peadar O'Donnell and Liam O'Flaherty were round and about, but I never met them.

Weber's prime enthusiasm, however, was for Thomas Kinsella, a Dubliner who had become fluent in Irish, had, though young, a senior and responsible job in the Civil Service, in the Ministry of Finance no less, and who was winning a reputation as a poet. His reputation had not yet quite reached his home town, which was preoccupied with other culture heroes; and, besides, in being a lyrical poet influenced by Auden, he was perhaps a little un-Irish. Abroad, of course, his qualities were seen as centrally Irish. Several persons told me of him and, although they were runners from several stables, their judgements seemed to run towards a pool of consensus: Ah, Kinsella's a grave one, a strange fellow. You never know what he's thinking behind those big pebbly glasses; he has the soul of a civil servant, I don't know if there's any nature in him at all; oh, no, he's no drinker, I don't know if he takes a drink at all, he won't have a drink with you, I doubt if he'll talk to you at all.

When I grew to know (and drink and talk with) Kinsella, I realized at once that none of my informants knew anything about him; even Weber had been confused by the pebbly glasses. Kinsella was not long married, he lived some miles out of Dublin in or near Killiney, and he didn't have time to engage in time-wasting; but he was very friendly, in an innocent and open way, although you could readily see that, when he moved back into the watchfully over-lapping circles of his compatriots, he would hoist the armour again, and deliberately give the impression that he carried his own motte-and-bailey keep around with him.

As a fairly cool but constant admirer of Clarke's poetry, Kinsella formed with Denis Donoghue, then a lecturer in English at UCD, and Donald Davie, then lecturing at Trinity, a trio of excellence and more than local ambition. The trio created, by sheer flair, the illusion of a culture metropolitan or even cosmopolitan in scope and feel. This was an illusion: Davie was a transient, after all, a little Englander seeking an English foothold in wider worlds. Donoghue was a mere lecturer, with a large and growing family, and he was going to have to move away at last; for it is a complex fate looking towards America, and it is almost though not quite impossible to look towards England at the same time. Kinsella took the same route, towards Ireland by way of America; it was an adventurous route at the time, which O'Faolain, for example, had taken before them, and which Montague, Brian Moore and Brian Coffey would at some time take (Montague like others came from there). By now it is a familiar furrow, and people grow blasé following it. Donoghue spent some time in England, at Cambridge, and, as he told me, went home because England was too degenerate a place in which to bring up a family. Kinsella seems still in two minds. 'Don't stay in this benighted country,' he told me in 1973, and his wife Eleanor chimed in, 'No, you're better off in England. They know how to live there. Go back there.' 'For God's sake,' I said, laughing, 'I've just got here. I haven't been in England, I've been in Canada. I don't want to go to bloody England.' I knew England far better than they did. Kinsella is in fact an incurable addict of Irishness; and at the time when I first knew him he and Weber and Donoghue remade Clarke, re-established him against the tearaways and countrymen who had nearly driven him out of the reckoning.

In the mid fifties, Weber's wanderings sometimes took him towards the official Dublin of Merrion Square, where the Ministry of Finance was. On occasions I went with him. One day, calling to see Kinsella in his office, we were interrogated by the Gardai on the front door, who were not impressed by Weber's cheerful greeting, 'Good morning, Guard', and so on, and who responded with 'Who? Who?' to the information, 'Kinsella. Mr Kinsella. Thomas Kinsella.' After three or four exchanges of this sort, Weber clicked his heels, stood to attention, and started to sing the National Anthem – in Irish. 'Sine Fianna Fail,' he yowled, staring straight out at the guards, who of course had been forced into standing to attention and giving whatever salutes were called for. Then in to see the embarrassed Kinsella. These useful japes became less common after Weber got his job as attendant in a children's playground at three pounds a week, becoming a bony and dedicated catcher in the concrete rye.

I would then occasionally meet Kinsella for lunch, and we would talk with whatever cultural workers turned up. Once there was Liam Miller, of the Dolmen Press, and I must have met that great rejuvenator of Irish traditional music, Sean O'Riada, who was a great friend of Kinsella. One day it was the Earl of Wicklow, whom Kinsella wanted to chat up about some project, and whom we failed to guide into a bar in Merrion Row, so that he was forced to stand murmuring on its threshold. His discourse was muted and masonic in quality; is this the man who, so I read the other day, is a member of the secret Catholic organization, *Opus Dei*?

With television, there has grown up in Ireland the phenomenon which I think of as endless recycling; nothing is left to go permanently to waste; everything is eventually used again. A lyric generates a painting, which suggests a ballet, which leads to a film, to which the music is provided by the Chieftains, who then cut a record, which leads to a ballet, a piece of sculpture, and endless interviews on television. There is the ancillary industry of receptions and launchings; and there is booze. Art works are in a sense the product of the drink-up, the drink-in, or the drink-over, in which star seeks out star to acknowledge star quality, and to make suggestions about recycling. This happens to a far greater extent than in other countries, and because the country is so small, the same names recur. To get into this system and process you must go to functions or be interestingly accessible in some other way to the right people. Heaney is the poet, Banville the novelist, McGahern the short story writer (interestingly inaccessible except to the right people), John Behan the sculptor, Friel the playwright; there is some dispute about the painter, and all this is in any case for the time being. Other circles intersect these with, for example, Kinsella or Montague as the poet, but there is a kind of consensus turning the wheel, and the effect is of constellations, the smaller and the larger, moving about one another.

This relevance to the élite has to be worked at; you can't afford to let someone else do your drinking for you; as one editor said to me, 'It would be as easy for me to live in Bandon, Co. Cork as in North Kildare; then I could catch the shuttle up and down twice a week, and be at work in about the same time.' Why didn't he do it, then? 'O, out of sight, out of mind. They'd assume I no longer existed, because they'd want me to disappear.' It's all quite true, I'm afraid. There is no system of regionalisms in Ireland as there is in Britain, or the US, or Canada, or Australia; there is no regional money, and there are no organizations. The media are in Dublin, and so is what money there is. Of this, more later. Some things, like the recent book, *An Duanaire* (edited by Thomas Kinsella and Sean O Tuama) are accepted as having a national dimension; but that was launched in Dublin, by bureaucrats based in Dublin who, to judge from their accents, came from all four provinces; the launching was recorded by Dublin cameras; the editors were interviewed by Dublin presenters. When a new system of arts grants (the Aos Dana) was announced, half the poets in the country set about working out how to get the grant as quickly as possible. Everyone wants to get on the TV books programme, *Folio*, which is worth any three launchings by itself. Harassed writers who are also academics will nevertheless drop everything to go to parties and launchings, where they will gather enough energy to act up. I have lunched with well-known poets who could not refrain from moving to three or four tables in the room; often these tables were occupied by media people. The sense is strong of a practised and habitual competitiveness.

Crucial to all this is the existence of North America. In the old

days America was there, but over there. Now, it is a constant concealed reference point. As Penelope said once, 'The Irish are not
interested in foreign writers, they are interested in foreign money.'
To that extent, the provincialism has gone sour; the visitor is quizzed
not for intrinsic interest but for his capacity to provide validation,
preferment, or escape. One Irish poet asked me if I would be willing
to go as the Irish delegate to a writers' conference in Louvain,
Belgium. 'Most intriguing,' I said. 'Mind you, you'd be an Irish
delegate, Vincent,' he said; and he must have revised his proprieties,
for I heard no more of it. Another writer offered to get me a plum
position at a week-long seminar in Innsbruck. 'Marvellous,' he said,
'a working holiday, but more holiday than work.' He was so used to
doing deals, and to thinking of foreigners as patrons and providers,
that he could think of nothing finer to offer me, and he was prepared
to make me an Irishman for the occasion. Denis O'Driscoll is
interested in foreign writers, and is always trying to create occasions
for getting them to Ireland. But, generally, Irish writers, and cultural
institutions, perceive themselves as the recipients, not the spenders,
of culture-money. The habit of recycling fits firmly, if obscurely,
into this syndrome; its arrangements have the complication of a page
in the Book of Kells.

The role of the reception, launching, and so on, is simple and
never declared: it is to pronounce an artistic fact an artistic event by
way of converting it immediately into a social event which, by
reason of its new standing, is reportable, and needs to be reported in
the press, usually with photos. In them we see Miss Philomena
O'Fitz of Blackrock, pictured with Mr FitzPhil O'Mena of
Whiterock at the opening last night of the Whatsit at the Soforth.
All of them look the same. They will be there again next year when
the paintings of George Russell (AE) . . . So we get in social mode
the expression of the generous, almost automatically hedonistic
response of the Irish to anything which appears before them, a
response that is combined with very watchful, unillusioned habits of
expectation.

If there is a love of 'diversion', there is also a love of style and personality. There is no premium on sounding, though there may be on being conventional. On the contrary, everyone has a way of insisting on quirks. They are likely to be extremely courteous, in a way that puts most of their English counterparts to shame, and one-upping in ordinary conversation is not regarded as a useful skill, though capping of jokes is spontaneous. Indeed, the Irish and the English intellectual styles differ completely; it is interesting versus right, entertainment versus solid probity, individual versus institutional. In both, there is a notion of the clubbable involved; but they are very different clubs. I suspect that English intellectual women are taught at school how not to burst out laughing in the presence of strangers; Irish women will laugh at the least excuse, and have been known to punch your arm by way of emphasis. This is intoxicating to visitors, and it conveys great charm. But Cambridge has charm, too; its charm consists in the pretence that everyone is agreeable, in both senses; the college porters and library attendants are exempt from this pretence, of course; but perhaps their role is that of the hard policeman who highlights the soft one.

Something of Dublin's sense of itself as permanent theatre came out during the Joyce centenary in 1982; this sense, and this interest, were not shared by the rest of the country, as I learned when I went to Cork later that year. Revisionism has been at work in literature as well as history, so that, while Yeats is down, Joyce is universally up. 1982 was Joyce's year. Contrary to what they often say, that nobody in Ireland gives Joyce the attention the Americans deserve, and that Ireland is thus a shame and scandal in the eyes of the world, or at least the paying part, the Irish went in big on Joyce year. RTE did a non-stop reading of *Ulysses*, which lasted thirty-six hours, starting early on Bloomsday and ending late the next day. A marvellous film was made for Joyce's birthday, with a script by Colbert Kearney. The Irish government struck a stamp. So far, so good. But 1982 is also the centenary, or something of the sort, of the composer John Field, the

Fenian novelist and balladist Charles Kickham, and the Gaelic story-teller Padraic O Conaire. What about them? So, special programmes for them too: stamps, indeed, for them, coming in on the back of Joyce, so that no merit may go unacknowledged and no interest-group unrecognized.

This impulse is generous, even lovable, but it is a small-town generosity ('and last, but not least . . .'), and the lovableness may be tinged with a certain resentment of genius. For no sense of scale is observed in these doings. It was not the greatness of Joyce that was at stake, but his currency. He had become journalists' property; it is they who say in what his significance consists ('What would James Joyce make of the arrangements to commemorate him at . . .'); it is they who invent ironies, and detect them everywhere; they imagine him laughing at the efforts of his devotees (a likely story, in my view). The significance consists in three facts; one, that he got Ireland to rights, and in his books made the largest obscene gesture of all time to his home and his people (Up you, Ireland!); that he provided, and continues to provide, work for many later workers in the cultural vineyard, ballet-dancers, song-writers, singers, radio-presenters, raconteurs, playwrights, television people, public relations people, people's relations and, of course, journalists and cultural secretaries; and, third, that he draws the Americans, drawing them especially in June of 1982, not on his own birthday but on Bloomsday, drawing them with ferocious ease, and he can be counted on to draw them for evermore. In the celebrations Dublin became (to paraphrase this poor used-up genius) a praiser of its own past.

Much of the commentary seems unable to tell *Ulysses* from *Finnegan's Wake*; the characters from his books are treated as more real than their author, and Bloom's house in Eccles Street, or his birthplace in Clanbrassil Street, is touted for preservation more ardently than Joyce's birthplace in Brighton Square. Padraic O Conaire can't draw the Americans in that way; and why shouldn't he have his due? But Joyce! whom a lot of us think the greatest novelist in his language – or languages.

So Dublin on Bloomsday was bubbling like a tarred street. People dressed up as characters from *Ulysses* and, timing themselves as carefully as any Irish person can, perambulated, sat, sang, winked and thought their way through the windings of the physical city, Dublin, in the manner prescribed by the omniscient experimenter. Dublin was filled, hour by hour, with people acting these fictional parts; and some people spoke as if this complexly simple device 'brought the book alive'. What was missing was its language, all its language; that was, at the very same time, being read out on another medium, the radio, where it could be heard but not seen. In the open city, the most language-smitten book of the century was spun out in perambulation and mime. A wonderfully charming and irrelevant conceit which, I am afraid, I was too curmudgeonly to go and witness. While the dozens of actors acted thus, they were watched, cheered, interrogated and heckled by hundreds of spectators, from posh tourists and entrepreneurs to cheeky Dublin street-kids. A delegation of scholars and seminar groupies went along to Bloom's birthplace, to set a plaque into its wall. The birthplace was in Clanbrassil Street, near which I used to live in 1957, and every inch of which I knew. But there are two Clanbrassil streets: Lower and Upper; the one I knew better, which runs down to Christchurch and St Patrick's cathedrals, and which is slightly the slummier, is Lower, and it is there that, in 1904 and earlier, and also in 1957, a close-built few hundred yards sustained a Jewish population. Upper Clanbrassil Street, in its brief stretch up to the Grand Canal, was probably of a slightly different social class, and not notable for Jewishness. Yet it was to Upper that the pilgrim-scholars went to attach their plaque. As they did so, the working-class women of the street came out to jeer and advise. 'No, it's not here. You've got it all wrong. Go down the road. There were never Jews here. Its Lower Clanbrassil Street you want.' And so on; until the leader of the delegation which had come to attach a real plaque to the 'birthplace' of an invented person, was irritated into crying out, 'O for goodness sake. He's only a character in a book. It's just a bit of fun.' Or words to that effect. A most Joycean moment.

And, so they explained, there was disagreement about the matter; a scholarly expert had established this as the true place; the plaque stayed. Leaving aside the oddities of logic in this retort (American rather than Irish logic, incidentally), we note two features of it all: Why did they not go to Lower? I would have, and I am no Dubliner. Ah, the address at Lower is no longer viable; the façade has been pulled down; there's nowhere to put the plaque ('Ah, put it wherever you bloody well like Seamus; he's only a feller in a book'); if no Clanbrassil exists, it will be necessary to invent one. And, isn't it remarkable how well read those working-class women were – to know where Leopold Bloom was born. They seem to have behaved in a far more authentically Joycean mode than the scholars, or the actors either: you don't have to wear fancy dress to be a character from *Ulysses*.

All this was staged in the midst of a national mood of dithering despair; for that's the way the country was that year. It had the rootless, small-scale vitality of a crossroads. I used to think of it as a deeply rooted, if provincial country, and there are still aspects of it which answer to that description. But not for most people, who are on the move, from this street to that, endlessly seeking change without difference, and letting their idealists die on hunger-strike without so much as a prayer.

Still, it is better to honour James Joyce than most other expatriate achievers. As it happened, his centenary fell at a time when almost all Irish writers had taken up his cause in various ways. It had become *de rigueur* to say that he was a 'socialist' (whatever that noble designation would mean in his case). He was generally preferred to Yeats, who had made the mistake of living too long in Ireland, and so was too well known to too many people. Whatever people said, nobody actually knew Joyce, or knew much about him; when a priest-writer discovered some interesting facts about Nora Barnacle, Joyce's wife, everyone behaved as if he had pulled off a scoop; yet his informants were there in Galway, available and ready for interview; the revelations were in no way secrets unearthed; it was just that no one had bothered before. So much for the omnivore, international scholarship.

Kinsella has made Joyce part of his own network of filiation; so, in a different way, has Heaney. Like the writers, they have fallen into the habit of quoting Joyce or using him as a point of reference. This is natural and inevitable for, apart from the fact that both poets are very attached to Joyce's works, Joyce-reference makes it easier to converse with American literary visitors. This network of filiations, with their implication of trips abroad and welcomes to overseas visitors, is a very important and obtrusive part of Irish literary life. I have the feeling that, whatever may be said about others, Americans are the people whose demands are not to be refused; yet most writers have silent phone numbers, allegedly to protect them from American minor scholars. The art thus becomes one of balancing – not a new challenge for the Irish; you are always available for the favoured visitor, so long as you know he is there; the art involves how to avoid knowing this. With male writers who have a large American clientele, wives become very important – their own wives, that is. The wife is a vibrant feature of the scene conceived, at the one extreme, as a matter of keeping life amenable, glad, and unforgettably Irish, and, at the other, as a power-situation. Irishwomen can play this role magnificently; it may be called the role of mystifying exhilaration. Sometimes a wife overplays the role, or adds too large an element of demand, but even these mistakes may have the good effect of making people talk about her and her husband.

When a number of writers, particularly poets, is together, the complexities of the poetry-game become incomprehensible. Not that there is anything which does not have its national version elsewhere, in Australia and Canada, for example; but in Ireland the contradictions are remarkable for drama and pace. Nowhere is this more obvious than at the Yeats summer school at Sligo, which I have attended twice, and where I have taken part in two public poetry readings.

The school is held in August, when you may get marvellous

weather (one year people were fainting in the heat), or you may be
faced by late-summer rain-storms from the Atlantic. This oddity in
the weather adds to the uncertainty generated by the poets; they may
come early, they may leave tomorrow, they may read, they may not,
they can't be certain, they are waiting for Godot to create an effect of
secretiveness and slow tension. In 1973, the reading was in the Sligo
townhall, and among the readers were Seamus Heaney, Michael
Longley, and the famous English poet Basil Bunting. We had been
given our places in the reading-order beforehand, and I had chanced
one of the two most favoured positions. I arrived on time, as did
Bunting; but with the crowd growing restive, two readers had still
not arrived, and the usual apologetic requests were made, 'Would
you mind going first?' and so on. I agreed, just as the slowcoaches
ambled in, to be told that they would now be reading in different
positions. All very well; but Bunting, who had originally had a
position of a sort which few poets like, overheard these re-
arrangements, and demanded testily if he too could have a better
place. At one stage, it looked as if I might have to read both first and
in the middle, to prevent anyone else having so discommodious a
place in the poetry universe.

Heaney read with his usual perfect pacing; but Bunting, reading
several of his lesser poems, was struggling in unfamiliar going. At
one point, just as he had announced that he was about to read a poem
written for the birthday of a young girl, a local woman rose in the
audience and cut across him loudly. It was a great thing to commemorate birthdays, but we should acknowledge all and not only some
birthdays; Mrs So-and-So, of Sligo, had her birthday this very day,
and the speaker would like Bunting to present the poem not just for
his own friend but also for the Sligo woman. This was marvellous
stuff, but Bunting seemed not to understand a word of it. 'What? I
beg your pardon?' he said carefully in his flat Geordic accent. This
was a mistake; for the woman, who had got some applause for her
first effort, struck once more, rising to commend a poet of the village
genius type who, so she said, had come all the way from Kilkenny to

be present. The reasons for celebration were getting more and more odd, and Bunting more and more bewildered. 'Oah,' he said slowly and detachedly, and read on as if nothing had happened.

Six years later, the visiting English poet and dignitary was Ted Hughes, who was down to give a reading of his favourite Yeats poems (which he did with remarkable empathy) and also to take part in a reading. Heaney is a close friend and associate of Hughes, and had come to Sligo to introduce and generally assist him; he too was to read. So was Michael Longley, who was present once more, and a couple of young southern poets. I was also included, and since the reading was to take place in the 'conference club', which would be full of roistering, since it would certainly start late, and since I had to give a paper the first thing next morning, I was careful to check how many readers there would be. Six or seven. Are you sure? Well, it could be eight, but I don't think so. Say six. Or perhaps seven.

That is a tolerable number, even in the smoky and autistic atmosphere of the club; any more is an excess. But there was a fly in the ointment, a contingency, an Unknown: Longley was accompanied by Paul Muldoon and two other poets from the Belfast establishment, Frank Ormsby and Ciaran Carson; there might even be others. They might want to read. 'Well, will they or won't they?' 'I don't know. We'll have to wait and see.' 'Well, why don't you bloody well ask them?' It was easy to find them; they sat almost permanently in their own corner of the bar, at their own table; they were the 'northern lads', and it was as the 'northern lads' that Gus Martin the organizer always referred to them. But he seemed apprehensive about disturbing them with a question about their intentions as they sat holding court. 'Can't you arrange two readings, Gus?' 'No, no.' And so, narrowing down from slow precedent to precedent, the list of readers grew to thirteen.

Of these, Heaney and Hughes had been taken to dinner and arrived back very late, just before it was time for them to read. Several others arrived on time but walked past the waiting audience and went to the bar, from which it would have been repugnant to Gaelic delicacy to dislodge them; they included one or two of the northern lads. Other, less experienced readers took the hint and absented themselves until a more congenial moment. It was the old ways, gnarled now into an impossible knot of indecision and self-will. The audience sat sweating shoulder to shoulder in the increasingly poisonous air while the MC, Lester Connor, called on this poet, then that, then any poet, any, to come forward. I volunteered, then listened to the next performer, Aidan Carl Matthews, and went home. Next morning poets were complaining of the idiocy of being required to read at midnight, which was unreasonable seeing that some of them had not arrived until eleven. I told Martin that I would never read in that building again; and I never will.

It is hard for organizers to know what time of the evening is best for a poetry reading, especially when part of the prospective audience, and almost all the prospective readers, will be needing a drink and a chat beforehand. In Listowel, where the annual writers week is rightly esteemed the pride of County Kerry, our reading in 1982 was due to start about eleven at night. The tiny theatre would not be free until then. So Muldoon and I read then, starting even later. The audience was understandably tiny; but Muldoon was, it seemed, gravely put out before he saw it. He is a man who looks even younger than his age, dresses stylishly, with a touch of the world snooker player about his use of the weskit, and walks and stands in a leaning, self-effacing manner, as if to emphasize the passive, wounded nature of his self in the world. He is also highly intelligent, with a mind that is combative rather than otherwise, which lies curled like a snake's head waiting to be stirred into strike. As Gabriel FitzMaurice ushered me into the hotel where I was to stay the night, and I walked into the centre, not of paralysis but of a roar like a cattle-sale, the first person I saw was Paul. He was seated, with the artist Mary Farl Powers, on the bottom step of the central stairway; they were forlornly drinking gin and tonic. About them swayed dozen upon dozen of Munstermen and women, and some Munsterkids, drinking and talking and roaring. There were snatches of songs of differing kinds. Every bar was full, every lounge, the television room, and the foyer. People passed for no apparent reason from one space to another, adding to the congestion. There was an air of much affluence combined with little poshness. Gracefulness was not insisted on. As soon as he saw us, Muldoon rose with an expression of great relief and offered drinks.

He had been, I imagine, experiencing culture-shock. This was the Kerry heartland *en fête*; it was rural shenanigans, and on a Sunday night at that; and although everyone there looked as if he or she had more money than I, that kind of joy can feel like the start of a peasants revolt combined with a takeover bid on the Stock Exchange, 'the bankers roaring like beasts on the floor of the Bourse', as Auden puts it. 'I don't think I'll read for very long,' said Paul, and he stubbornly kept his word. He read, as Heaney does, with a highly developed negative capability, letting the words and phrases fall towards and away from one another, but in a much lighter voice than Heaney. Later, we had the obligatory argument about the hunger-strikers.

Irish poets seem in constant co-operation, filiation, with certain intellectuals who, though not themselves poets, are central to the poetic economy, which, as I have said, is one of social and pro-motional activity. Such a man is Sean O'Reamoinn, an RTE exe-cutive, Irish enthusiast, lay theologian, and helper of causes that founder in pubs; he seems to run like a thread through the doings of the past three decades, and is always present when others are doing. In this, he possibly follows an earlier though much less organized guru, Eoin O Mahony, known everywhere as 'the Pope'. O Mahony was an SC (equivalent to a QC) who did not practise his art very much. I first met him casually in the gate of Trinity in 1956 and after some chat four of us, including the historian, Florence O Donoghue, sauntered up Grafton Street to Davy Byrne's pub, stopping at three or four stations in the street while O Mahony filled in the new chum on various features of the culture. These features were mostly visible, and chiefly human. The Pope's treatment of them was backward-looking and anecdotal, not to say sardonic.

For example: 'See that fellow there, across the street, walking away from us. That's Dick Mulcahy. *General* Richard Mulcahy. He doesn't want to have to notice me. Do you see the way he's walking: very stiff, upright. A picture of uprightness. Perhaps a bit scared. He doesn't know who's going to have a go at his back. Of course, he was a soldier. But he's afraid to look over his shoulder at the ghosts. When they executed the seventy-seven Republicans at the end of the Civil War, he was in the inner Cabinet; and Desmond FitzGerald was the only one of them who knew any theology, moral or otherwise; and FitzGerald got upset and said, 'No, you can't kill them like that, it's against the moral law; St Thomas says that God . . .'; and your man there yelled, "Ah, don't bring God into it, for God's sake".'

There were many stories like this, and I heard some of them on that and subsequent occasions. Both O Mahony and O Donoghue were Munstermen, and my own Munster provenance may have been the reason for their indulging me. O Mahony was chief of Clan O Mahony ('The O Mahony', I suppose), and he held regular clan hostings in the ancient clan territory of Kerry or West Cork. He did sometimes appear in court in defence of the benighted. Everyone knows the story of how, when the sixteen-year-old Brendan Behan was in jail in Liverpool, O Mahony was got to defend him, and the Protestant warders were impressed and horrified to see Behan receiving a telegram which began, 'The Pope arriving . . .' I saw the Pope one day walking ahead of me down Grafton Street, dressed in a suit, and with proper black shoes, but with no socks. I surmised that he had given them to one less fortunate; but that was mere sentiment, and no doubt he had merely forgotten or lost them.

He was a famous man, and 'character': rightly so. But in another sense, he was one of a fairly large class, of Cork and Kerry geniuses adrift in Dublin. Other places yielded geniuses, too, but those two counties produce quite noticeable specimens. Inherent in this character, which the Pope played, and in terms of which he was perceived, is the presumption of saintliness: the person is not only genius but 'saint'; even his mischievousness, his bloody-mindedness, is a saint's vice (one good definition of a saint would be 'an immortal bloody mischief'). Mac Reamoinn is also credited, or debited, with this characterization. Unfortunately, for most people, saintliness entails not making a fuss, in the long run (whatever about the short) not causing a nuisance, not speaking ill of any but those which consensus has declared to be proper targets, such as vulgarians, aunts, supermarket tycoons, and archbishops; this list now includes members and supporters of provisional, but not of official, Sinn Fein. Of others, exempt from satire, it is said, 'Sure, there's no harm in him'; but to this is frequently added, with a look of hypocritical ferocity, 'but that other feller now!' Saintliness, in short, is in these terms a system of 'human respect'. Mac Reamoinn puts himself out; he fronts up. It is arguable that the best thing the courageous man or woman can do is front up, and shut up; but in Ireland that formula is simply not on; concealment is not the same as silence.

One day Neil Courtney and I were having a pint in Wicklow Street when I discovered that he had known Mac Reamoinn a few years earlier in Rome. We walked down past Trinity discussing him when, just as we completed the crossing from the Bank of Ireland, I spied the man himself, beginning the crossing in the other direction. I said, 'Hullo, Sean', but he had left the kerb, so we called after him; and as he speeded up we chased after him, calling louder. It was not until we caught him, and I slapped him on the shoulder, that I noticed that he was close to collapse from physical effort and apprehension, and that he was carrying in one hand a laden linen bag which, if it did not contain blessed oils, surely held money. So it did; the behaviour of the man was explained, as the flight from a supposed pursuit by bandits; the look on his face told its own story. But what was this money? He explained; he had been talking (in a pub?) to the organizers of some charity, and had undertaken to free them to some other duty by carrying and depositing in the Bank of Ireland their week's takings, which amounted to thousands of pounds. It was not a job he often did; he was running late; and imagine the addition to his existing fear, suspicion, panic, and self-mistrust of repeated and pursuing greetings in foreign voices from two men he had barely noticed. SAS? The Littlejohn brothers (for these intrepid British adventurers had but recently been at work robbing banks in this very area)! Republicans? Loyalists? Or merely a cabal motivated by the ideology of anit-Mac Reamoinn?

His offer to help, his punctiliousness, his haste, his panic, all of these were Irish of the Irish; and somewhere inside or behind them a notion of saintliness was no doubt at work. With O Mahony, as with Sean MacBride, this emerged as an aspiration to fight, and win, lost causes. MacBride, son of Major John MacBride, shot by the British in 1916, and shot again in Yeats's poem *Easter 1916*, and of Maud Gonne, ceaseless Republican and humanitarian idealist, is himself a figure of great authority. He founded and led Amnesty International, he has acted as mediator in a hundred quarrels, he will probably have a share in whatever solution is found to the present terror of life in the six counties; and he appears in court for Republican prisoners. Decades ago he was an IRA leader, at the end of the forties he was leader of a political party in office. He holds many awards. I have never heard any of the traditionally satirical Dublin commentators say a slighting word about him; they are too in awe of him to mention him much at all. This authority is the high-ascetic equivalent to the personal quality which O Mahony had in a high-comic, and Mac Reamoinn has in a high-genial mode. It is something moral, and it is something mystical. You could perhaps say of MacBride, you could certainly say of Mac Reamoinn, that like Martha he is busy about many things; you could not say that he is self-serving or petty.

The voiceless feeling for the mystical lives at point after point of Irish culture. Kinsella and Heaney both have it; O Riada had it; it permeates Irish music; it creeps in the short story as a peculiar melancholy; it drives thousands of missionaries to fruitful homesickness in the most remote of foreign lands. It is the most effective, the most practical, strain in the creative imagination. I know this claim was once the dominant cliché in the typecasting of the Irish, and that the Irish themselves now vigorously disclaim it, but I have few doubts about its presence and power.

But it cannot prevail against cowardice. Whatever praise we give, whatever sympathy we extend, to Irish writers and intellectuals, there remains Section 31 of the Broadcasting Act, and the demeaning puzzle of their acquiescence in it. This section was first introduced in 1973; it is always attacked as intolerable by whoever is in opposition, who then quietly endorses it the next year, when the inevitable election has somersaulted him into the impotence called power in Irish government circles. It forbids members of the Republican movement, of its legal as well as of its illegal components, to speak or be interviewed on national radio or TV. This by itself means that the prime national debate cannot be conducted, because there is no way of mounting it. In addition, successive ministers for Posts and Telegraphs (the ministry which covers broadcasting) have interpreted the section so broadly that no members of Sinn Fein are ever presented talking about anything; and if the ministers neglect to do it, their subordinate executives will. Dr Conor Cruise O'Brien, one of the most brilliant men in the country, brought to a fine art the administration of this embargo; under him, embargo came to seem the natural state of affairs. If a free thinker objected, he would be waved aside with the *hauteur* of a duchess waving aside a smell. Ireland was under the rule of, 'But surely you don't . . .', which, if it spreads widely enough, will eliminate the need for both morality and legislation. O'Brien can be testy; later in the seventies he made remarks that suggested some desire to extend his censoring powers to the newspapers as well; too many pro-Republican letters had been appearing in the letters columns of the *Irish Press*. But its editor, Tim Pat Coogan, took this attack as a signal honour, offered to meet the threat, and won the encounter.

What is depressing is not that bureaucrats (including intellectuals like O'Brien in their bureaucratic role) want to stop debate. Of course they do. What good did debate ever do them? If you encourage debate, only the wrong people will benefit; and so on. What is depressing is that the writers and intellectuals accept it, indeed make an odd virtue of it by suggesting that, if they ever did want to speak for a unified Ireland, they certainly would want the law to prohibit the wrong sort from speaking on the same side. An aesthetic view, basically.

To judge from the general silence about Section 31, the fighting Irish must keep their pugnacity for the bedroom or the bank manager's office. Most journalists simply accept it as part of nature, and creative artists always seem surprised to be reminded that it exists; the analysts and commentators must be a bit shamefaced at having some of their occupational material (the cobbler's scraps of leather, so to speak) denied to them; but they do not often say so. There is now a committee, set up this year, to work for the repeal of Section 31, and it is a group of highly reputable workers in the cultural vineyard; but, since some of them have supported republican or civil rights causes or both for years, no doubt they will be easily dismissed as pro-Provo.

The carelessness of civil liberties, the simple not-noticing of institutional denials of such liberties, has reached in Ireland the stage which it was at in Australia thirty years ago. Ireland is no more undemocratic or anti-democratic than any other Western country; in some senses it is an unusually free country; but analysis of social wrongs free of all restraints is not common there; when undertaken, it is with some self-consciousness; it is not habitual, as it is in England, France, or America. As in the Australia of the past, and leaving aside a Section 31 here or there, in Ireland the civil liberties exist, but their existence is concealed by mystifications of one kind or another. When a friend of mine was running for Dail Eireann on a minority republican ticket, I told him I thought he should raise the question of access to contraception as a matter of civil rights. He said, no, the voters in my constituency aren't interested in that sort of thing. That can't be true, I said; and of course it is not. But the assumption that it is prevents the matter ever being discussed except in a scratchy and partisan way.

Although the Irish speak wittily and sardonically about public leaders, they will not attack them in public. I was told one story about an occasion when de Valera, as chancellor of the National University, was chairing a meeting of senate or assembly, at which a former president of the Republic and his wife, both well-known scholars but in widely separated fields, were to be given academic awards. The assembly was to endorse the decision of its committee, which was that he should get an LLD and she a Litt.D; the endorsement was a formality. But the arrangment did not please The Boss who, so my informant says, growled, 'No. They'll both be given LLDs.' There was complete silence, then he added: 'I take it you all agree.' More silence, before a lone (indeed, invisible) voice at the back of the room said that it didn't. De Valera looked up sharply, and gazed sternly over the company before saying, 'Did I hear someone say something?' Of course, he had not.

One cause which was approved, and still is approved, was the preservation of the Viking remains at Woodquay, near the river Liffey, in the core of the oldest part of Dublin. Some buildings had been demolished, and excavation produced an unexpected store of artefacts left by the Vikings. Discovery could go on for years, maybe for decades. But it is prime commercial land, that stretch of old bank (or Bank), and the corporation wanted it as the base for an office-block, the remains of which some thwarted archaelogists will no doubt discover in the blackened mud in some future century. Out with the foreign scourings, in with the modern native foundations. Who ever heard anything good about a Viking, anyway? Plunderers and looters, snorted the land developers.

Here was a cause on which almost everyone could agree. Huge protest marches were held, with a poet and a priest (Kinsella and F.X. Martin) at their head; excellent speeches were made; petitions were presented; publicity was got; but the corporation would not yield, for it was led, if Kinsella is to be believed, by a lord mayor who was 'ignorant, and proud of it'. The battle was arduous, and not at all amusing; groups of volunteers, heavily garbed rather than heavily armed, occupied the site, and had to be removed. Legal cases were taken and threatened; and in the end the soul of Ireland had to retreat, while officialdom started to provide bits of a new body. The irony is that, after the building had progressed a fair way, evidence was found that the Viking remains are far richer than anyone had thought. And there they are, still, in the ground, where no doubt God intended them to be (otherwise he would not have kicked out the Norsemen in such a hurry); some hidden, some exposed.

This splendid campaign was not approved by everyone; for example, not all republicans are sound on Viking Dublin. To every archeological wisdom there is a counter-wisdom, and there may have been some feeling that, in building his dwellings, the Viking had obliterated our own. One commentator snarled that Woodquay protests were a middle-class sport, and that there are better causes. Of course there are; but in my view all these causes, for Viking coins and dispossessed workers and free speech and men on hunger-strike, support rather than oppose one another. Perhaps the commentator was recalling with some bitterness the way in which so much snobbery was brought out by the campaign to save 'Georgian Dublin', a campaign led by a titled Guinness. Certainly the Woodquay exercises were aided by the expertise gained in earlier campaigns by preservationists. Kinsella is a veteran of such campaigns; his own house in Percy Place is not Georgian, but nineteenth century, and he once said to me, 'No, I don't want an eighteenth-century house; I wouldn't like always to be reminding myself that I was living in something built on slave labour'; the area, on the Grand Canal, has been threatened for years, and the Kinsellas have fought the threats with resource and vehemence. Then, too, better Georgian than anti-Georgian Dublin; and better the nineteenth century than no century at all.

Cork is relatively free from these worries, although parts of Limerick, a handsome city, are devastated, and Galway seems always agitated by its endemic problems. One of these is the presence of 'tinkers' (or travellers, travelling people) in Eyre Square, specially during the 'tourist season'. How, for example, to stop them sitting on the seats in the square? 'I suggest,' said one councillor, 'that an electric current be passed through the seats, a very mild one, so that any of them who sits down will get a slight shock.' Any of them? What about any of us? Irish good sense and Christian compassion prevailed.

Anyway, Cork writers regard Dublin as a strange, half-mad place, much as San Franciscans regard New York. Further, from my limited experience they seem to have towards one another (and I hope they do not take this amiss) a certain charity, a fellow-feeling, such as you often get in Adelaide, or Melbourne, or Perth, but which is regarded in Sydney as pansy moralism.

Several of the important writers of the Irish Renaissance came from Cork, among them Sean O'Faolain and Frank O'Connor; and it was Daniel Corkery who awakened these and later writers to the power of Gaelic literature, expressed in and growing from the Gaelic tongue. But they were chiefly writers of prose fiction, even though O'Connor became a translator of immense influence, providing material for Yeats, among others. Now Cork is home for John Montague, laureate of and expatriate from Co. Tyrone, whom many literary people in Cork regard as the best poet in the country; it has Sean Lucy, poet, translator, former captain in the British army, and insatiable singer; and it has Sean O Tuama, who with Kinsella produced the texts and translations for the anthology *An Duanaire* which, as Heaney said to me, will be as important for this and the next generation as Corkery was for earlier ones. Thomas McCarthy, Paul Durcan and Theo Dorgan also live there. The interesting point is that all the three older men are teachers at University College, Cork, though nobody ever directs towards them the neatly Australian sneer of 'academic'; and the younger ones are in a close if intermittent association with them. There is an atmosphere of mutual care and relaxation about them; well, up to a point.

The night I read with Sean Lucy in Cork last August we held an impromptu party which led Dorgan to say, 'I'm told that's what Dublin was like in the fifties.' 'No, it wasn't,' I said, 'but it's what Melbourne was like in the fifties.'

Chapter Eleven

STYLES ABOUT POETRY

What do Irish poets hope for? To be thought number one. America. What do they fear? To fall down the competition table. Never to be thought number one. To be denied America.

Irish poets in general are like ambitious youngsters trying to escape from the working class. America is the upper-middle class. Their vertu, however, the source of their energy and appeal, is in the Irishness which they are trying to escape; they have therefore to emphasize this or some version of it. Their destiny, their complex fate, is not to become Americans, but to be Irish in relation to America.

This was not so in the mid fifties. Then, Ireland itself, an ideal of Ireland combined with an ideal of the form of the poem, were activating a new poetry, through Kavanagh and Kinsella and Austin Clarke. Kinsella, at that time a young poet, barely known outside Ireland, was a devotee of Auden, but also kept as a reference-point Clarke, whom he regarded as 'a major poet'. He took little notice of Patrick Kavanagh, whose haunting but surely insubstantial figure has gained much greater substance since then. Of course, he is dead now; but though he was then thought a countryman, a 'Culchie', hating and resenting Dublin, many Dubliners now see him as a laureate of their Dublin, the sleazy, resonant, attractive, petrol-smelling Dublin of Baggot and Leeson streets, of the Grand Canal, near which Kinsella has lived for many years in Percy Place. In the fifties, this was also the Dublin of Behan and of my friends Weber and Kinsella, although Kinsella lived well out of the city, by the seaside at Killiney. Now it is the walking-ground of Liam O'Flaherty and Francis Stuart, a giant's model and a giant's shadow. Kavanagh in the fifties was widely and bitterly excoriated as a bum, a sponger, and an unpleasant drunk; which may all have been the most envious calumnies. Now he is spoken of in the literary pages and on the wireless as 'a lovely man'. So are they all, all lovely, lovely men.

Whence comes this adoration? Not from America, surely; but in any case from an ambiguous, part-cynical, part-nostalgic and indulgent attitude to the old bohemia of that past, the years in which the young radio-presenters, now fresh from their universities, were carefully arranging their own births. In those decades, in one generation, Dublin bohemia has devolved into Dublin saloon-bar society, where nearly all the drinkers have incomes of some sort, the source of most incomes is 'cultural', and most of them have homes to go to. Where once you would drink in The Pearl, or other bars down near the quays and the newspaper offices (poet being to journo close allied), now you might frequent Madigan's, or other bars up near Ranelagh and Donnybrook, near the radio and television stations, University College, and the red brick terraces of flatland. Both base and superstructure have changed since Kavanagh's day and Kinsella's poetic youth.

But why is Kavanagh now a lovely man? Well, he makes no demands; he is not political, his poetry is not difficult, he is against rural obscurantism, and finally he reassures everyone that there is not much left for them to do.

But Kavanagh is not among those who looked first to America. Other poets have a deep and productive relation with that country. John Montague, for instance, was born in Brooklyn, and has lived in Paris, a city which he still visits. He has also lived and worked in America, and is well known all over North America from his visits on the reading-circuits. 'Why am I never regarded as an American poet?' he said to me. 'Why would an American poem by me never get into an American anthology?' It is a question worth asking. Montague's Irish publisher, Dolmen Press, which is also Kinsella's, has an American affiliate, which enables them both to be published in dual editions. In their reading tours they are actually following their books, which would be studied in 'Anglo-Irish' literature courses in dozens of North American places; and Montague at any

rate publishes in American and Canadian journals (Kinsella is reti-
cent with journals).

All this gives a direct link and an important source of income.
Kinsella actually teaches in Philadelphia, and spends four months
there every year; another four months are taken up teaching
American students in Ireland, the course a broad and highly imaginative study of Irish culture. Sometimes he speaks as if America has
absorbed him: 'America's our home now,' he said once. But that
remains to be seen; Kinsella is deeply, quintessentially Irish, and he
has a most powerful pull towards the West, the Gaeltacht, where his
great friend Sean O'Riada settled, studied his music, and died. More
and more I think Kinsella is drawn to the West, even now O'Riada is
gone – to the isles of the blest, or of the young, or of the voyages, or
of the discoveries, or Hy-Brasil, or, it may be, just America. But
Kinsella is both laconic and impulsive in speech, and you would
never know what he most deeply desires.

An American university feeds him, and a Cork one feeds
Montague, who also has a house in the West, in West Cork. Both
poets have jumped the English reference-hurdle, which marks out
the bounds of the civilized world for so many people; yet both have
edited anthologies for famous English publishers. Their position in
this is quite unlike that of Derek Mahon or Michael Longley, both
northern Protestants educated at a Dublin university; they have
largely an English point of reference. Their work, like that of the
southerner Richard Murphy, educated at Oxford, is said to exhibit
'tension'. Good lord; as though there is no tension between compet-
ing cultures in Kinsella or Montague. Murphy is an important
member of an Irish literary establishment; an issue of the *Irish
University Review* was devoted to him; he reads to good audiences at
the approved places, and can count on full-scale reviews of each of his
books. He publishes with an English publisher, and has close links
with England. He is an old friend of Ted Hughes, as Kinsella and
Seamus Heaney also are. Yet Murphy too has his link with, his
reliance on, America. He has held temporary teaching jobs there, in

universities, and has at various times relied on the reading-circuit.

The whole business of travelling to America for the reading-circuit is very much like the seasonal life of the old tatie-hokers, travelling every year from Donegal to Scotland to harvest the potato-crop. It is one of the basic images of Ireland and the Irish: the riches, the resources, are always somewhere else, and the chief resource of the Irish is their labour-power, which they will use to harvest the fields of others. And, since it works both ways, it is from elsewhere that the Irish keep on drawing the ability to renew their labour-power and in some sense their very identity; for America is a mirror, in which you shine more grandly than at heart you feel. This life has its occupational hazards, of drink, disorientation, and cultural inversion; but, to judge from the cases of Montague and Kinsella (who teaches there regularly), the Irish base is unbroken, and the Irish genes are strong. The only thing is, these poets have a link with the North American teachers of 'Anglo-Irish' literature, with Robert O'Driscoll in Canada, Thomas Flanagan and Eoin McKiernan in America. Irish poets and American academics oblige each other. These men organize associations for the study of their subject, run conferences, import readers, circulate reading-lists and anthologies. McKiernan gives an award each year to a selected Irish writer, while Flanagan spent the whole of each summer in Ireland while he was writing *The Year of the French*. This complex connection is essential for both parties. It is in itself an intellectual and social economy.

Derek Mahon, who is popular everywhere in the south, particularly in Cork, now lives in London. His fellow northerners, Longley, Paul Muldoon and Ciaran Carson, are members of a formal Belfast establishment; while he is a semi-exile. All would have their American contacts, circuits, and opportunities. Muldoon, for example, has written 'American' poems. In Tucson, Arizona, I heard that a local poet had visited Belfast, in hopes no doubt of coming across the real thing in the way of death, destruction, drama, agony, and hence of poetry. She asked about Heaney. 'Och, Heaney,' she was told, 'no, he's not an Irish poet; he's a Yank now.' She went home repeating this mysterious formula, and evidently convinced she had been meeting the authentic native object. The means and manner of Heaney's transformation, whether by shape-changing or by deed poll, were unclear. The charge too is ironic: Irish Amerigophiles want to have a continental sophistication (and, above all, experience and income), but they also want to be 'native', because it is that quality which attracts the tourist attention; subsidized scholars are the tourists of our time. How Heaney could be thought to lack native quality beggars the imagination; fifty years of America could never make him a Yank (I am not so sure about his critics). But what is interesting is the withdrawal of approval on those grounds.

Poetry in Ireland is not an art, but a sub-culture, which is attached in the manner of a client to the media-culture. Writing is easy, but apart from the best poets is not accomplished; and there is not a great deal of it. Publishing too is easy but not accomplished; for the most part the books are small, and full of smallish poems; there is a poor but intensive cultivation of the market, and bookshops like the Eblana in Grafton Street, which very gallantly stocked all books of Irish poetry, including some not in print, have gone out of business. The life, the vivacity, the meaning, are at the point of reception, and it is a social point. I mean reception literally, for the Irish poetry sub-culture is characterized less by poetry than by receptions, launchings, prizes, readings (at festivals and outside them), reviews, broadcasts, and old-fashioned photographs. Poets write that they may be interviewed in the papers. There is a whole network of these occasions ('functions', to use a handy Irishism), and although none by itself is remarkable, the literary life in Ireland consists in attendance at all of them, and participation (if only by vocal non-attendance) in their spin-offs, general publicity, public controversy (both of them got with astonishingly little effort), and further radio. The smallness of material rewards is compensated for by their systematic promulgation; and full participation in the system opens up the way to that fuller life, that social life in which the literary life properly speaking gets its completion, the life of drinking and gossip. We thus have an odd phenomenon: there is a scarcity economy, but also an incentive to full participation, so that the fullest advantage is taken of the available goods. Perhaps it is a technique for survival of the art itself.

But of course the whole thing is very competitive, and here the gossip serves its essential neutralizing function; and (if we exclude Belfast, which I do not know at first hand) it is an affair of one centre, Dublin; literary life in Ireland is literary life as practised in Dublin, since that is where the newspapers and radio are. That is where the 'projects' can be presented and discussed; I say projects, for it seems to me that there is very little of deep impulse in the initiatives of most Irish poets; they take on projects, translations or semi-dramatic works, editing, something to keep them up front even when the creative flow is not at the full. This is the other aspect which matches the fey, America-oriented aspect of Cargo-Celt. This is, for its best practitioners anyway, the traditional literary life; it involves meetings with visitors of all sorts, travellings, launchings, and correspondence (not that that ever bothered any Irish man or woman).

Woman. I'm glad I mentioned that word. For Irish poetry is a male preserve. There are well-known women poets, such as Eilean ni Chuilleanain, Eavan Boland and Medbh McGuckian, and also Maire Mac Entee, who writes in Irish; but they are not growth-points for the art. Maybe the concerns of the ruling poets do not interest women, since they involve too overt and persistent a concern with status, position, placement. 'I'm glad I'm not a poet,' the short story writer Catherine Coakley said to me. 'Poets seem to talk about nothing except who's best, who's up, who's down. I couldn't live like that.' It may be that women need to develop a new poetic form (for the ruling Irish ones are, by and large, unenterprising ones); if so, they will need to get out and about more, de-provincialize their concepts and their language, discover, it may be, their actual emotions.

They have already a large achievement in prose fiction: in modern times, not only Somerville and Ross but Elizabeth Bowen, Kate O'Brien (whom I saw given a standing ovation when she walked slowly to the lectern at a conference in Montreal), Mary Lavin, who has a similar stature to Sean O'Faolain, Jennifer Johnston, Edna O'Brien. The Irish sadness, and the Irish story by which it may be defined, seems to come readily to their thoughts; while the half-formal shapes of poetry, with their light rhetoric and stiff stinging line, do not. This excellence at fiction, in its desire to tell it the way it was, is, and always will be, goes with an even more striking excellence in journalism.

Even if you leave out Maeve Binchy, a novelist who is also a gently comic columnist, a writer whose *comedie humaine* is constructed with a remarkable sense for speech rhythms and idioms, there is a group of women journalists who are probably better than their male counterparts, good as they are; I mean Elgy Gillespie, Fionnuala O'Connor, Olivia O'Leary, and Nell McCafferty. O'Leary's forte is political and socio-political analysis, and she is particularly good at it because her stylish and shapely prose rejects cant, nonsense and doubletalk, and always thinks to ask the central questions; she has reported from various centres of disturbance; her paper had her in Buenos Aires for the Falklands war; she can see through male Irish politicians without winking. Nell McCafferty, who is from Derry, as O'Leary is from the midlands, is a marvellous reporter of the deprived, sordid and unjust assaults on members of the working class from which she herself comes: a reporter of the sub-licensed life. Her compassion comes out as a quiet scorn and a stringent refusal to press the point; her forte is compression, economy, the epiphany. Her vignettes of the Dublin courts and the Dublin poor are marvels of economy, yet each could have been written in five minutes, in addition, that is, to the longer hours spent anguished inside and outside the court.

Neither of these is an 'investigative journalist', a breed of which Ireland has had some notable examples for many years. They are composers of worlds of analysis; O'Leary is obviously trusted by many figures in Irish political life, but she takes from them what she needs for her analysis of the issue under discussion; she does not probe, compute and depose in the way of Vincent Browne, the quite remarkable journalist who founded and edited the monthly journal *Magill*, and now edits the weekly *The Sunday Tribune*. Browne, who is frighteningly outspoken, has an awesome range of 'sources', and he should always be listened to on any matter concerning the views and actions of Republican groups, or developments in the north. Though not himself a northerner, he learned the north painfully and knows it well. But his aim is typically to unearth, to show things up, to persuade people into fundamental change; there is behind his revelations a steady, harsh, mocking anger, very different from Nell McCafferty's more impulsive, exuberant framing of incidents by which to show in one glance the evils of the society. But, as T. S. Eliot said, 'there is no competition' here, as there is among the poets; these five journalists are on the same side, and it is not the side of hypocrisy.

The visitor gets a general impression that the Irish have a weakness for poetry; and it may be true; equally, it may be that we are confusing it with a love of song. Some bookshops have shown great loyalty to Irish poetry, but at the cost of almost total lack of interest in poetry from anywhere else, even the fabled America. At the launching of *An Duanaire: Poems of the Dispossessed*, translated by Kinsella and Sean OTuama, the invited guests numbered a couple of hundred, and they were palpably excited by the book and its coming out; a bookseller on Baggot Street Bridge claimed later that she had sold 3,000 copies of this book which, subsidized as it is by the Irish government, is a great bargain at the price. Yet when I took a class of advanced honours students in modern poetry at Trinity College in 1973, they knew no Kinsella or Heaney; only one had even seen Heaney, and they were introduced to his person by me. That is extraordinary in a city like Dublin. But these students possessed few books of poetry, and evidently could not see why they should do so. The Irish poets whose work they knew were Louis MacNeice,

Brendan Kennelly, and Kavanagh, the second of whom was their
professor and the other two commended to them by him and Terence
Brown.

So, while there is a certain love of poetry, it has to do with habit,
publicity, and the use of set texts. They like those they are expected
to like. Few turn up to poetry readings by strangers, and will consider
them at all only under special recommendation; of course, they are
not alone in this; English and American audiences are subject to the
same laws of ebb and flow. Power lies in small pools. *The Sunday
Independent* publishes one poem per month, and pays a hundred
pounds for it. The forces at work are a highly social array. Yet there
are some curious inhibitions about it. When everyone was talking
about *An Duanaire*, it astonished me to see how many poets and intellectuals treated well-known poems as if the new translations had
revived some fancy of their youth, something that had once troubled
them but which they had long forgotten; in short, they did not know
these poems. They had learned Irish, and I had not; but earlier
translations, which I knew and loved, seemed unknown to them. The
poems survived in them not as part of their cultural liberation in
youth, but as items in their school bonding.

This inhibition goes back, I suppose, to the use of poetry in the
nationalist training of sensibility, connected in this with compulsory
Irish in schools. It is also connected with expectations about singing.
A great number of Irish people can sing, even if it is only a party
piece. But, then, how did they come to have a party piece? They were
made to, by specific elements in the social context; I am told that
social pressures lead to such oddities as one man's singing with his
face to the wall, another from under the table, and another from
behind his hand. Do we conclude that singing is subliminally regarded as a childish accomplishment and activity? I would not think
so; it might equally be argued that those who have talents use them;
but I have often noticed that an individual will show a barely released
excitement as he sings. Singing is something that both the extrovert
and the inhibited may do.

But other kinds of Irish people read poetry too. According to

Thomas McCarthy, the books which are always stolen from the Cork libraries as soon as they are shelved are 'the paranormal, drugs, guns, magic, Beat poets, and books on hypnotism'. Singing up against one's hand would be a good way to inducing the last.

Poetry readings are frequent, but inclined to the *déjà vu*; young as they are, the reigning poets are old favourites. Audiences turn out for any one of perhaps eight poets, all Irish. When I asked Marion FitzGibbon who had most drawing-power in Limerick (for I had been struck by the enthusiasm in Cork for Derek Mahon, as well as John Montague, who lives there), she began by saying that Mahon was a special favourite; then, as I mentioned each poet in turn, Kinsella, Murphy, and so on, I was told O yes, he has a great following; and most of all, perhaps, Brendan Kennelly, who comes from Kerry, the neighbouring county, and despite his Trinity professorship still acts (and probably thinks) like a countryman. 'He gets a great crowd of school students', she said. 'The nuns love Brendan.' Lovable, original, irreverent, foul-mouthed Brendan; it is the nuns of his native Munster who love him most.

For visitors like myself, in the country the audiences are small, and the organizers always unreasonably ashamed. I expect nothing else; it is not poetry that such people love, but the familiar contract between themselves and the poet, the illusion of poetry in a sense. Not even good organizers, like Marion in Limerick or Theo Dorgan in Cork, can drum them up. Why should they go? The attractiveness of the 'reading' is itself something of an illusion; just as the *aficionado* of even the most advanced Irish music cannot be expected to go to a whole concert of (say) Turkish music thought to resemble it. But the Irish audiences are modest even for large international figures, such as John Ashbery; it is unnecessary to be more particular.

In Ireland, as in other Western countries, the 'reading' is an art-form developed in the past thirty years. In the fifties, although I went to concerts in Dublin, I do not remember there being a single poetry reading. In the sixties, there may have been such things (for the American connection had been strengthened in the intervening ten years), but if so I was nowhere near them. 1966 was in any case the sesqui-centenary of Easter Week, and most poetry would have been concerned with that, as film and music were. They were beginning to form up by the start of the seventies, at the very time Seamus Heaney was entering on his first period of fame, which came from his appealing to a hitherto deeply unsatisfied nerve in English taste. With the shocking start of the northern struggle, with the British army bulling in thousands inside the Catholic areas, the IRA split and revitalized, the Protestant paramilitaries planning their ambiguous campaigns, explosions all over the six counties, and then in Dublin, internment of supposed republicans, torture of suspects, the murder of thirteen civilians in Derry in early 1972, with all that, other northern poets, including Mahon and Longley, gained an alert audience throughout Ireland, and in Britain too. Their publishers were London ones. Montague and Kinsella were published by a Dublin press, Dolmen; and they were still international, both spending more time in America.

By now, Kinsella, a fine poet never given his due in Britain, was hardly part of the Irish contact-system at all. He maintained regular production, was very much part of Dublin life, chose new poetry for Dolmen Press, gave his periodic readings dutifully, and as the Baggot Bridge bookseller said to me, 'We think a lot of him round here'; he was the leading Irish poet, if there can be such a being; yet he was somehow outside the reassurances of this system. He was not a willingly co-operative part of the sub-culture as such; he was a little reserved and foreign, as his demeanour had always threatened he would become; with his personal agonies behind him, or maybe still with him, he lived a very private life, 'away with his family', as it might be, trying to keep his corner of Dublin from the destroyers called 'developers', and, of course, setting up his own venture, Peppercanister Books, to publish his own poems as pamphlets before, combined, they would be published as books by his friend Liam Miller of Dolmen. He had become, up to a point, a businessman, whose business involved preventing the alienation of the poet from his own work; but, since he was marketing his books rather than himself, he was no longer to be seen nearly so much in the areas where poets play.

In 1973 I found myself somewhere near the set of activities lovingly known as poetry, but not near their centre, if they had such a thing. I had come to Dublin from Canada at mid year, and was lucky enough to find Kinsella in town, and his usual helpful self; it was not the last time he helped me find a flat, though I have a feeling that, while his wife Eleanor enjoys the slightly absurd dance of profit and loss between owner and supplicant, it causes Kinsella distaste and discomfort, not to mention boredom. You've seen one landlord, you've seen the lot.

The two readings which I can remember giving that year were arranged by the Australian Embassy. The ambassador, Keith Brennan, who had an unusual understanding of Irish thought-patterns, had pulled off a coup by arranging an enormous shimmering exhibition of paintings by Sidney Nolan, an exhibition so big that the paintings could be accommodated nowhere but in the RDS building at Ballsbridge, where the annual horse show is held. I rushed from Canada so that I could see it, and there ran into Brennan and Nolan, whom I had met before. Brennan's triumph had been so striking, and his sympathetic flair so evidently superb, that he wanted to keep the effect of Australian competence going; and, since Nolan you have not always with you, he asked me to give some readings. Being a diplomat, he arranged one for each Dublin university. The first was at UCD, with a partly invited and partly casual audience; and it was held on a night on which I had been invited to travel to Derry City to read in the Bogside with Seamus Heaney and Seamus Deane, with Planxty and another group of traditional musicians also performing. There was and is nothing I would love more than to do that, but duty was in Dublin at Belfield. Deane later told me that they had read to the intermittent noise of explosions, all around them, and bursts of gunfire; there had been a crowd of thousands, very enthusiastic. Afterwards, he had walked out with an old friend to feel the streets (for he is a Derry man), and tasted almost more than he wanted; for they ran into repeated clashes in the dark with the occupying British troops.

While this was going on, I was battling it out in Belfield. But that reading was merely a curtain-raiser for the next, which was held in Trinity. The embassy had invited an audience, as usual, but had put on drinks for them before the reading. Brendan Kennelly warned me solemnly against this arrangement. It was a mistake; they would all get drunk and 'slag' me while I was reading. His warnings were baseless. No one interrupted me; what nearly undid me was a lapse on my own part. My brief was to give a reading of selections from the literature of our distant country, prose and verse, ending up with a long thunderclap of my own work. It was not until I was getting ready to face the audience, including Heaney, Deane, their wives, and Eileen O'Casey, Sean's widow, most of whom were beaming slightly and ready to listen to anything for a brief while, that I realized most of my few texts were back in my flat at Donnybrook. All I had with me was a novel by Patrick White and a certain amount of cheek. The embassy chauffeur, Paddy, was given my keys and asked to pick up the missing material from my flat in Donnybrook. He arrived back just in time. This audience was like all the Irish audiences I have seen, alert, receptive, neither fulsome nor captious, lacking in the narcissism that afflicts many North American audiences, the minginess of some English ones, and the studied indifference of some Australian ones. They care about the sort of thing they take a poetry reading to be, whether or not they much like what they are hearing from moment to moment; and it is true that they have an ease with the combination of oral and print cultures. It is not merely courtesy. I noticed, when I was taking some guest tutorials at UCD, that even students who showed a certain shyness about giving their views, or indeed answering any questions, could fairly easily be induced to read, and most of them would read even poetry they did not know with an accurate emphasis and some sense of its particular music. They see no virtue, no advantage, in being clodhopperish.

But poetry readings, in my experience, go best with music. The trick is to choose music which does not wipe out the poetry, for it is a truth of racing that a good song will always beat a good poem. Ireland is full of musicians, most of them among the laboring classes and men of no property; and they love the music so much that, where the arts are not subsidized, they will often play for nothing. Similarly, poets will often read for nothing, although they will try to get something for their pains (reading one's own poems not being so enjoyable as playing someone else's tunes), and I think they sometimes pretend to have been paid when they have not. I do know that famous poets who could get $1,000 minimum in America will cheerfully read for fifty or sixty Irish pounds.

If your reading is sponsored by the local outpost of the Arts Council, you will get the agreed fee, and the friendliest hospitality, but someone may forget to pay you the train-fare. Other readings are locally organized, but, oddly, seem to need approval from someone in Dublin. Where money is so scarce, it is essential that everyone try not to waste it. A few enthusiasts try bravely to finance their own functions. One day in 1981, for example, Michael Hartnett rang me from Newcastlewest in County Limerick, and asked would I read there. Certainly. What pay would I ask? I didn't know, and said so, and was surprised when Michael mentioned eighty pounds. How would he get that? Well, there was a thriving arts committee in the town, and they would expect to get a good crowd. He would read with me, unpaid, and local musicians would play.

Newcastlewest is Hartnett's hometown, a substantial smallish town on the main road south from Limerick to Tralee. As many such towns were, it was once a British garrison town, and at the time of the famine, three quarters of its population of several thousand were paupers; it was the poor law centre for the area. Such things give a town a permanent underlying sickness of will, and Newcastlewest seemed to have some traces of such a sickness, although it has a good library and a certain prosperity coming from the industrial development on the river Shannon, some miles to the north.

Anyway, Hartnett comes from there, and he had gone back there to write poetry in the onset of early middle age. Having written a *Farewell to English*, he now writes in Irish, a language which he also speaks with congenial companions like Gabriel FitzMaurice. He reserves English for the odd ballad on local events, and these he publishes and circulates locally. He is an amusingly intense man. As we walked to the hotel where we were to attend some meeting, he said, 'Don't say anything against Heaney in this town.' 'I wouldn't dream of it,' I said. 'Why do you mention it?' It appeared that, some months earlier, Heaney had given a reading there, and had then stayed at the bar until very late drinking with his local admirers and other clean-minded types. Among these was the town bore, who as the night wore on annexed Heaney more and more. Heaney coped courteously with all this, but the speaker was so boring that the other drinkers moved slowly away from him. At last, in the middle of a sentence, the poor bore collapsed, and slid slowly down the bar to lie at Heaney's feet. He, looking around, called to the nearest deserter, 'Would you mind giving me a hand?' and, with the volunteer thus chosen by the Chinese system, carried the man over and laid him carefully on a couch. 'They've never stopped talking about it,' said Hartnett. 'Heaney's king around here.'

It must have been on this occasion that, when he was signing copies of his works, Heaney was presented with a photocopy of a whole volume. Pirated. 'What did you do?' I asked him when I heard of it. 'O I signed it,' he said. 'Why not?' Then he brooded awhile, and added, 'It often happens in the States.' You could not deny to impoverished Limerick what you had granted to Louisville or Omaha.

I was to read in the building which gives the town its name, the banqueting hall of the now destroyed castle of the Fitzgeralds, Earls of Desmond and Norman magnates of this whole area. The hall is very handsome, but very dilapidated. If some mad, lovable, posterity-infatuated millionaire would do it up, it would be the greatest place in the world for a poetry reading, especially with musicians. As it is,

you read seated in a stone window embrasure; the acoustics are
excellent; the possibilities are great, and the local people who serve
on the committee see them clearly even if, like most Irish people,
they are unwilling to promise themselves too much.

On the appointed night, nobody had arrived fifteen minutes after
starting-time; there were doors to be opened, lights to be turned up, a
hundred chairs to be brought and set up; so Gabriel FitzMaurice's
wife Brenda kept me company in Lynch's bar next to the hall while
these things were done. It was a small dark friendly bar, and we sat
and chatted as the time wore on. Every so often Gabriel would enter,
looking fierce, and start on a pint of stout; then he would dash off,
and Michael would enter looking quite distracted, and toss down a
whiskey. An hour and a half after starting-time, I said to him, 'What
does it matter, Michael? Let's call it off. I don't mind.' But that was
psychologically impossible; and there was a further complexity,
which I never fully understood, and which Michael felt he had to
deal with: musicians had been engaged to play, but only one had
turned up, characteristically, in the pub, had said to us, 'Are there no
musicians here? I was told there would be musicians here' and
ignored all Gabriel's bluff suggestions that, if only he gave a lead, the
others would gather. Giving a lead is not a Limerick sport. I could see
the man's attitude quite clearly, and I said to Gabriel and Michael, 'O
leave him alone. He doesn't want to play. Forget it.' He kept smiling
slyly, and watching everyone.

Michael became sick of this, and rushed off, returning with two
teenagers, a banjoist and an accordion player. They were Munster
junior champions in their instruments; they would play. They did;
they were marvellous, and played with enormous vitality to the
audience of about a dozen, whom I read at as vigorously as I could.
Even the second point of honour that was bothering Hartnett was
cleared up; for I said to him, 'Forget money; 'I'll read for the train
fare,' and, later, 'Look, I'll read for nothing.' It wouldn't have been
the first time. But he would not have it. He rushed off fiercely once
more, and returned to shove into my hand a roll of pound notes,

every one of which I swear had passed across a bar counter that night. He must have gone to every place in town. I knew without counting how many would be in the bundle. It was a quintessentially Irish gesture, solution, and sense of honour. But it was also an Irish problem, that of the promises not kept, the suspicious doubts allowed to run ahead of performance, the earlier engagement quietly discovered.

At reading's end, it was back to Lynch's bar, now crowded with jovial people who had failed to attend the reading, were full of curiosity about it, and of congratulations to those of us who had survived it. The young musicians took one orange juice each, and played tune after tune until after midnight. The banjoist sat on one side of the narrow door to the outside lavatory, and I sat on the other; everyone who wanted to use it had to push between us, and as each passed, the banjoist, without casting a single glance anywhere but at his own brimming soul, would flick the banjo upright, so that part of the time he played vertical, and part diagonal. Once going, and once coming. Gabriel FitzMaurice played along with them. One after another, charming people approached me and enquired of genealogy, poetry, music, and of course Australia. Each had 'heard I was in town'. They could not be described as poetry groupies, for they were far more interested in the idea of poetry than in the reality. But they were interested in the idea. This could be seen in the way they treated Michael Hartnett as a local laureate, and solicited comments from visiting strangers on his wider fame.

In this, they were representative of the whole culture, in all its ambivalence. Poetry was treated with reverence and neglect. And that expressed itself in many ways.

Several times, I was surprised and shocked to hear the complaints by young poets about how the reigning poets ignored them. These complaints were voiced always after I had read and made criticisms of poems they had shown me. The leading Irish poets would not do this, said the plainants. Why not? They didn't know. At first I did not believe them; later I could see for myself that they were right. The leading poet might read some poems, and he might vaguely commend them, but he would not criticize them or comment on them in any detail.

This looks like simple lack of generosity; but I wonder; it may be one more expression of the Irish scarcity economy. It implies, for one thing, a reluctance to presume on someone else's creative life; this feeling varies greatly from poet to poet, so that, whereas Heaney will happily swap 'technical' criticisms and suggestions (very delicately), Kinsella proceeds on the basis that one's own poem is one's own task. To use an expression of his, arising from a quite different situation, 'He's where no man can help him.'

Then, there is a reluctance to criticize in private, face to face; he who does that is on a hiding to nothing. I read a typescript volume of one young poet, and suggested some sweeping cuts. He was taken aback, and I said, 'Why are you so surprised? Have you shown them to someone else?' He had, to a leading poet, who had said nothing by way of criticism. Later, I asked *him* why he had been so recessive. What could I say? he said. They had to live near each other. Fatalism was at work again, quietly, slyly, cordially getting rid of the available challenges.

And it it also true that the leading poets are too busy for such prolonged civilities, too busy in the sense that going to the place, giving the reading, talking at large, having a drink, making several appointments, is as much of a commitment as they can make to these colleagues at this time. There is, it must now be clear, a sense in which being a leading poet in Ireland is a business, set up as such, to be conducted as systematically as the world allows. Young Ireland may be ripe for discipleship, but the master-poets are giving a reading in Leeds or editing a special supplement for the Havana Arts News. It is better to ignore than to analyse. Say nothing.

Nor are there any poetic 'schools' to set up those workshop activities which the young poets so clearly see to be necessary. There are some groups; for example, that which publishes *Cyphers*, or the working-class poets at the Raven Arts Press, or the group emerging around the *Cork Review* before it sadly died. Whatever the fellowship among poets (and I saw plenty, both in Cork and in Dublin), there is no way for any of them to learn a tradition, a traditional thing, method, ethos, skill, such as every young musician begins to learn from his or her seniors as soon as the first tin whistle touches the lips. If Ireland is a source country, as I believe, it is so for the traditional musician in a way which it seemingly cannot be for the poet; and the sources, it seems, cannot be articulated by their guardians, the poets.

These follow the national ethos, conformist individualism, doing the prescribed thing with variations and grace-notes. It seems to work. I have noticed with interest that each strong poet keeps his or her reputation fresh, and does not have to recreate it, to woo or persuade his audience, every time he goes somewhere to read. Hostility in Ireland is not expressed in that way.

Nor is it expressed, by and large, in published criticisms. There is almost no full-scale criticism of a forthright sort published at all; critical essays are gentle commendations. There are plenty of reviews, but, with two or three exceptions, reviewers speak as members of a fellowship which they are not about to betray, or expose to hostile view. The bigger poets exercise a sort of *droit de seigneur* with newspapers and their reviewers, while the smaller ones plunge their hands in their pockets and hopefully read the *Irish Times*. Bigger poets have no hesitation in chastizing a critic by letter, public or private; some get their friends to follow suit; here wives come in handy, and take reviewers to task, the more severely the more vulnerable they are; I know of attempts to get reviewers sacked. This is the self-protective infighting of a small and oddly politicized country, in which no critical comment is assumed to be without its malicious intent or hostile background; unfavourable reviews are assumed to be paybacks; the bitchiness which spreads in public gets greater purchase on people's imaginations by means of these wounds and scratched scabs. Editors are approached in protest, or to grant special favour to this or that poet; and I know two cases where capricious patronage by editors of non-literary journals has led, eventually, to poetry's being driven permanently out of their papers. Everything is local, particular, and enforced by habit; everything is matter for gossip and speculation; there is little sense of world trends or of international standards. When the government founded an intriguing system of subsidy called the *Aos Dana*, which among other things involves a practising artist being chosen for subsidy by a permanent committee of his peers, each of them elected in the first place by his or her peers, a large number of poets rushed to secure the grant. One friend of mine, approaching another, to ask for sponsorship, was greeted by such an immediate and withering tirade about the racketeers and chancers who had set up the scheme in the first place that he forbore to mention the reason for his visit, and went sadly away. It is a constricted but loose society.

In all this, the tension and attraction between north and south come into play. Michael Longley's wife, Edna, herself originally a southerner, has an abiding distaste for Kinsella and his poetry, and puts them down at every chance. For her, and the group she represents, it is the northern poets who are producing the really exciting stuff. Heaney, do you mean? No, no longer, for he is now in the south, and some English writers have even speculated that he may be a republican; so Heaney too becomes an enemy in some strange adversary system of blame and promotion.

For some young southern poets, this northern-ness of mien and valuation is a great if foreign virtue; 'They are a *comitatus*', one of them said to me of a group of northern poets; 'Far stronger than we are,' said another. The northerners are exotically tough; they are also productive, and apparently interested in technique.

There is little politics in all this, in the ordinary sense of 'politics', though among a few poets there is a subliminal concern for or with the British link, the British endorsement. It is hard to be accurate about this. Heaney's case is instructive, however; the neurotic English worry about his 'republicanism' could not be more misplaced. He is, in almost every ordinary public sense, non-political. He is non-political by nature, fundamentally. This non-political nature increases the need for him to live a political life in a different sense. All Irish poets who have any views on the northern struggle have to do this to some extent, which shows how far their very stature is governed by others. But in Heaney's case this behaviour is the pathway to a pit of contradictions from which he has escaped only in the past few years, carrying the pit-awareness inside him, a finer poet than ever. Deane and Montague are republican in one or another sense, and can espouse that cause if they wish (they cannot be said to do that very much in their poetry). Muldoon and Paul Durcan are anti-republican, and the same truth applies to them. Heaney is in a different situation. He cannot present his own case, or that of his people, without invoking, and indeed without translating into verbal shape and event, the politics in which he does not believe, and which he is secretly notable for not believing in.

But it is only those who have used politics who can survive them.

Chapter Twelve

BLESSED ARE THE POOR

In 1956 we were drinking in a pub one night when a man put his head around the door and called out to the man next to me, 'Are you going to Bodenstown Sean?' Then he addressed the company at large, 'All republican Ireland will be there. Will you be there?' It was one of those evangelical moments that float for ever in the detached memory. In Bodenstown churchyard, in Kildare, Wolfe Tone is buried, 'father of Irish republicanism', wry separatist political anti-sectarian, collaborator with the all-conquering but incompetent French in the 1790s; various groups of differing degrees of Republican authenticity make pilgrimages to his grave every year. I started to talk to Sean, who proved to have strong opinions about where we should go, and what we should visit. On the way to Cork, we should diverge and go to Gougane Barra, heart of the West Cork Gaeltacht; there, in Coolea or in Ballingeary, we would find and hear and learn the real Ireland. He gave us the name of a woman who would give us bed and board. But what, by comparison, was there to see in Cork city?

In the midst of this educational session, pipes were heard in the street. This was not surprising, since it was an Irish national festival. We went outside; a pipe band went swinging down Grafton Street, in Irish uniform; they were playing 'Scotland the Brave'. Hardly had they disappeared than another band swung down a side street; they too were in saffron and green; they too were playing 'Scotland the Brave'.

We set off by train for Cork, and sure enough we never reached there, not because we went off to Gougane Barra and its eeerily beautiful lake, but because we were waylaid by hospitality in the middle of Tipperary. Brian Ryan, the GP from my home town of Romsey, was living in a small village called Bansha with his six small children and his wife, who was justly much liked and admired by my mother; so we got off the Cork train at the old Butler town of Cahir, were met by Mrs Ryan, and driven to the place in which they were renting a flat, Bansha Castle; we left, with great difficulty, about two weeks later.

It was a nineteenth-century castle, built for or inhabited by a well-known painter of imperial military feats, disasters, and ventures, Lady O'Brien-Butler. Its modern incumbent was an elderly bachelor, Tom Givens, who himself had served the British imperium in the capacity of commander of police intelligence in Shanghai, now, alas, in other hands. Despite his life's work, he was a Tipperary countryman, who had been born in the Glen of Aherlow in a small house from which you could see this grander residence. His mother's people had lived there for generations; he told me their faction-cry; he recounted how, as a boy, he had looked on Bansha Castle and lusted after it; yet, recounting his feelings on every return from abroad, he remembered how his heart had nearly leapt through his breast as soon as the train turned the green corner on to the bridge. He moved between proprietor and aspirant, and in the end it was less important to him to have this home than to be at home here.

Republican Ireland, of which this was a crucial place, for out-lawed rebels had taken refuge in the wooded glen for generations, meant little to him; but neither did titled Anglo-Ireland, though he spoke often of its denizens. He belonged neither to revolutionary purpose nor to social class, but to the rhythm of the land and of his remaining days. Every morning I would stump with him through the unbelievably lush grass of his meadows, looking at his beeves, acknowledging his workmen, who touched their antiquated caps and called him sir; for his part, he greeted them not so much with masterful authority as with the hesitancy of mute will. His stretch of the river had fish with distinctive markings. He gave us whiskey before dinner, and carried the blackthorn of the squire.

Yet, fine as he was in his incompletely tamed primitivism, this memory is not about him; for my theme is poverty, and he was not poor. There was, however, a kind of poverty everywhere: the castle that was not a castle, the squire who had not title or connections, the stone indoor space which no furniture aggrandized, the stocky and strong-smelling cook who was, in a friendly way, a menial rather than the ruler of her own domain, the memory that was merely personal, not ancestral, and which fed elsewhere than here; all these, and the charming awkward young man whom he brought into the drawing-room to meet us the first day, introducing him, 'This is my kinsman, Ned Cosgrove.' For Ned, whom I talked with a lot, looked like a priest, thought like a literary journalist, smelled like a cattleman, and was treated as a poor relation. In Britain, everything depends on imperial wealth; in Ireland, everything nests in poverty. Ned would be given a whiskey, but he had no rights over it.

It was he who introduced me to the local priests and the local parson. The parish priest, who was the founder of a thriving organization called Muintir na Tire, and a famous man, lived in one house; each curate lived in another; they shared a fairly big congregation and were the chief professional men in the district. The Church of Ireland rector had a tiny congregation, was too Irish to be accounted an important man by the Anglo-Irish, and consorted often with the priests. Fishing, speculation and imaginative gossip went on at their own pace, as seemed inevitable.

In this lush land, the men of God were suffering from loneliness; their purposes for their people could not be fulfilled; the land, the social land, did not burgeon. One purpose of Muintir na Tire was the restoration of rural society; but Irish society continued to sink invisibly into the grass. The mill was ruined, the church hall as I went past it echoed with the lonely sounds of a single rudimentary piper, the children strolled aimlessly, the drinking-shops (for there were no hotels) were tiny and dark (one of them owned by the schoolteacher, who thus created envy, scandal, and aesthetic distaste). One curate, who did not drink himself, and who took literally the expression 'a glass of whiskey', gave me my first 'glass' of *poitin*: illegal whiskey. 'I'm told that retailing *poitin* is a reserved sin,' I said as

I accepted the glass. 'Only in the next diocese,' he said as he handed it over. 'Ah,' I said, and drank it memorably down. It was years before I was to risk another.

The vicar had the loneliness of the abandoned; his congregation, he told me, was four or five on Sunday, and maybe three times that on the imperial feasts, when regimental flags stood in the parish church and his parishioners wore their (imperial) medals. He too wore his medal, that of the Irish defence forces placed along the border to resist a threatened British attack from the six counties during World War II. 'I'm afraid my co-religionists do not understand my pride,' he said. He was a republican on Mondays, Wednesdays, and Fridays; the rest of the time . . . He had heard that the Anglican church in Australia was Romish in its dress and practices; indeed, his friend Tommy from the next parish had felt obliged to protest at the overweening robes of the prelate to whose diocese he had come; Protestantism must be kept up, even in mannerisms. He had all the eccentricities of the Anglo-Irish gentry without their provenance and their snobbery. He would cure ailments, and diagnose pregnancies, by suspending a wedding-ring; this he called 'the box'; he adhered erratically to a notion of ESP, and would rove restlessly all over Ireland whenever he got the chance. He was a subject for Chaucer. But the sociology of his religion had combined with the intransigence of his class to leave him there, a trout beached on the green bank.

The poverty of the rural working class had issued in migration or in a range of expressions of the despair which coloured the religion of so many. Canon Hayes was heading an organization which, if it could develop in its members the initiative aimed at, would make redundant the paternalism inherent in its foundation; my sense was that, while much was done, nothing changed. The interesting people in the neighbourhood raged quietly against inertia. One, Sean McCarthy, was a farmer who painted fine 'primitive' pictures; he was a quiet, self-contained man who looked strangely like the 'small dark man' of Maurice Walsh's book; more than once we stood chatting in the evenings as the sun brushed itself to one side and the mountains, the Galtees, suddenly came a step closer, almost as close as our hands. 'You feel you could touch them,' he'd say, and so you did. Yet it was said of him that, when his brother died, the local poet who subscribed himself Seamus McCarthy Mor, Sean was so maddened with grief that he stood at the window of the farmhouse with a hunting-gun and dared them to remove the body.

Then there was Philly O'Dwyer, who is now, I believe, a race-horse trainer. Anyway, he drove us to the races at Tramore, a long way away, on the Waterford coast. At every landmark he sang a song, very tunefully; he spoke of the state of the country and the language and suddenly, in disgust of the government's ever doing anything to help the latter, he removed the *fainne*, the gold pin which he wore in his lapel to signify that he was a fluent speaker of Irish, and handed it to my wife, saying, 'It's no use to me now. You have it.'

Tom Givens was pressing us to stay, not to go to Cork. Every day there would be a new reason. The most effective was the races at Limerick Junction, where only a few days before Brian Ryan had fallen into an altercation with the station master and knocked him down. To the Junction we went, among a crowd of tinkers and gentry which would have gladdened Yeats's heart; there I saw what the rural poverty was like in full fig; and there I backed a horse which won at twelve to one only because all its rivals took the wrong turning out of the straight, and after waiting twenty minutes heard the stewards declare it no race. Ah well. And there I reflected that, colourful as it all was, the countryside was holed with a peculiar loneliness, which their ardent religion made worse rather than better.

But this chapter set out to be about living in working-class Dublin; and for that, the vintage year was 1957. We had come over from Cambridge sometime in the spring; my prose book was just about finished, and a draft of several chapters had very likely been sent to the publishers; I was finishing off a book of poems for Leonard Woolf at the Hogarth Press (too tardily, as it turned out, to my eventual relief; by it I learned the immortal lesson, The English Won't Wait). I was anxious to see close at hand the development of the Sinn Fein campaign which we had seen starting the previous year. In August we were to go back to Australia.

The trouble was, I had no money, no ways of earning any, and was writing begging letters as a result of which I was to be in debt for years. Dublin rents were high, too, which was disconcerting when Dublin landlords seemed to have extraordinarily high standards of character, morality, financial security and general attractiveness, at least for their tenants. Our landlord rooked us, as usual, and the rent kept us pinned down inside South Dublin more than I wanted. The place was a flat, the downstairs one of three, at 19 Emorville Avenue, a short street which runs north from South Circular Road very close to and parallel with Clanbrassil Street. It was my beloved South Side of Dublin once again:

> On our bed no linen
> and on our arms no silk;
> we ate our meat on stone floors
> and drank the gritty milk
> and walked outside at nightfall
> to let the low sun in,
> living with my body's pleasure
> on the South Side of Dublin.

> At dusk the sluttish children
> wandered down the Grand Canal
> smoking butt-ends by green water:
> who'll catch them when they fall?
> The streets were hatched with shadows
> and down them came the din
> of music ticking like a watch
> across the South Side of Dublin.

At night lunatic voices
would crowd the narrow hall.
They breathed like bees. By midnight
I scraped slugs from the wall
that, humid as the earth itself,
grew fidgety and thin;
and the damp grew live on every surface
on the South Side of Dublin.

For many years, looking back, I thought the place a slum; but I now realize it was not; it was a small house without amenities in a cramped neighbourhood; but houses in that neighbourhood are now being restored for sale as middle-class *pieds a terre* or transitional dwellings. It was in, or very near, a slum. If you turned left out the door, took twenty paces, and turned left again, you would be on the way to Blackpitts and The Coombe by way of Lower Clanbrassil Street, and all of that, including the depressing shops, was slum. It was also a Jewish quarter. Around the corner was a tiny synagogue. Our next door neighbour was a Jewish solicitor, but although I greeted him often, he never answered. Although Dubliners called the area Little Jerusalem, there were only a few dozen Jewish families in it; the great vowel change was already shifting them a group of miles further south, to Terenure. The population at large was conventionally Irish, and if it worried about affiliation, did so in terms religious rather than ethnic.

On the corner of Lower Clanbrassil Street and South Circular Road was Farney's pub, a foursquare rectangle based on the principle that, the less furniture you have, the more bodies you can fit into the available space. The pub was one long bar, with a completely straight counter, and at one end a small enclosed area (less a room than a way of life), with a kind of serving hatch or trapdoor, from which you might hear from time to time the sound of female laughter and opinion. This was the 'snug', the 'ladies' parlor', as the culture allowed it. Whenever I went in on my own, I would converse with whoever stood next to me at the bar; none of these was a woman. One was a retired police sergeant who worshipped Archbishop Mannix, and extorted from me complimentary tales about him. Another was a young fellow of gloomy but intelligent conversation who, on hearing that I had been to a Sinn Fein street meeting in College Green, asked immediately, 'How many did they get?' 'About 4,000 I suppose', I said. 'Is that all they can bring out these days?' he sneered. He believed in no political system, and eventually announced to me, with obvious misgiving, that he was Jewish; he was a factory worker, and his workmates insulted him. We talked about the politics of Israel. Everyone else in the pub thought him a Gael.

It was a tough pub, and its clientele ranged from proletariat to lumpen. Not that I spent much time there. Sinn Fein was having its meetings two or three nights a week in College Green, and I would often go to them. The Green was then a large clear space at the foot of Dame Street opposite the entrance to Trinity and beside the Bank of Ireland. They would let down the back of a large lorry, mount amplifiers, and the speakers would address the crowd from the lorry top. Every bus would let off people coming to the meeting, which would invariably start with a gramophone recording of 'The Mountains of Pomeroy'. At the song's end, the crowd would give a great cheer, and the speakers would get going.

The mountains of Pomeroy are in Co. Tyrone, in the north, and the playing of the song was a notice that that was where the guerrilla fight was being conducted, by an independent Republican unit, if I remember rightly, which later became associated with the IRA. The speeches were given by a group of star speakers, and, while they did not incite to violence, were rousing in a traditional mode; from time to time they would briefly and obliquely advert to the fighting in the northern counties. The most common speakers were Tomas MacGiolla, a pedantic looking man who is now senior strategist of the Workers Party, and quite anti-Republican (a hostile journalist always calls him the Mantis), Seoirse Dearle, who a few years ago stood for the Labour Party, Sean Cronin, and (most affecting of all)

Tomas MacCurtain, whose father, succeeding the martyred McSwiney as Lord Major of Cork, had been murdered by the Black and Tans during the gutting of that city. MacCurtain's high voice, impersonal stare, and nervous passionate introverted emotion made him a very considerable orator. I never met him, but I briefly met MacGiolla and Cronin; and, learning that Dearle worked in a chemist's shop in Grafton Street, I visited him there, and had a couple of conversations with him. He plainly did not know how to deal with me, and sent me on to the offices of the *United Irishman*; and it may be there that I met Cronin. It was not, however, until I read J. Bowyer Bell's book on the IRA that I realized that at the time Cronin was chief of staff of the IRA, and Dearle its training officer.

The meetings would close with the playing of the national anthem which, as 'The Soldier's Song', is also the anthem of the northern nationalists. The uniformed gardai in the crowd would be forced by protocol to stand rigidly to attention, as though Richard Weber himself was confronting them; so would the special branch men; and the republicans surrounding them would laugh and jeer at them, for they were well known. It was obvious to me, too, on my visits to the *United Irishman*, that police agents were watching the building from across the street.

One meeting was held outside the still more hallowed portals of the GPO, where Pearse had summoned Cuchullain to his side; after it, we marched to Mountjoy, led by pipers, to salute the political prisoners. A couple of the College Green meetings had people from the crowd climbing on the platform and singing; and one of them ended with a caelidh on the lorry top, with young men and women dancing set dances, and singing joyfully to the tune of 'Whack Fol the Diddle':

> And so we say, Hip Hooray,
> God Bless England so we say,
> Come and join the IRA.

This song was always sung by Joe McEvoy, a blind Sinn Fein member, who became a friend of mine. He had a splendid voice, and the crowd would applaud while he was singing. This contact of the heart meant a great deal to him; he believed in the Republican ideal and movement in the most free-hearted way, and never commended violence. More than once I called for him in his home on the north side, in one of the once-beautiful tenement buildings which the whole tribe of rack renters and barbarians had turned into a cross between a ruin and a prison: black graffiti, broken fanlights, stinking hallways, fouled doorsteps. There Joe wove his hopes. Everyone knew him, and knew that if he wanted help of any kind he would ask for it; he was an unusual blind man in some ways; his blindness was no more than a squint to him, at least in that respect.

He would drink with me, too, in any of the pubs on the north or on the south side, or at my place. One Friday night we were in Farney's with the crowd roaring and buzzing around us, when I noticed a young lad, with the usual eager idealist's face, selling the *United Irishman*, working the bar. While describing his progress to Joe, I watched him with some interest, for I wanted to see if he met any hostility. He met none, and when he reached us, we hailed him (Joe in Irish) and bought him a pint. He and Joe did not know each other, but 'I've seen you, of course', he said. He had sold six dozen copies in that pub (an unbelievable number), he left us to sell the few he had left, and then came up to my place for a few drinks. He was eighteen, he was waiting to go 'up north'; he was looking forward to it in the way that I had looked forward to it during the war, when we too called it 'up north'. I hope he got home safely.

Twice Joe took me as his guest to a meeting of a branch (cumann) of Sinn Fein. I now think it could not have been his cumann, for it was on the south side, in or near Merrion Square, and I think it may have been a meeting of more than one cumann. The meeting was packed on each occasion; dozens of people were there, most of them of a quite unmilitary cast, although I recognized two or three from the caelidh. There was no talk of war, no fund-raising; the business was debate and preparations for further meetings. No one objected to my presence; Joe's word was good enough for everyone. They were totally working-class occasions.

One Sunday that year the Irish government interned Republicans. They moved everywhere, dragging in hundreds of them. I had just heard of it on the wireless when Joe rang: 'I don't suppose they'll be on to you, but better get out.' I was leaving Ireland the next day anyhow, and there was nothing for them to be on to me for, but I thanked him; I was feeling that panic-toned sadness I always feel before I leave Ireland. 'You'll be all right yourself, Joe?' Well, they hadn't taken to interning blind men yet, though fifteen years later the British in the north were not so delicate; John McGuffin says that among those forcibly interned in 1971 were a blind man and a dog. For any Dublin regime, a blind interne would be too much trouble, and would cause them too much shame.

Many years later, in 1977, he came to a poetry reading I gave at Trinity. It had been advertised in the papers, and someone had read out the notice to him. I grabbed him, and he sat in a group drinking Australian wine for an hour. My poems, he said, were written as if especially for blind people; I led people through the poems as if I were leading blind people. He turned to a girl, 'We were in it when it was dangerous.' What it, Joe? What danger? 'You're still a Republican, Joe?' I asked. 'I don't know what you'd think of the kind of republican, Vincent.' Ah. IRSP? Surely not the bloody officials. Don't ask. There he sits, re-wording my poems to make them the expressions of a blind consciousness. Perhaps that's what they are. He grasps the girl's thigh. She looks dazedly at me. What is the vision that meanders in his head? Years ago. We wore the easter lily. And risked nothing. He gave me his address, and I lost it. But I'll meet him again, perhaps when this chapter is published.

Brigid had started school, at the National School run by the Dominican nuns in Blackpitts, a few hundred yards down Lower Clanbrassil Street, almost to the Coombe. Dean Swift would have known those alleys well; so would Kinsella, for he was brought up in an adjacent area; so, God help us, would Leopold Bloom. It was a perfectly ordinary school, but it suffered, as all inner-city Catholic schools do, from the dirt and sordidness caused by overcrowding and lack of resources. The children at playtime were jammed into the yard, trampling crusts of bread and other, less identifiable objects; although it was mid year, there was a constant impression of damp, coming from the unusual degree of enclosure the geography of the streets created; it was a cul de sac within a cul de sac. Most of the lessons were supposed to be conducted in Irish ('through the medium', as they put it); but religion and arithmetic were exempt, and it was these Brigid was supposed to be present for. Actually, she was there for longer periods than that, and became friendly with some of the kids. It was in the aftermath of the Hungarian national uprising, and Ireland had taken a number of refugees; so the kids were familiar with the name, Hungarian, if not with the thing. Brigid was about as foreign a person as they could conceive. 'Isn't Brigid a regular little Hungarian, Sister', one of them said one day. The teacher, who had renounced her own family name when becoming a nun, nevertheless wanted to convey to me that her name, too, was Buckley; and she contrived this by a system of indirections such as, 'You'd have a Cork connection, I suppose. Buckley is a common name down there. They say of the Buckleys ... I remember my father ...', and so on, in a delightful fashion, while around us crept the small human life of devastate Dublin, where no life but theirs would ever grow again.

The landlord lived in Co. Kildare, where he had a small business making furniture, and from which he issued regularly to see to his property, investments, and 19 Emorville Ave. He specialized in cupboards, and he needed somewhere in Dublin to store a couple of samples of his art, to show to prospective customers. Would we be likely minders of the objects? We won't be here long enough, I said, there's really very little space in this flat, and by the way can I show you ... The house was bothered by damp, and every night I would scrape the slugs off the kitchen walls and carry them outside; there was no heating, and the turf which we burned acted to produce even more humidity in the closed space; the back yard was tiny, and you could feel it as though entering the house, especially when you were dealing with the irritatingly resistant slugs (question for mockers: how *do* you kill a slug, short of poisoning yourself?) He was a poor landlord, for he was on the make. Anyhow, he decided to use for his agent the young fellow who lived on his own in the better of the two upstairs flats. This was reached through the front door and up the hallway which gave on to our flat, and the phone (a coinbox one, cunning man from Kildare) which he deemed necessary for the conducting of his business, to warn us that he'd be coming up the following day, and generally for trying to keep us in order, was in this hallway. In the Dublin of the widowed phone, this was a bonus; so I did not mind answering the phone to breathless voices pursuing the cabinet maker's bargains.

The lad upstairs, the agent, proved to be a quare one indeed. A couple of times we went down to Farney's and he explained his situation. He had been a corporal in the RAF, but had come home; armies were not for him (invalided out, I deduced; or maybe discharged as unsuitable; still, he'd been a corporal). He lived on some bit of a pension and some part of a dole; and 'people helped him'. He had a secret, however; he was of demon-stock, and on his thirtieth birthday he would become of God-stock. This would be in a few weeks, so with any luck I would be around for the event. Now don't ask me to explain what he said, for some of it was in response to my sympathetic and cunning questioning. For now, he was (a) under the control of the devil, (b) possessed by the devil, (c) the devil. With his transformation, he would become (a) within the power of the Holy Spirit, (b) possessed by the Holy Spirit, (c) Christ. I cast some doubt on all this, but knew better than to mock or provoke. So far as I know, Christ was never in the RAF; I don't know about the devil. This poor devil, as my father would have called him, decided that it was important to show me, to prove to me, that what he said was right, even if I could never understand it. He had a large abscess or infected weal on one cheek; I came to think of it, in Chaucerian terms, as 'the mormal'. It was the devil's mark. Diet, I murmured; skin specialists. No. He knew what it was; I could take it or leave it; we had another pint. He went up to Rathmines municipal library, and came back with more proof. It was a book by some theologian on the seven sacraments. I opened it and read a few pages leaning on Farney's bar; 'I don't think much of this, mate,' I said. 'I don't see what this dry old stuff has to do with you.' 'No, no,' he said vehemently, 'it's a message, don't you see? I'm the only one who can understand it; and I'm telling you, because I want you to understand what's happening.' No chance of that, I thought. 'Look.' He had marked passages, and begun a commentary on them in the margin. I read away, contradicting in what I hoped would be a reassuring manner.

It wasn't. He grew impatient at my thickness, and decided to play a bigger trump. 'How do you think it happens that I have the three Maries?' he said secretively. 'Have you indeed?' I said. 'Yes, I've seen you with the girls, and there *are* three. Are they all named Mary?' 'Near enough,' he said, and he reeled off their names with a kind of conversion table added on, so that they all ended up as Mary. 'Do they understand what is happening?' I asked, but no, of course they didn't understand it all, they merely had an inkling, but they would play their part when it became necessary. I had awful visions of suicide by crucifixion, and of my being forced to watch while the three Maries engaged in a deposition scene, ending in a regular Pieta. The situation was too delicate for me to ask him about such matters as the view which each of the Maries took of the others; for him, their only relation was to him, and he saw them not as persons engaged in discourse but as an iconic grouping which he by his ambiguous spirit blessed (or cursed).

Naturally I wondered if he was a con man; and I think he was that as well, like the psychotic who pretends to neurotic symptoms. The landlord had no choice but to let him collect money on his behalf;

and at any given time he would be likely to have in his care some goods or money (at most, a few pounds) belonging to the landlord. One day, he approached me in perturbation; this was the great day, and he expected the change at midnight; the mormal would go from his face, and he would pass from one inner realm to the other. He was going down to the pubs on the Liffey to have a few drinks; would I come with him? I couldn't, I said; Brigid had a fever, and I had to be on hand to see if it worsened or broke. Could I lend him a couple of quid, then? I lent him what I could, and off he went.

Early the next morning, after midnight in any case, I heard heavily running footsteps, and banging at the front door, with ancillary pantings and exclaimings. Himself, of course. I got up and let him in. He rushed past me and up the stairs, pointing to the mormal and crying out, 'Fooled again.' The change had not occurred. That day he was not to be seen, and I grew concerned. The next day, too, silence, and by the third day I began to wonder if he had committed suicide. The door to his flat was locked. I roused the third lodger, and shamed him into accompanying me as I climbed out a window and into the devilman's window, where a curtain moved lightly in the breeze. He had absconded, and the flat was cleared out, including the landlord's money. A day or two later, one of the Maries called and handed me a note. In this he thanked me, asked me not to speak of the arcane matters I had all but witnessed, and said he was leaving Dublin. It only remained to keep telling the landlord that I knew nothing about anything.

Now, there was a character for you: an Irish parable, down to the ambiguous service of England and the manipulative dependence upon a group of women. But how *did* he get the women? Such cogitations still amaze the troubled midnight and the noon's repose. Or, if you want to look at it from my point of view, how does it come about that I attract so many paranoiacs?

Brigid's condition did get worse, and even the doctor grew obviously worried. This man, Doctor O'Leary, had his house and surgery in South Circular Road, near the big Harrington Road

Catholic church. He was from Cork, and was such a magnificent GP
that Cork people would make the trip to Dublin to consult him; so
that, if you went to the afternoon surgery, you would find yourself at
the bottom of a staircase on which patients waited before going into
the waiting-room. And as we slowly ascended the stairs, it would
grow so late that one or other of his daughters would emerge from
some other door to ask anxiously when he would be ready for his
dinner. The conversation you would have on the stairs would likely
be with country people; but, if Dr O'Leary was good with southerners, he was uneasy with foreigners, and wore a perpetual look of
not knowing what on earth to say to you next. I could not see how he
could have any hour safe from demands; and I knew that every year
he took part of his annual holidays by making the pilgrimage to the
penitential island of Lough Derg. 'Sure, he's a saint', his patients said;
and so he was, although not necessarily because of Lough Derg. He
was not unique; it is impossible to make it clear to you how rootedly,
how absolutely religious the best of Ireland was in those days. Indeed,
although the mode and the manners have changed a great deal, that
game of commitment is not over yet. In 1981 I had to consult Dr
Brendan Deasy, of Rathfarnham, over a skin condition which he
cured eventually by frankly admitting that he was bewildered by the
failure of the known solutions. He is a burly, redheaded, offhand
man, who speaks frankly and informally, never presumes, yet
projects the image of a Jesuit-educated, rugby-playing, beer-drinking
insouciant. He told me on one visit that he'd be away for his annual
holiday. The west? I asked. No, abroad. Oh, where? Lourdes,
actually. He had got into the habit of taking his sceptical and
enquiring mind to that nest of miracles, to act as one of the medical
assessors. He had no word of piety about it, but found it fascinating,
wouldn't miss it, and thought it had changed his attitude to the
world. Memories of Dr O'Leary.

The day on which Brigid's fever came to its crisis, the latter said to
me, 'If she starts vomiting, or if her condition changes at all, ring me
at once. Never mind what time. Tell them I asked you to ring.'

'Certainly,' I said, 'but why? What are you expecting?' No answer; but when I had to make the call, he was at dinner, and rushed straight around. As I opened the front door, he rushed in, vehement as the devilman, ran into the bedroom, rolled Brigid in a blanket, and ran out to lay her in his little car. Sweat was pouring down his face, and he was quite distraught. 'Where are you taking her?' I shouted. 'Ballyfermot.' 'What are you scared of?' 'Meningitis.' And off he went, the poor weak old tyres squealing on the roadway, to drive her to the infectious hospital.

Now, it was meningitis all right, or the next best thing; and Brigid was in the hospital for several days. During them, the locals prayed for her; and I went up to the local church, next to O'Leary's surgery, to ask for a Mass to be said for her. A burly priest opened the door, and accepted the commission. Then I said, 'Can I give you something for that, Father?' 'That will be two half-crowns, my friend,' he answered, without a second's pause for reflection or computation, thus giving me one of those rare but invaluable sentences which we can remember all our lives. From then onwards, I tended to do my praying myself, keeping it in the family as it were.

Dr O'Leary kept his patient under close attention, and did us many other services; and he had not yet received a penny; it therefore embarrassed me a lot to have to go to him at the end of our stay and tell him that we were leaving Ireland, ask for a bill, and tell him that I would have to send him the money from Australia. He thought long and hard, blinking away at me as if unsure that I existed, and then said, 'O say two guineas. Would that be all right?' 'Two guineas!' I said, 'Fifty would be more like it.' No, no. Only too pleased. Say a prayer for me. Cork people are said to be the money-grabbers of Ireland. Dr O'Leary did not see why he should be rewarded for saving people; salvation is not a marketable commodity.

Indeed, you'd need to have a heart of granite to make money out of the devout misery of the local people. That was the time when the unemployed elected a member to parliament and held large demonstrations in the streets, or joined Sinn Fein, or trudged on to the migrant boats; and small children would stop you in the street and ask, 'Have ya got a cigarette mister?' When Brian Ryan and I went to a Cistercian monastery in England for a few days' retreat, the guest-master, an Irish monk, for whom Brian had wickedly brought a bottle of whiskey, spoke passionately for hours about the Irish poor, and how he had written to every TD, and what hope was there? None, I said; for nobody wants to change.

But the generosity persisted, and was everywhere. On the other side of us lived a widow with one son, a young man who had a minor job in the public service. Before we left, she held a party for us, and plied us with food of a quality none of us could afford. Although neither of them drank, she had bought a half-bottle of whiskey for me. I was enormously touched by such feckless thoughtfulness. It turned out that she was a first cousin of Michael Collins, and hated the party of his opponents ('and murderers', she would add); she took no part in politics, and did not spread abroad the news of her relationship; but, speaking with me, and to the obvious embarrassment of her son, she expressed fascination with certain details of the recent death in action of the IRA man, Sean South, who would surely be even more hateful to her than the constitutionalists of Fianna Fail. 'They say that when he died, his blood ran down on both sides of the border. Do you think that's true?' I don't know, I said, but it's quite a thought.